Walden Edition

THE WRITINGS OF
HENRY DAVID THOREAU

Along the Old Marlborough Road in November

THE WRITINGS OF
HENRY DAVID THOREAU

JOURNAL

EDITED BY BRADFORD TORREY

XIV

AUGUST 1, 1860–NOVEMBER 3, 1861

BOSTON AND NEW YORK

HOUGHTON MIFFLIN COMPANY

The Riverside Press, Cambridge

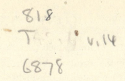

CONTENTS

ILLUSTRATIONS

JOURNAL

VOLUME XIV

THE JOURNAL OF
HENRY DAVID THOREAU

VOLUME XIV

I

AUGUST, 1860 (ÆT. 43)

Aug. 1. P. M. — To Cliffs.

The earliest corn has shed its pollen, say a week or ten days. Rye, wheat, and oats and barley have bloomed, say a month.

I stand at the wall-end on the Cliffs and look over the Miles meadow on Conantum. It is an unusually clear day after yesterday's rain.

How much of beauty — of color, as well as form — on which our eyes daily rest goes unperceived by us! No one but a botanist is likely to distinguish nicely the different shades of green with which the open surface of the earth is clothed, — not even a landscape-painter if he does not know the species of sedges and grasses which paint it. With respect to the color of grass, most of those even who attend peculiarly to the aspects of Nature only observe that it is more or less dark or light, green or brown, or velvety, fresh or parched, etc. But if you are studying grasses you look for another and different beauty, and you find it, in the wonderful variety of color, etc., presented by the various species.

Take the bare, unwooded earth now, and consider the beautiful variety of shades (or tints?) of green that clothe it under a bright sun. The pastured hills of Conantum, now just imbrowned (probably by the few now stale flowering tops of the red-top which the cows have avoided as too wiry), present a hard and solid green or greenish brown, just touched here and there delicately with light patches of sheep's fescue (though it may be only its radical leaves left), as if a dew lay on it there, — and this has some of the effect of a watered surface, — and the whole is dotted with a thousand little shades of projecting rocks and shrubs. Then, looking lower at the meadow in Miles's field, that is seen as a bright-yellow and sunny stream (yet with a slight tinge of glaucous) between the dark-green potato-fields, flowing onward with windings and expansions, and, as it were, with rips and waterfalls, to the river meadows.

Again, I sit on the brow of the orchard, and look northwest down the river valley (at mid-afternoon). There flows, or rests, the calm blue winding river, lake-like, with its smooth silver-plated sides, and wherever weeds extend across it, there too the silver plate bridges it, like a spirit's bridge across the Styx; but the rippled portions are blue as the sky. This river reposes in the midst of a broad brilliant yellow valley amid green fields and hills and woods, as if, like the Nanking or Yang-ho (or what-not), it flowed through an Oriental Chinese meadow where yellow is the imperial color. The immediate and raised edge of the river, with its willows and button-bushes and polygonums, is a light green, but the immediately adjacent low meadows, where the sedge prevails, is a brilliant and cheerful yellow, intensely, incredibly bright, such color as you never see in pictures; yellow of various tints, in the lowest and sedgiest parts deepening to so much color as if gamboge had been rubbed into the meadow there; the most cheering color in all the landscape; shaded with little darker isles of green in the midst of this yellow sea of sedge. Yet it is the bright and cheerful yellow, as of spring, and with nothing in the least autumnal in it. How this contrasts with the adjacent fields of red-top, now fast falling before the scythe!

When your attention has been drawn to them, nothing is more charming than the common colors of the earth's surface. See yonder flashing field of corn through the *shimmering* air. (This was said day before yesterday.)

The deciduous woods generally have now and for a long time been nearly as dark as the pines, though, unlike the pines, they show a general silveriness.

For some days have seen stigmas of what I have called *Cyperus dentatus*, but it is evidently later than the *diandrus*.

See a berry (not ripe) of the two-leaved Solomon's-seal dropped at the mouth of a mouse or squirrel's hole, and observe that many are gone from these plants, as if plucked by mice.

The sphagnum shows little black-balled drumsticks now. The nuthatch is active now. Meadow-haying commenced. *Cinna arundinacea* (?) almost.

Looked in two red maple swamps to find the young plants. If you look carefully through a dense red maple swamp now, you find many little maples a couple of inches high which have sprung up chiefly on certain spots alone, especially where the seed has fallen on little beds of sphagnum, which apparently have concealed the seed at the same time that they supplied the necessary moisture. There you find the little tree already deeply rooted, while the now useless winged seed lies empty near by, with its fragile wing half wasted away, as if wholly unrelated to that plant, — not visibly attached, but lying empty on one side. But so far as I look, I see only one maple to a seed, but, indeed, I see only a single seed at a time. You do not find dense groves of them generally, as you might expect from the abundance of seed that falls.

Nevertheless, you will be surprised, on looking through a large maple swamp which two months ago was red with maple seed falling in showers around, at the very small number of maple seeds to be found there, and probably every one of these will be empty. The little maples appear oftenest to have sprung from such as fell into crevices in the moss or leaves and so escaped. Indeed, almost every seed that falls to the earth is picked up by some animal or other whose favorite and perhaps peculiar food it is. They are daily busy about it in the season, and the few seeds which escape are exceptions. There is at least a squirrel or mouse to a tree. If you postpone your search but for a short time, you find yourself only gleaning after them. You may find several of their holes under every tree, if not within it. They ransack the woods. Though the seed may be almost microscopic, it is nuts to them; and this apparently is

one of the principal ends which these seeds were
intended to serve.

Look under a nut tree a month after the nuts have
fallen, and see what proportion of sound nuts to the
abortive ones and shells you will find ordinarily. They
have been dispersed, and many effectually planted, far
and wide by animals. You have come, you would
say, after the feast was over, and are presented with
shells only. It looks like a platform before a grocery.
These little creatures must live, and, pray, what are
they to eat if not the fruits of the earth? — *i. e.* the
graminivorous [*sic*] ones.[1]

Aug. 2. The wing of the sugar maples is dry and ripe
to look at, but the seed end and seed are quite green. I
find, as Michaux did, one seed always abortive.

P. M. — Up Assabet.

The young red maples have sprung up chiefly on the
sandy and muddy shores, especially where there is a
bay or eddy.

At 2 P. M. the river is twelve and seven eighths above
summer level, higher than for a long time, on account
of the rain of the 31st. Seed of hop-hornbeam not ripe.
The button-bush is about in prime, and white lilies considerably past prime. Mikania begun, and now, perhaps, the river's brink is at its height. The black
willow down is even yet still seen here and there on
the water.

The river, being raised three or four inches, looks
quite full, and the bur-reed, etc., is floating off in con-

[1] *Vide* below.

siderable masses. See those round white patches of eggs on the upright sides of dark rocks.

There is now and of late a very thin, in some lights purplish, scum on the water, outside of coarser drift that has lodged, — a brown scum, somewhat gossamer-like as it lies, and browner still on your finger when you take it up. What is it? The pollen of some plant?

As we rest in our boat under a tree, we hear from time to time the loud snap of a wood pewee's bill overhead, which is incessantly diving to this side and that after an insect and returning to its perch on a dead twig. We hear the sound of its bill when it catches one.

In huckle-berry fields I see the seeds of berries recently left on the rocks where birds have perched. How many of these small fruits they may thus disseminate!

Aug. 3. The knotty-rooted cyperus out some days at least.

Aug. 4. 8.30 A. M. — Start for Monadnock.[1]
Begins to rain at 9 A. M., and rains from time to time thereafter all day, the mountain-top being constantly enveloped in clouds.

Notice in Troy much of the *cyperinus* variety of wool-grass, now done, of various heights. Also, by roadside, the *Ribes Cynosbati*, with its prickly berries now partly reddened but hardly ripe. Am exhilarated by the pecul-iar raspberry scent by the roadside this wet day — and of the dicksonia fern. Raspberries still quite common,

---

[1] [See account of the Monadnock excursion in *Familiar Letters*, pp. 368–372; Riv. 428–433.]

though late. The high blackberries, the mulberry kind, all still green and red; and also on the 9th, except one berry on a rock.

There was a little sunshine on our way to the mountain, but the cloud extended far down its sides all day, so that one while we mistook Gap Monadnock for the true mountain, which was more to the north.

According to the guide-board it is two and one fourth miles from Troy to the first fork in the road near the little pond and schoolhouse, and I should say it was near two miles from there to the summit, — all the way up-hill from the meadow.

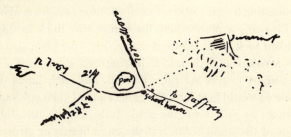

We crossed the immense rocky and springy pastures, containing at first raspberries, but much more hard-hack in flower, reddening them afar, where cattle and horses collected about us, sometimes came running to us, as we thought for society, but probably not. I told Bent of it, — how they gathered about us, they were so glad to see a human being, — but he said I might put it in my book so, it would do no harm, but then the fact was they came about me for salt. "Well," said I, "it was probably because I had so much salt in my constitution." Said he, "If you had had a little salt with you [you]

could hardly have got away from them." "Well," said
I, "[I] had some salt in my pocket." "That's what they
smelt," said he. Cattle, young and old, with horns in all
stages of growth, — young heifers with budding horns,
— and horses with a weak [?] Sleepy-David look, though
sleek and handsome. They gathered around us while
we took shelter under a black spruce from the rain.

We were wet up to our knees before reaching the
woods or steep ascent where we entered the cloud. It
was quite dark and wet in the woods, from which we
emerged into the lighter cloud about 3 p. m., and proceeded to construct our camp, in the cloud occasionally
amounting to rain, where I camped some two years ago.

Choosing a place where the spruce was thick in this
sunken rock yard, I cut out with a little hatchet a space
for a camp in their midst, leaving two stout ones six
feet apart to rest my ridge-pole on, and such limbs of
these as would best form the gable ends. I then cut four
spruces as rafters for the gable ends, leaving the stub
ends of the branches to rest the cross-beams or girders
on, of which there were two or three to each slope; and
I made the roof very steep. Then cut an abundance of
large flat spruce limbs, four or five feet long, and laid
them on, shingle-fashion, beginning at the ground and
covering the stub ends. This made a foundation for
two or three similar layers of smaller twigs. Then made
a bed of the same, closed up the ends somewhat, and all
was done. All these twigs and boughs, of course, were
dripping wet, and we were wet through up to our mid-
dles. But we made a good fire at the door, and in an
hour or two were completely dried.

Mt. Monadnock from the Troy Road

The most thickly leaved and flattest limbs of the spruce are such as spread flat over the rocks far and wide (while the upper ones were more bushy and less flat); not the very lowest, which were often partly under the surface and but meagrely leafed, but those close above them.

Standing and sitting before the fire which we kindled under a shelving rock, we could dry us much quicker than at any fireside below, for, what with stoves and reduced fireplaces, they could not have furnished such blaze or heat in any inn's [?] kitchen or parlor. This fire was exactly on the site of my old camp, and we burned a hole deep into the withered remains of its roof and bed.

It began to clear up and a star appeared at 8 P. M. Lightning was seen far in the south. Cloud, drifting cloud, alternated with moonlight all the rest of the night. At 11.30 P. M. I heard a nighthawk. Maybe it hunted then because prevented by the cloud at evening.

I heard from time to time through the night a distant sound like thunder or a falling of a pile of lumber, and I suspect that this may have been the booming of nighthawks at a distance.

Aug. 5. The wind changed to northerly toward morning, falling down from over the summit and sweeping through our camp, open on that side, and we found it rather cold!

About an hour before sunrise we heard again the nighthawk; also the robin, chewink, song sparrow,

Fringilla hyemalis; and the wood thrush from the woods below.

Had a grand view of the summit on the north now, it being clear. I set my watch each morning by sunrise, and this morning the lichens on the rocks of the south-ernmost summit (south of us), just lit by the rising sun, presented a peculiar yellowish or reddish brown light (being wet) which they did not any morning afterward. The rocks of the main summit were olive-brown, and C. called it the Mount of Olives.

I had gone out before sunrise to gather blueberries, — fresh, dewy (because wet with yesterday's rain), almost crispy blueberries, just in prime, much cooler and more grateful at this hour, — and was surprised to hear the voice of people rushing up the mountain for berries in the wet, even at this hour. These alternated with bright light-scarlet bunchberries not quite in prime.

The sides and angles of the cliffs, and their rounded brows (but especially their southeast angles, for I saw very little afterward on the north side; indeed, the cliffs or precipices are not on that side), were clothed with these now lively olive-brown lichens (umbilicaria), alike in sun and shade, becoming afterward and generally dark olive-brown when dry. *Vide* my specimens. Many of the names inscribed on the summit were produced by merely rubbing off the lichens, and they are thus distinct for years.

At 7.30 A. M. for the most part in cloud here, but the country below in sunshine. We soon after set out to walk to the lower southern spur of the mountain. It is chiefly a bare gray and extremely diversified rocky sur-

face, with here and there a spruce or other small tree
or bush, or patches of them, or a little shallow marsh
on the rock; and the whole mountain-top for two miles
was covered, on countless little shelves and in hollows
between the rocks, with low blueberries of two or more
species or varieties, just in their prime. They are said
to be later here than below. Beside the kinds (black
and blue *Pennsylvanicum*) common with us, there was
the downy *Vaccinium Canadense* and a form or forms
intermediate between this and the former, *i. e.* of like
form but less hairy. The *Vaccinium Canadense* has a
larger leaf and more recurved and undulating on its
surface, and generally a lighter green than the common. There were the blue with a copious bloom, others
simply black (not shiny, as ours commonly) and on
largish bushes, and others of a peculiar blue, as if with
a skim-coat of blue, hard and thin, as if glazed, such as
we also have. The black are scarce as with us.

These blueberries grew and bore abundantly almost
wherever anything else grew on the rocky part of the
mountain, — except perhaps the very wettest of the
little swamps and the thickest of the little thickets, —
quite up to the summit, and at least thirty or forty people came up from the surrounding country this Sunday
to gather them. When we behold this summit at this
season of the year, far away and blue in the horizon,
we may think of the blueberries as blending their color
with the general blueness of the mountain. They grow
alike in the midst of the cladonia lichens and of the
lambkill and moss of the little swamps. No shelf amid
the piled rocks is too high or dry for them, for every-

where they enjoy the cool and moist air of the mountain. They are evidently a little later than in Concord,
— say a week or ten days later. Blueberries of every
degree of blueness and of bloom. There seemed to be
fewer of them on the more abrupt and cold westerly and
northwesterly sides of the summit, and most in the hollows and shelves of the plateau just southeast of the
summit.

Perhaps the prettiest berry, certainly the most novel
and interesting to me, was the mountain cranberry,
now grown but yet hard and with only its upper cheek
red. They are quite local, even on the mountain. The
vine is most common close to the summit, but we saw
very little fruit there; but some twenty rods north of
the brow of this low southern spur we found a pretty
little dense patch of them between the rocks, where we
gathered a pint in order to make a sauce of them. They
here formed a dense low flat bed, covering the rocks
for a rod or two, some lichens, green mosses, and the
mountain potentilla mingled with them; and they rose
scarcely more than one inch above the ground. These
vines were only an inch and a half long, clothed with
small, thick, glossy leaves, with two or three berries
together, about as big as huckleberries, on the recurved
end, with a red cheek uppermost and the other light-
colored. It was thus a dense, firm sward [?] of glossy
little leaves dotted with bright-red berries. They were
very easy to collect, for you only made incessant dabs
at them with all your fingers together and the twigs and
leaves were so rigid that you brought away only berries and no leaves.

I noticed two other patches where the berries were thick, *viz.* one a few rods north of the little rain-water lake of the rocks, at the first, or small, meadow (source of Contoocook) at northeast end of the mountain, and another not more than fifty rods northwest of the summit, where the vines were much ranker and the berries larger. Here the plants were four or five inches high, and there were three or four berries of pretty large huckleberry size at the end of each, and they branched like little bushes. In each case they occupied almost exclusively a little sloping shelf between the rocks, and the vines and berries were especially large and thick where they lay up against the sloping sunny side of the rock.

We stewed these berries for our breakfast the next morning, and thought them the best berry on the mountain, though, not being quite ripe, the berry was a little bitterish — but not the juice of it. It is such an acid as the camper-out craves. They are, then, somewhat earlier than the common cranberry. I do not know that they are ever gathered hereabouts. At present they are very firm berries, of a deep, dark, glossy red. Doubtless there are many more such patches on the mountain.[1]

We heard the voices of many berry-pickers and visitors to the summit, but neither this nor the camp we built afterward was seen by any one.

[1] Brought some home, and stewed them the 12th, and all thought them quite like, and as good as, the common cranberry. Yet George Emerson speaks of it as "austere" and inferior to the common cranberry.

P. M. — Walked to the wild swamp at the northeast spur. That part is perhaps the most interesting for the wild confusion of its variously formed rocks, and is the least, if at all, frequented. We found the skull and jaws of a large rodent, probably a hedgehog, — larger than a woodchuck's, — a considerable quantity of dry and hard dark-brown droppings, of an elliptical form, like very large rat-droppings, somewhat of a similar character but darker than the rabbit's, and I suspect that these were the porcupine's.

Returned over the top at 5 P. M., after the visitors, men and women, had descended, and so to camp.

Aug. 6. The last was a clear, cool night. At 4 A. M. see local lake-like fogs in some valleys below, but there is none here.

This forenoon, after a breakfast on cranberries, leaving, as usual, our luggage concealed under a large rock, with other rocks placed over the hole, we moved about a quarter of a mile along the edge of the plateau eastward and built a new camp there. It was [a] place which I had noticed the day before, where, sheltered by a perpendicular ledge some seven feet high and close to the brow of the mountain, grew five spruce trees. Two of these stood four feet from the rock and six or more apart; so, clearing away the superfluous branches, I rested stout rafters from the rock-edge to limbs of the two spruces and placed a plate beam across, and, with two or three cross-beams or girders, soon had a roof which I could climb and shingle. After filling the inequalities with rocks and rubbish, I soon had a sloping floor on

which to make our bed. Lying there on that shelf just
on the edge of the steep declivity of the mountain, we
could look all over the south and southeast world without raising our heads. The rock running east and west
was our shelter on the north.

Our huts, being built of spruce entirely, were not noticeable two or three rods off, for we did [not] cut the
spruce amid which they were built more than necessary,
bending aside their boughs in order to enter. My companion, returning from a short walk, was lost when
within two or three rods, the different rocks and clumps
of spruce looked so much alike, and in the moonlight
we were liable to mistake some dark recess between two
neighboring spruce ten feet off for the entrance to our
house. We heard this afternoon the tread of a blueberry-
picker on the rocks two or three rods north of us, and
saw another as near, south, and, stealing out, we came
round from another side and had some conversation
with them, — two men and a boy, — but they never
discovered our house nor suspected it. The surface is
so uneven that ten steps will often suffice to conceal the
ground you lately stood on, and yet the different shelves
and hollows are so much alike that you cannot tell if
one is new or not. It is somewhat like travelling over a
huge fan. When in a valley the nearest ridge conceals
all the others and you cannot tell one from another.

This afternoon, again walked to the larger northeast swamp, going directly, *i. e.* east of the promon-
tories or part way down the slopes. Bathed in the small
rocky basin above the smaller meadow. These two
swamps are about the wildest part of the mountain and

most interesting to me. The smaller occurs on the northeast side of the main mountain, *i. e.* at the northeast end
of the plateau. It is a little roundish meadow a few rods
over, with cotton-grass in it, the shallow bottom of a
basin of rock, and out the east side there trickles a very
slight stream, just moistening the rock at present and
collecting enough in one cavity to afford you a drink.
This is evidently a source of the Contoocook, the one I
noticed two years ago as such.

The larger swamp is considerably lower and more
northerly, separating the northeast spur from the main
mountain, probably not far from the line of Dublin. It
extends northwest and southeast some thirty or forty
rods, and probably leaked out now under the rocks at
the northwest end, — though I found water only half
a dozen rods below, — and so was a source probably of
the Ashuelot. The prevailing grass or sedge in it, growing in tufts in the green moss and sphagnum between
the fallen dead spruce timber, was the *Eriophorum vaginatum* (long done) and the *E. gracile.* Also the *Epilobium palustre*, apparently in prime in it, and common
wool-grass (*Scirpus Eriophorum*). Around its edge grew
the *Chelone glabra* (not yet out), meadow-sweet in bloom,
black choke-berry just ripening, red elder (its fruit in
prime), mountain-ash, *Carex trisperma* and *Deweyana*
(small and slender), and the fetid currant in fruit (in a
torrent of rocks at the east end), etc., etc.

I noticed a third, yet smaller, quite small, swamp, yet
more southerly, on the edge of the plateau, evidently
another source of a river, where the snows melt.

At 5 p. m. we went to our first camp for our remaining baggage. From this point at this hour the rocks of the precipitous summit (under whose south side that camp is placed), lit by the declining sun, were·a very light gray, with reddish-tawny touches from the now drying *Aira flexuosa* on the inaccessible shelves and along the seams. Returned to enjoy the evening at the second camp.

Evening and morning were the most interesting seasons, especially the evening. Each day, about an hour before sunset, I got sight, as it were accidentally, of an elysium beneath me. The smoky haze of the day, suggesting a furnace-like heat, a trivial dustiness, gave place to a clear transparent enamel, through which houses, woods, farms, and lakes were seen as in [a] picture indescribably fair and expressly made to be looked at. At any hour of the day, to be sure, the surrounding country looks flatter than it is. Even the great steep, furrowed, and rocky pastures, red with hardhack and raspberries, which creep so high up the mountain amid the woods, in which you think already that you are half-way up, perchance, seen from the top or brow of the mountain are not for a long time distinguished for elevation above the surrounding country, but they look smooth and tolerably level, and the cattle in them are not noticed or distinguished from rocks unless you search very particularly. At length you notice how the houses and barns keep a respectful, and at first unaccountable, distance from these near pastures and woods, though they *are* seemingly flat, that there is a broad neutral ground between the roads and the mountain; and yet when the truth flashes upon you, you have to imagine the long, ascending path through them.

To speak of the landscape generally, the open or cleared land looks like a thousand little swells or tops of low rounded hills, — tent-like or like a low hay-cap spread, — tawny or green amid the woods. As you look down on this landscape you little think of the hills where the traveller walks his horse. The woods have not this swelling look. The most common color of open land (from apex at 5 P. M.) is tawny brown, the woods dark green. At midday the darker green of ever-greens amid the hardwoods is quite discernible half a dozen miles off. But, as the most interesting view is at sunset, so it is the part of [the] landscape nearest to you and most immediately beneath the mountain, where, as usual, there is that invisible gelid haze to glass it.

The nearest house to the mountain which we saw from our camp — one on the Jaffrey road — was in the shadow even of the low southern spur of the mountain which we called the Old South, just an hour before the sun set, while a neighbor on a hill within a quarter of a mile eastward enjoyed the sunlight at least half an hour longer. So much shorter are their days, and so much more artificial light and heat must they obtain, at the former house. It would be a serious loss, methinks, one hour of sunlight every day. *We* saw the sun so much longer. Of course the labors of the day were brought to an end, the sheep began to bleat, the doors were closed, the lamps were lit, and preparations for the night were made there, so much the earlier.

The landscape is shown to be not flat, but hilly, when the sun is half an hour high, by the shadows of the hills.

But, above all, from half an hour to two hours before
sunset many western mountain-ranges are revealed,
as the sun declines, one behind another, by their dark
outlines and the intervening haze; i. e., the ridges are
dark lines, while the intervening valleys are a cloud-
like haze. It was so, at least, from 6 to 6.30 P. M. on the
6th; and, at 5 P. M. on the 8th, it being very hazy still,
I could count in the direction of Saddleback Mountain
eight distinct ranges, revealed by the darker lines of the
ridges rising above this cloud-like haze. And I might
have added the ridge of Monadnock itself within a quarter of a mile of me.

Of course, the last half of these mountain-ridges appeared successively higher and seemed higher, all of
them (i. e. the last half), than the mountain we were
on, as if you had climbed to the heights of the sky by a
succession of stupendous terraces reaching as far as
you could see from north to south. The Connecticut
Valley was one broad gulf of haze which you were soon
over. They were the Green Mountains that we saw,
but there was no greenness, only a bluish mistiness, in
what we saw; and all of Vermont that lay between us
and their summit was but a succession of parallel ranges
of mountains. Of course, almost all that we mean com-
mercially and agriculturally by Vermont was concealed
in those long and narrow haze-filled valleys. I never
saw a mountain that looked so high and so melted away
at last cloud-like into the sky, as Saddleback this eve,
when your eye had clomb to it by these eight successive terraces. You had to begin at this end and ascend
step by step to recognize it for a mountain at all. If you

had first rested your eye on *it*, you would have seen it for a cloud, it was so incredibly high in the sky.

After sunset the ponds are white and distinct.[1] Earlier we could distinguish the reflections of the woods perfectly in ponds three miles off.

I heard a cock crow very shrilly and distinctly early in the evening of the 8th. This was the most distinct sound from the lower world that I heard up there at any time, not excepting even the railroad whistle, which was louder. It reached my ear perfectly, to each note and curl, — from some submontane cock. We also heard at this hour an occasional bleat from a sheep in some mountain pasture, and a lowing of a cow. And at last we saw a light here and there in a farmhouse window. We heard no sound of man except the railroad whistle and, on Sunday, a church-bell. Heard no dog that I remember. Therefore I should say that, of all the sounds of the farmhouse, the crowing of the cock could be heard furthest or most distinctly under these circumstances. It seemed to wind its way through the layers of air as a sharp gimlet through soft wood, and reached our ears with amusing distinctness.

Aug. 7. Morning — dawn and sunrise — was another interesting season. I rose always by four or half past four to observe the signs of it and to correct my watch. From our first camp I could not see the sun rise, but only when its first light (yellowish or, rather, pink-

[1] At 5 P. M. the 5th, being on the apex, the small pond by the schoolhouse is mostly smooth plated, with a darker rippled portion in the middle.

ish) was reflected from the lichen-clad rocks of the southern spur. But here, by going eastward some forty rods,
I could see the sun rise, though there was invariably a
low stratum or bar of cloud in the horizon. The sun
rose about five. The tawny or yellowish pastures about
the mountain (below the woods; what was the grass?)
reflected the auroral light at 4.20 A. M. remarkably, and
they were at least as distinct as at any hour.

There was every morning more or less solid white
fog to be seen on the earth, though none on the mountain. I was struck by the localness of these fogs. For
five mornings they occupied the same place and were
about the same in extent. It was obvious that certain
portions of New Hampshire and Massachusetts were
at this season commonly invested with fog in the morning, while others, or the larger part, were free from it.
The fog lay on the lower parts only. From our point of
view the largest lake of fog lay in Rindge and southward;
and southeast of Fitzwilliam, *i. e.* about Winchendon,
very large there. In short, the fog lay in great spidery
lakes and streams answering to the lakes, streams, and
meadows beneath, especially over the sources of Miller's
River and the region of primitive wood thereabouts;
but it did [not] rest on lakes always, *i. e.*, where they
were elevated, as now some in Jaffrey were quite clear.
It suggested that there was an important difference, so
far as the health and spirits of the inhabitants were concerned, between the town where there was this regular
morning fog and that where there was none. I shall
always remember the inhabitants of State Line as dwellers in the fog. The geography and statistics of fog have

not been ascertained. If we awake into a fog, it does
not occur to us that the inhabitants of a neighboring
town which lies higher may have none, neither do they,
being ignorant of this happiness, inform us of it. Yet,
when you come to look down thus on the country every
morning, you see that here this thick white veil of fog
is spread and not there. It was often several hundred
feet thick, soon rising, breaking up, and drifting off, or
rather seeming to drift away, as it evaporated. There
was commonly such a risen fog drifting through the
interval between this mountain and Gap Monadnock.

One morning I noticed clouds as high as the Peterboro Hills, — a lifted fog, — ever drifting easterly but
making no progress, being dissipated. Also long rolls
and ant-eaters of cloud, at last reduced by the sun to
mere vertebræ. That morning (the 8th) the great and
general cloud and apparently fog combined over the
lowest land running southwest from Rindge was apparently five hundred or more feet deep, but our mountain was above all.

This forenoon I cut and measured a spruce on the
north side the mountain, and afterward visited the
summit, where one of the coast surveyors had been
signalling, as I was told, to a mountain in Laconia, some
fifty-five miles off, with a glass reflector.

After dinner, descended into the gulf and swamp
beneath our camp. At noon every roof in the southern
country sloping toward the north was distinctly revealed, — a lit gray.

In the afternoon, walked to the Great Gulf and

meadow, in the midst of the plateau just east of and under the summit.

Aug. 8. *Wednesday.* 8.30 A. M. Walk round the west side of the summit. Bathe in the rocky pool there, collect mountain cranberries on the northwest side, return over the summit, and take the bearings of the different spurs, etc. Return to camp at noon.

Toward night, walk to east edge of the plateau.

Aug. 9. At 6 A. M., leave camp for Troy, where we arrive, after long pauses, by 9 A. M., and take the cars at 10.5.

I observed these plants on the rocky summit of the mountain, above the forest: —

Raspberry, not common.
Low blueberries of two or three varieties.[1]
Bunchberry.
Solidago thyrsoïdea.
Fetid currant, common; leaves beginning to be scarlet; grows amid loose fallen rocks.
Red cherry, some ripe, and handsome.
Black choke-berry.
Potentilla tridentata, still lingering in bloom.
Aralia hispida, still lingering in bloom.
Cow-wheat, common, still in bloom.
Mountain cranberry, not generally abundant; full grown earlier than lowland ditto.[2]
Black spruce.
Lambkill, lingering in flower in cool and moist places.
Aster acuminatus, abundant; not generally open, but fairly begun to bloom.

[1] *Vide* p. [11].   [2] *Vide* p. [12].

Red elder, ripe, apparently in prime, not uncommon.

Arenaria Grœnlandica, still pretty common in flower.

Solidago lanceolata, not uncommon; just fairly begun.

Epilobium angustifolium, in bloom; not common, however.

Epilobium palustre, some time, common in mosses, small and slender.

Wild holly, common; berries not quite ripe.

Viburnum nudum, common; berries green.

White pine; saw three or four only, mostly very small.

Mountain-ash, abundant; berries not ripe; generally very small, largest in swamps.

Diervilla, not uncommon, still.

Rhodora, abundant; low, *i. e.* short.

Meadow-sweet, abundant, apparently in prime.

Hemlocks; two little ones with rounded tops.

Chelone glabra, not yet; at northeast swamp-side.

Yarrow.

Canoe birch, very small.

Clintonia borealis, with fruit.

Checkerberry.

Gold-thread.

One three-ribbed goldenrod, northwest side (not *Canadense*).

Tall rough goldenrod, not yet; not uncommon.

Populus tremuliformis, not very common.

Polygonum cilinode, in bloom.

Yellow birch, small.

Fir, a little; four or five trees noticed.

Willows, not uncommon, four or five feet high.

Red maple, a very little, small.

Water andromeda, common about the bogs.

Trientalis.

Pearly everlasting, out.

Diplopappus umbellatus, in bloom, not common (?); northeast swamp-side, also northwest side of mountain.

Juncus trifidus.

Some *Juncus paradoxus ?* } about edge of marshes.
Some *Juncus acuminatus ?* }

CYPERACEÆ

Eriophorum gracile, abundant, whitening the little swamps.

Eriophorum vaginatum, abundant, little swamps, long done,
(this the coarse grass in tufts, in marshes).

Wool-grass, not uncommon, (common kind).

Carex trisperma (?) or *Deweyana*, with large seeds, slender and
drooping, by side of northeast swamp. *Vide* press.

Carex scoparia? or *straminea?* a little.

C. debilis.

Carex, small, rather close-spiked, *C. canescens*-like (?), common.

A fine grass-like plant very common, perhaps *Eleocharis tenuis;*
now without heads, but marks of them.

GRASSES

Aira flexuosa.

Glyceria elongata, with appressed branches (some purplish), in
swamp.

Blue-joint, apparently in prime, one place.

Festuca ovina, one place.

Cinna arundinacea, one place.

Agrostis scabra (?), at our spring, *q. v.*

FERNS AND LICHENS, ETC.

A large greenish lichen flat on rocks, of a
peculiarly concentric growth, *q. v.*

Some common sulphur lichen.

The very bright handsome crustaceous yellow lichen, as on White
Mts., *q. v.*

Two or three umbilicaria lichens, *q. v.*, giving the dark brown to
the rocks.

A little, in one place, of the old hat umbilicaria, as at Flint's Pond
Rock.

Green moss and sphagnum in the marshes.

Two common cladonias, white and greenish.

Stereocaulon.

Lycopodium complanatum, one place.

Lycopodium annotinum, not very common.

Common polypody.

Dicksonia fern, *q. v.*

Sensitive fern, and various other common ones.

I see that in my last visit, in June, '58, I also saw here Labrador tea (on the north side), two-leaved Solomon's-seal, *Amelanchier Canadensis* var. *oligocarpa* and var. *oblongifolia*, one or two or three kinds of willows, a little mayflower, and chiogenes, and *Lycopodium clavatum*.

The prevailing trees and shrubs of the mountain-top are, in order of commonness, etc., low blueberry, black spruce, lambkill, black choke-berry, wild holly, *Viburnum nudum*, mountain-ash, meadow-sweet, rhodora, red cherry, canoe birch, water andromeda, fetid currant.

The prevailing and characteristic smaller plants, excepting grasses, cryptogamic, etc.: *Potentilla tridentata*, *Solidago thyrsoidea*, bunchberry, cow-wheat, *Aster acuminatus*, *Arenaria Grœnlandica*, mountain cranberry, *Juncus trifidus*, *Clintonia borealis*, *Epilobium palustre*, *Aralia hispida*.

Of *Cyperaceæ* the most common and noticeable now were *Eriophorum gracile* and *vaginatum*, a few sedges, and perhaps the grass-like *Eleocharis tenuis*.

The grass of the mountain now was the *Aira flexuosa*, large and abundant, now somewhat dry and withered, on all shelves and along the seams, quite to the top; a pinkish tawny now. Most would not have noticed or detected any other. The other kinds named were not common. You would say it was a true mountain grass. The only grass that a careless observer would notice. There was nothing like a sod on the mountain-top. The tufts of *J. trifidus*, perhaps, came the nearest to it.

The black spruce is the prevailing tree, commonly six or eight feet high; but very few, and those only in the most sheltered places, as hollows and swamps, are of regular outline, on account of the strong and cold winds with which they have to contend. Fifteen feet high would be unusually large. They cannot grow here without some kind of lee to start with. They commonly consist of numerous flat branches close above one another for the first foot or two, spreading close over the surface and filling and concealing the hollows between the rocks; but exactly at a level with the top of the rock which shelters them they cease to have any limbs on the north side, but all their limbs now are included within a quadrant between southeast and southwest, while the stem, which is always perfectly perpendicular, is bare and smooth on the north side; yet it is led onward at the top by a tuft of tender branches a foot in length and spreading every way as usual, but the northern part of these successively die and disappear. They thus remind you often of masts of vessels with sails set on one side, and sometimes one of these almost bare masts is seen to have been broken short off at ten feet from the ground, such is the violence of the wind there. I saw a spruce, healthy and straight, full sixteen feet without a limb or the trace of a limb on the north side. When building my camp, in order to get rafters six feet long and an inch and a half in diameter at the small end, I was obliged to cut down spruce at least five inches in diameter at one foot from the ground. So stout and tapering do they grow. They spread so close to the rocks that the lower branches are often half worn away for a foot in length by their rubbing on the rocks in the wind, and I sometimes mistook the creaking of such a limb for the note of a bird, for it is just such a note as you would expect to hear there. The two spruce which formed the sides of my second camp had their lower branches behind the rock so thick and close, and, on the outsides of the quadrant, so directly above one another perpendicularly, that they made two upright side walls, as it were, very convenient to interlace and make weather-tight.

I selected a spruce growing on the highest part of the plateau east of the summit, on its north slope, about as high as any tree of its size, to cut and count its rings. It was five feet five inches high. As usual, all its limbs except some of the leading twigs extended toward the south. One of the lowermost limbs, so close to the ground that I thought its green extremity was a distinct tree, was ten feet long. There were ten similar limbs (though not so long) almost directly above one another, within two feet of the ground, the largest two inches thick at the butt. I cut off this tree at one foot from the ground. It was there five inches in diameter and had forty-four rings, but four inches of its growth was on the south side the centre and only one inch on the north side. I cut it off again nineteen inches higher and there there were thirty-five rings.

Our fuel was the dead spruce — apparently that which escaped the fire some forty years ago!! — which lies spread over the rocks in considerable quantity still, especially at the northeast spur. It makes very good dry fuel, and some of it is quite fat and sound. The spruce twigs were our bed. I observed that, being laid bottom upward in a hot sun, as at the foot of our bed, the leaves turned pale-brown, as if boiled, and fell off very soon.

The black spruce is certainly a very wild tree, and loves a primitive soil just made out of disintegrated granite.

After the low blueberry I should say that the lamb-kill was the commonest shrub. The black choke-berry also was very common, but this and the rhodora were both dwarfish. Though the meadow-sweet was very common, I did not notice any hardhack; yet it was exceedingly prevalent in the pastures below. /

The *Solidago thyrsoidea* was the goldenrod of the mountain-top, from the woods quite to the summit. Any other goldenrod was comparatively scarce. It was from two inches to two feet high. It grew both in small swamps and in the seams of the rocks everywhere, and was now in its prime.

The bunchberry strikes one from these parts as much as any, — about a dozen berries in a dense cluster, a lively scarlet on a green ground.

Spruce was the prevailing tree; blueberry, the berry; *S. thyrsoidea*, the goldenrod; *A. acuminatus*, the aster (the only one I saw, and very common); *Juncus tri-fidus*, the juncus; and *Aira flexuosa*, the grass, of the mountain-top.

The two cotton-grasses named were very common and conspicuous in and about the little meadows.

The *Juncus trifidus* was the common grass (or grass-

like plant) of the very highest part of the mountain, —
the peak and for thirty rods downward, — growing on
the shelves and especially on the edges of the *scars*
rankly, and on this part of the mountain almost alone
had it fruited, — for I think that I saw it occasionally
lower and elsewhere on the rocky portion without
fruit.

The apparently common green and white cladonias,
together with yet whiter stereocaulon, grew all over the
flat rocks in profusion, and the apparently common
greenish rock lichen (*q. v.* in box) grew concentricwise
in large circles on the slopes of rocks also, not to mention the common small umbilicaria (*q. v.*) of one or
two kinds which covered the brows and angles of the
rocks.

The berries now ripe were: blueberries, bunchberries, fetid currant, red cherry, black choke-berry (some
of them), mountain cranberry (red-cheeked and good
cooked), red elder (quite showy), *Clintonia borealis*,
raspberry (not common). And berries yet green were:
Aralia hispida (ripe in Concord, *much* of it), wild holly
(turning), *Viburnum nudum* (green), mountain-ash.

The birds which I noticed were: robins, chewinks,
F. hyemalis, song sparrow, nighthawk, swallow (a few,
probably barn swallow, one flying over the extreme
summit), crows (sometimes flew over, though mostly
heard in the woods below), wood thrush (heard from
woods below); and saw a warbler with a dark-marked
breast and yellowish angle to wing and white throat,

and heard a note once like a very large and powerful nuthatch. Some small hawks.

The bird peculiar to the mountain was the *F. hyemalis*, and perhaps the most common, flitting over the rocks, unless the robin and chewink were as common. These, with the song sparrow and wood thrush, were heard regularly each morning. I saw a robin's nest in one of the little swamps. The wood thrush was regularly heard late in the afternoon, its strain coming up from the woods below as the shadows were lengthening.

But, above all, this was an excellent place to observe the habits of the nighthawks. They were heard and seen regularly at sunset, — one night it was at 7.10, or exactly at sunset, — coming upward from the lower and more shaded portion of the rocky surface below our camp, with their *spark spark*, soon answered by a companion, for they seemed always to hunt in pairs, — yet both would dive and boom and, according to Wilson, only the male utters this sound. They pursued their game thus a short distance apart and some sixty or one hundred feet above the gray rocky surface, in the twilight, and the constant *spark spark* seemed to be a sort of call-note to advertise each other of their neighborhood. Suddenly one would hover and flutter more stationarily for a moment, somewhat like a kingfisher, and then dive almost perpendicularly downward with a rush, for fifty feet, frequently within three or four rods of us, and the loud booming sound or rip was made just at the curve, as it ceased to fall, but whether voluntarily or involuntarily I know not. They appeared to be diving for their insect prey. What eyes they must

have to be able to discern it *beneath* them against the
rocks in the twilight! As I was walking about the camp,
one flew low, within two feet of the surface, about me,
and lit on the rock within three rods of me, and uttered
a harsh note like *c-o-w, c-o-w,* — hard and gritty and
allied to their common notes, — which I thought ex-
pressive of anxiety, or to alarm me, or for its mate.

I suspect that their booming on a distant part of the
mountain was the sound which I heard the first night
which was like very distant thunder, or the fall of a pile
of lumber.

They did not fly or boom when there was a cloud or
fog, and ceased pretty early in the night. They came
up from the same quarter — the shaded rocks below —
each night, two of them, and left off booming about
8 o'clock. Whether they then ceased hunting or withdrew to another part of the mountain, I know not. Yet
I heard one the first night at 11.30 p. m., but, as it had
been a rainy day and did not clear up here till some time
late in the night, it may have been compelled to do its
hunting then. They began to boom again at 4 a. m.
(other birds about 4.30) and ceased about 4.20. By
their color they are related to the gray rocks over which
they flit and circle.

As for quadrupeds, we saw none on the summit and
only one small gray rabbit at the base of the mountain,
but we saw the droppings of rabbits all over the mountain, and they must be the prevailing large animal, and
we heard the motions probably of a mouse about our
camp at night. We also found the skull of a rodent

larger than a woodchuck or gray rabbit, and the tail-bones (maybe of the same) some half-dozen inches long, and saw a large quantity of dark-brown oval droppings (*q. v.*, preserved). I think that this was a porcupine, and I hear that they are found on the mountain. Mr. Wild saw one recently dead near the spring some sixteen years ago. I saw the ordure of some large quadruped, probably this, on the rocks in the pastures beneath the wood, composed chiefly of raspberry seeds.

As for insects: There were countless ants, large and middle-sized, which ran over our bed and inside our clothes. They swarmed all over the mountain. Had young in the dead spruce which we burned. Saw but half a dozen mosquitoes. Saw two or three common yellow butterflies and some larger red-brown ones, and moths. There were great flies, as big as horse-flies, with shining black abdomens and buff-colored bases to their wings. Disturbed a swarm of bees in a dead spruce on the ground, but they disappeared before I ascertained what kind they were. On the summit one noon, *i. e.* on the very apex, I was pestered by great swarms of small black wasps or winged ants about a quarter of an inch long, which fluttered about and settled on my head and face. Heard a *fine* (in the sod) cricket, a dog-day locust once or twice, and a *creaking* grasshopper.

Saw two or three frogs, — one large *Rana fontinalis* in that rocky pool on the southwest side, where I saw the large spawn which I supposed to be bullfrog spawn two years ago, but now think must have been *R. fontinalis*

spawn; and there was a dark pollywog one inch long.
This frog had a raised line on each side of back and was
as large as a common bullfrog. I also heard the note
once of some familiar large frog. The one or two smaller
frogs which I saw elsewhere were perhaps the same.

There were a great many visitors to the summit, both
by the south and north, *i. e.* the Jaffrey and Dublin
paths, but they did not turn off from the beaten track.
One noon, when I was on the top, I counted forty men,
women, and children around me, and more were constantly arriving while others were going. Certainly more
than one hundred ascended in a day. When you got
within thirty rods you saw them seated in a row along
the gray parapets, like the inhabitants of a castle on a
gala-day; and when you behold Monadnock's blue
summit fifty miles off in the horizon, you may imagine
it covered with men, women, and children in dresses of
all colors, like an observatory on a muster-field. They
appeared to be chiefly mechanics and farmers' boys and
girls from the neighboring towns. The young men sat
in rows with their legs dangling over the precipice,
squinting through spy-glasses and shouting and halloo-
ing to each new party that issued from the woods below.
Some were playing cards; others were trying to see
their house or their neighbor's. Children were running
about and playing as usual. Indeed, this peak in pleasant weather is the most trivial place in New England.
There are probably more arrivals daily than at any of the
White Mountain houses. Several were busily engraving
their names on the rocks with cold-chisels, whose inces-

sant clink you heard, and they had but little leisure to look off. The mountain was not free of them from sunrise to sunset, though most of them left about 5 P. M. At almost any hour of the day they were seen wending their way single file in various garb up or down the shelving rocks of the peak. These figures on the summit, seen in relief against the sky (from our camp), looked taller than life. I saw some that camped there, by moonlight, one night. On Sunday, twenty or thirty, at least, in addition to the visitors to the peak, came up to pick blueberries, and we heard on all sides the rattling of dishes and their frequent calls to each other.

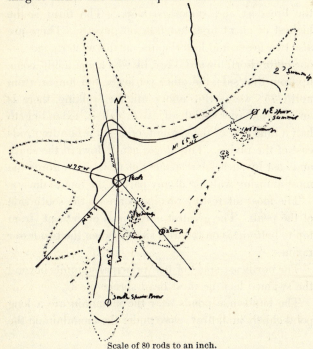

Scale of 80 rods to an inch.

The rocky area — or summit of the mountain above the forest — which I am describing is of an irregular form from a mile and a half to two miles long, north and south, by three quarters to a mile wide at the widest part, in proportion as you descend lower on the rocks.

There are three main spurs, *viz.* the northeast, or chief, one, toward Monadnock Pond and the village of Dublin; the southerly, to Swan's [?]; and the northerly, over which the Dublin path runs. These afford the three longest walks. The first is the longest, wildest, and least-frequented, and rises to the greatest height at a distance from the central peak. The second affords the broadest and smoothest walk. The third is the highest of all at first, but falls off directly. There are also two lesser and lower spurs, on the westerly side, — one quite short, toward Troy, by which you might come up from that side, the other yet lower, but longer, from north 75° west. But above all, for walking, there is an elevated rocky plateau, so to call it, extending to half a mile east of the summit, or about a hundred rods east of the ravine. This slopes gently toward the south and east by successive terraces of rock, and affords the most amusing walking of any part of the mountain.

The most interesting precipices are on the south side of the peak. The greatest abruptness of descent (from top to bottom) is on the west side between the two lesser ravines.

The northeast spur (of two principal summits beyond the swamp) has the most dead spruce on it.

The handsome ponds near the mountain are a long pond chiefly in Jaffrey, close under the mountain on the

east, with a greatly swelling knoll extending into it on
the east side; Monadnock Pond in Dublin, said to be
very deep, about north-northeast (between the northeast spur and Dublin village); a large pond with a very
white beach much further off in Nelson, about north
(one called it Breed's?); Stone Pond, northwesterly,
about as near as Monadnock Pond. Also large ponds
in Jaffrey, Rindge, Troy; and many more further off.

The basis of my map was the distance from the summit to the second camp, measured very rudely by casting
a stone before. Pacing the distance of an easy cast, I
found it about ten rods, and thirteen such stone's throws,
or one hundred and thirty rods, carried me to the camp.
As I had the course, from the summit and from the
camp, of the principal points, I could tell the rest nearly
enough. It was about fifty rods from the summit to the
ravine and eighty more to the camp.

It was undoubtedly Saddleback Mountain which I
saw about S. 85° W. What was that elevated part of
the Green Mountains about N. 50° W., which one
called falsely Camel's Hump? — the next elevated
summit north of Saddleback.

It would evidently be a noble walk from Watatic to
Goffstown perchance, over the Peterboro mountains,
along the very backbone of this part of New Hampshire,
— the most novel and interesting walk that I can think
of in these parts.

They who simply climb to the peak of Monadnock
have seen but little of the mountain. I came not to look
off from it, but to look *at* it. The view of the pinnacle
itself from the plateau below surpasses any view which

you get from the summit. It is indispensable to see the
top itself and the sierra of its outline from one side. The
great charm is not to look off from a height but to walk
over this novel and wonderful rocky surface. Moreover,
if you would enjoy the prospect, it is, methinks, most
interesting when you look from the edge of the plateau
immediately down into the valleys, or where the edge of
the lichen-clad rocks, only two or three rods from you,
is seen as the lower frame of a picture of green fields,
lakes, and woods, suggesting a more stupendous precipice
than exists. There are much more surprising effects of
this nature along the edge of the plateau than on the summit. It is remarkable what haste the visitors make to get
to the top of the mountain and then look away from it.

Northward you see Ascutney and Kearsarge Mountains, and faintly the White Mountains, and others
more northeast; but above all, toward night, the Green
Mountains.

But what a study for rocks does this mountain-top
afford! The rocks of the pinnacle
have many regular nearly right-
angled slants to the southeast, covered with the dark-brown (or oli-
vaceous) umbilicaria. The rocks which you walk
over are often not only worn smooth and slippery,
but grooved out, as if with some huge rounded tool,
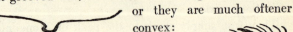 or they are much oftener
convex:
You see huge buttresses or walls
put up by Titans, with true joints,
only recently loosened by an earthquake as if ready to

topple down. Some of the lichen-clad rocks are of a rude brick-loaf form or small cottage form:
You see large boulders, left just on the edge of the steep descent of the plateau, commonly resting on a few small stones, as if the Titans were in the very act of transporting them when they were interrupted; some left standing on their ends, and almost the only convenient rocks in whose shade you can sit sometimes. Often you come to a long, thin rock, two or three rods long, which has the appearance of having just been split into underpinning-stone, — perfectly straight-edged and parallel pieces, and lying as it fell, ready for use, just as the mason leaves it. Post-stones, door-stones, etc. There were evidences of recent motion as well as ancient.

I saw on the flat sloping surface of rock a fresher white space exactly the size and form of a rock which was lying by it and which had lately covered it. What had upset it? There were many of these whitish marks where the dead spruce had lain but was now decayed or gone.

The rocks were not only coarsely grooved but finely scratched from northwest to southeast, commonly about S. 10° E. (but between 5° and 20° east, or, by the true meridian, more yet).[1] I could have steered myself in a fog by them.

Piles of stones left as they were split ready for the

[1] Hitchcock, p. 387, calls the rock of Monadnock granite, and says the scratches are north and south, nearly, and very striking. *Vide* three pages forward.

builder. I saw one perfect triangular hog-trough —

except that it wanted one end — and
which would have been quite portable and
convenient in a farmer's yard. The core,
four or five feet long, lay one side.

The rocks are very commonly in terraces with a
smooth rounded edge to each. The most remarkable
of these terraces that I noticed was between the second
camp and the summit, say some forty rods from the
camp. These terraces were some six rods long and six
to ten feet wide, but the top slanting considerably back
into the mountain, and they were about four or five feet
high each. There
were four such in
succession here,
running S. 30°
E. The edges of
these terraces, here and commonly, were rounded and
grooved like the rocks at a waterfall, as if water and
gravel had long washed over them.

Some rocks were   shaped like
huge doughnuts: The edges
of cliffs were frequently lumpishly rounded, covered with
lichens, so that you could not stand near the edge. The
extreme east and northeast parts of the plateau, especially near the little meadow, are the most interesting
for the forms of rocks. Sometimes you see where a
huge oblong square stone has been taken out from the
edge of a terrace, leaving a space which looks like a
giant's grave unoccupied.

On the west side the summit the strata ran north and

south and dipped to east about 60° with the horizon. There were broad veins of white quartz (sometimes one foot wide) running directly many rods.

Near the camp there was a succession of great rocks, their corners rounded semi-circularly and grooved at the same time like the capital of a column reversed. The most rugged walking is on the steep westerly slope.

We had a grand view, especially after sunset, as it grew dark, of the *sierra* of the summit's outline west of us, — the teeth of the sierra often turned back toward the summit, — when the rocks were uniformly black in the shade and seen against the twilight.

In Morse's Gazetteer (1797) it is said, "Its base is five miles in diameter north to south, and three from east to west. . . . Its summit is a bald rock." By the summit he meant the very topmost part, which, it seems, was always a "bald rock."

There were all over the rocky summit peculiar yellowish gravelly spots which I called scars, commonly of an oval form, not in low but elevated places, and looking as if a little mound had been cut off there.  The edges of these, on the very pinnacle of the mountain, were formed of the *Juncus trifidus*, now gone to seed. If they had been in hollows, you would have said that they were the bottom of little pools, now dried up, where the gravel and stones had been washed bare. I am not certain about their origin. They suggested some force which had suddenly cut off and washed or blown away the surface there, like a thunder-spout [*sic*], or lightning, or a hurricane. Such spots were very numerous, and had the appearance of a fresh scar.

Much, if not most, of the rock appears to be what Hitchcock describes and represents as graphic granite (*vide* his book, page 681).

Hitchcock says (page 389) that he learns from his assistant, Abraham Jenkins, Jr., that "on the sides of and around this mountain [Monadnock] [1] diluvial grooves and scratches are common; having a direction about N. 10° W. and S. 10° E. The summit of the mountain, which rises in an insulated manner to the height of 3250 feet, is a naked rock of gneiss of several acres in extent, and this is thoroughly grooved and scored. One groove measured fourteen feet in width, and two feet deep; and others are scarcely of less size. Their direction at the summit, by a mean of nearly thirty measurements with a compass, is nearly north and south."

According to Heywood's Gazetteer, the mountain is "talc, mica, slate, distinctly stratified," and is 3718 feet high.

Though there is little or no soil upon the rocks, owing apparently to the coolness, if not moisture, you have rather the vegetation of a swamp than that of sterile rocky ground below. For example, of the six prevailing trees and shrubs — low blueberry, black spruce, lamb-kill, black choke-berry, wild holly, and *Viburnum nudum* — all but the first are characteristic of swampy and low

[1] [The brackets are Thoreau's.]

ground, to say nothing of the commonness of wet mosses, the two species of cotton-grass, and some other plants of the swamp and meadow. Little meadows and swamps are scattered all over the mountain upon and amid the rocks. You are continually struck with the proximity of gray and lichen-clad rock and mossy bog. You tread alternately on wet moss, into which you sink, and dry, lichen-covered rocks. You will be surprised to see the vegetation of a swamp on a little shelf only a foot or two over, — a bog a foot wide with cotton-grass waving over it in the midst of cladonia lichens so dry as to burn like tinder. The edges of the little swamps — if not their middle — are commonly white with cotton-grass. The *Arenaria Grœnlandica* often belies its name here, growing in wet places as often as in dry ones, together with eriophorum.

One of the grandest views of the summit is from the east side of the central meadow of the plateau, which I called the Gulf, just beneath the pinnacle on the east, with the meadow in the foreground.

Water stands in shallow pools on almost every rocky shelf. The largest pool of open water which I found was on the southwest side of the summit, and was four rods long by fifteen to twenty feet in width and a foot deep. Wool- and cotton-grass grew around it, and there was a dark green moss and some mud at the bottom. There was a smoother similar pool on the next shelf above it. These were about the same size in June and in August, and apparently never dry up. There was also the one in which I bathed, near the northeast little meadow. I had a delicious bath there, though the water was warm, but there was a pleasant strong and drying wind blowing over the ridge, and when I had bathed, the rock felt like plush to my feet.

The cladonia lichens were so dry at midday, even the day after rain, that they served as tinder to kindle our fire, — indeed, we were somewhat troubled to prevent the fire from spreading amid them, — yet at night, even before sundown, and morning, when we got our supper and breakfast, they would not burn thus, having absorbed moisture. They had then a cool and slightly damp feeling.

Every evening, excepting, perhaps, the Sunday evening after the rain of the day before, we saw not long after sundown a slight scud or mist begin to strike the summit above us, though it was perfectly fair weather generally and there were no clouds over the lower country.

First, perhaps, looking up, we would see a small scud not more than a rod in diameter drifting just over the apex of the mountain. In a few minutes more a somewhat larger one would suddenly make its appearance, and perhaps strike the topmost rocks and invest them for a moment, but as rapidly drift off northeast and disappear. Looking into the southwest sky, which was clear, we would see all at once a small cloud or scud a rod in diameter beginning to form half a mile from the summit, and as it came on it rapidly grew in a mysterious manner, till it was fifty rods or more in diameter, and draped and concealed for a few moments all the summit above us, and then passed off and disappeared northeastward just as it had come on. So that it appeared as if the clouds had been attracted by the summit. They also seemed to rise a little as they approached it, and endeavor to go over without striking. I gave this account of it to myself. They were not attracted to the summit, but simply generated there and not elsewhere. There would be a warm southwest wind blowing which was full of moisture, alike over the mountain and all the rest of the country. The summit of the mountain being cool, this warm air began to feel its influence at half a mile distance, and its moisture was rapidly condensed into a small cloud, which expanded as it advanced, and evaporated again as it left the summit. This would go on, apparently, as the coolness of the mountain increased, and generally the cloud or mist reached down as low as our camp from time to time, in the night.

One evening, as I was watching these small clouds forming and dissolving about the summit of our mountain, the sun having just set, I cast my eyes toward the dim bluish outline of the Green Mountains in the clear red evening sky, and, to my delight, I detected exactly over the summit of Saddleback Mountain, some sixty miles distant, its own little cloud, shaped like a parasol and answering to that which capped our mountain, though in this case it did not rest on the mountain, but was considerably above it, and all the rest of the west horizon for forty miles was cloudless. I was convinced that it was the local cloud of that mountain because it was directly over the summit, was of small size and of umbrella form answering to the summit, and there was no other cloud to be seen in that horizon. It was a beautiful and serene object, a sort of fortunate isle, — like any other cloud in the sunset sky.

That the summit of this mountain is cool appears from the fact that the days which we spent there were remarkably warm ones in the country below, and were the common subject of conversation when we came down, yet we had known nothing about it, and went warmly clad with comfort all the while, as we had not done immediately before and did not after we descended. We immediately perceived the difference as we descended. It was warm enough for us on the summit, and often, in the sheltered southeast hollows, too warm, as we happened to be clad, but on the summits and ridges it chanced that there was always wind, and in this wind it was commonly cooler than we liked. Also our water, which was evidently rain-water caught in the rocks and retained by the moss, was cool enough if it were only in a little crevice under the shelter of a rock, *i. e.* out of the sun.

Yet, though it was thus cool, and there was this scud or mist on the top more or less every night, there was, as we should say, no dew on the summit any morning. The lichens, blueberry bushes, etc., did not feel wet, nor did they wet you in the least, however early you walked in them. I rose [?] to observe the sunrise and picked blueberries every morning before sunrise, and saw no dew, only once some minute dewdrops on some low grass-tips, and that was amid the wet moss of a little bog, but the lambkill and blueberry bushes above it were not wet. Yet the Thursday when we left, we found that though there was no dew on the summit there was a very heavy dew in the pastures below, and our feet and clothes were completely wet with it, as much as if we had stood in water.

I should say that there were no true springs (?) on the summit, but simply rain-water caught in the hollows of the rocks or retained by the moss. I observed that the well which we made for washing — by digging up the moss with our hands — half dried up in the sun by day, but filled up again at night.

The principal stream on the summit, — if not the only one, — in the rocky portion described, was on the south-east side, between our two camps, though it did not distinctly show itself at present except a little below our elevation. For the most part you could only see that water had flowed there between and under the rocks.

I fancied once or twice that it was warmer at 10 P. M. than it was immediately after sunset.

The voices of those climbing the summit were heard remarkably far. We heard much of the ordinary conversation of those climbing the peak above us a hundred rods off, and we could hear those on the summit, or a hundred and thirty rods off, when they shouted. I heard a party of ladies and gentlemen laughing and talking there in the night (they were camping there), though I did not hear what they said. We heard, or imagined that we heard, from time to time, as we lay in our camp by day, an occasional chinking or clinking sound as if made by one stone on another.

In clear weather, in going from one part of the summit to another it would be most convenient to steer by distant objects, as towns or mountains or lakes, rather

than by features of the summit itself, since the former are most easily recognized and almost always in
sight.

I saw what I took to be a thistle-down going low over
the summit, and might have caught it, though I saw no
thistle on the mountain-top nor any other plant from
which this could have come. (I have no doubt it was a
thistle by its appearance and its season.) It had evidently come up from the country below. This shows
that it may carry its seeds to higher regions than it
inhabits, and it suggests how the seeds of some mountain plants, as the *Solidago thyrsoidea*, may be conveyed
from mountain to mountain, also other solidagos, asters,
epilobiums, willows, etc.

The descent through the woods from our first camp
to the site of the shanty is from a third to half a mile.
You then come to the raspberry and fern scented region.
There were some raspberries still left, but they were fast
dropping off.

There was a good view of the mountain from just
above the pond, some two miles from Troy. The vary-
ing outline of a mountain is due to the crest of different
spurs, as seen from different sides. Even a small spur,
if you are near, may conceal a much larger one and
give its own outline to the·mountain, and at the same
time one which extends directly toward you is not
noticed at all, however important, though, as you travel
round the mountain, this may gradually come into view
and finally its crest may be one half or more of the outline presented. It may partly account for the peaked or
pyramidal form of mountains that one crest may be

seen through the gaps of another and so fill up the line.

Think I saw leersia or cut-grass in bloom in Troy.

I carried on this excursion the following articles (beside what I wore), *viz.* : —

One shirt.
One pair socks.
Two pocket-handkerchiefs.
One *thick* waistcoat.
One flannel shirt (had no occasion to use it).
India-rubber coat.
Three bosoms.
Towel and soap.
Pins, needles, thread.
A blanket (would have been more convenient if stitched up in the form of a bag).
Cap for the night.
Map and compass.
Spy-glass and microscope and tape.
Saw and hatchet.
Plant-book and blotting-paper.
Paper and stamps.
Botany.
Insect and lichen boxes.
Jack-knife.
Matches.
Waste paper and twine.
Iron spoon and pint dipper with handle.
    All in a knapsack.
Umbrella.

N. B. — Add to the above next time a small bag, which may be stuffed with moss or the like for a pillow.

For provision for one, six days, carried : —

2½ lbs. of salt beef and tongue.   Take only salt beef next time, 2 to 3 lbs.

18 hard-boiled eggs.	Omit eggs.
2½ lbs. sugar and a little salt.	2 lbs. of sugar would have done.
About ¼ lb. of tea.	⅔ as much would have done.
2 lbs. hard-bread.	The right amount of bread,
½ loaf home-made bread and a piece of cake.	but might have taken more home-made and more *solid* sweet cake.

N. B. — Carry salt (or some of it) in a wafer-box. Also some sugar in a small box.

N. B. — Observe next time: the source of the stream which crosses the path; what species of swallow flies over mountain; what the grass which gives the pastures a yellowish color seen from the summit.

The morning would probably never be ushered in there by the chipping of the chip-bird, but that of the *F. hyemalis* instead, — a dry, hard occasional chirp, more in harmony with the rocks. There you do not hear the *link* of the bobolink, the chatter of red-wings and crow blackbirds, the wood pewee, the twitter of the kingbird, the half [*sic*] strains of the vireo, the passing goldfinch, or the occasional plaintive note of the blue-bird, all which are now commonly heard in the lowlands.

That area is literally a chaos, an example of what the earth was before it was finished.[1]

Do I not hear the mole cricket at night?

Aug. 10. 2 p. m. — Air, 84°; Boiling Spring this afternoon., 46°; Brister's, 49°; or where there is little or no

[1] *Vide* Aug. 26 and 28, and Sept. 1.

surface water the same as in spring. Walden is at surface 80° (air over it 76).

Aster dumosus and pennyroyal out; how long? Sand cherry is well ripe — some of it — and tolerable, better than the red cherry or choke-cherry. *Juncus paradoxus*, that large and late juncus (tailed), as in Hubbard's Close and on island above monument and in Great Meadows, say ten days.

Saw yesterday in Fitzwilliam from the railroad a pond covered with white lilies uniformly about half the size of ours!

Saw this evening, behind a picture in R. W. E.'s dining-room, the hoary bat. First heard it fluttering at dusk, it having hung there all day. Its rear parts covered with a fine hoary down.

Aug. 11. *Panicum capillare;* how long? *Cyperus strigosus;* how long?

Aug. 12. The river-bank is past height. The button-bush is not common now, though the clethra is in prime. The black willow hardly ceases to shed its down when it looks yellowish. *Setaria glauca*, some days. *Elymus Virginicus*, some days. *Andropogon furcatus* (in meadow); how long? Probably before *scoparius.* Zizania several days.

River at 5 p. m. three and three quarters inches below summer level.

Panicum glabrum (not *sanguinale?* — our common); how long? The upper glume equals the flower, yet it has many spikes.

Aug. 13. P. M. — To Great Meadows and Gowing's Swamp.

Purple grass (*Eragrostis pectinacea*), two or three days. *E. capillaris*, say as much. *Andropogon scoparius*, a day or two. *Calamagrostis coarctata*, not quite. *Glyceria obtusa*, well out; say several days.

Some of the little cranberries at Gowing's Swamp appear to have been frost-bitten. Also the blue-eyed grass, which is now black-topped.

Hear the steady shrill of the alder locust.

Rain this forenoon; windy in afternoon.

Aug. 14. Heavy rain.

Aug. 15. Fair weather.

See a blue heron.

Aug. 16. 2 P. M. — River about ten and a half inches above summer level.

Apparently the Canada plum began to be ripe about the 10th.

Aug. 17. We have cooler nights of late.

See at Pout's Nest two solitary tattlers, as I have seen them about the muddy shore of Gourgas Pond-hole and in the Great Meadow pools. They seem to like a muddier shore than the peetweet.

Hear a whip-poor-will sing to-night.

Aug. 18. The note of the wood pewee sounds prominent of late.

Aug. 19. Examine now more at length that smooth, turnip-scented brassica which is a pest in some grain-fields. Formerly in Stow's land; this year in Warren's, on the Walden road. To-day I see it in Minot Pratt's, with the wild radish, which is a paler yellow and a rougher plant. I thought it before the *B. campestris*, but Persoon puts that under brassicas with *siliquis tetraedris*, which this is not, but, for aught that appears, it agrees with his *B. Napus*, closely allied, *i. e.* wild rape. Elliot speaks of this as introduced here. *Vide* Patent Office Report for 1853 and "Vegetable Kingdom," page 179. The *B. campestris* also is called rape.[1]

Leersia (cut-grass) abundantly out, apparently several days.

Aug. 21. Soaking rains, and in the night.
A few fireflies still at night.

Aug. 22. P. M. — Row to Bittern Cliff.
Now, when the mikania is conspicuous, the bank is past prime,[2] for lilies are far gone, the pontederia is past prime, willows and button-bushes begin to look the worse for the wear thus early, — the lower or older leaves of the willows are turned yellow and decaying, — and many of the meadows are shorn. Yet now is the time for the cardinal-flower. The already, *methinks*, yellow-ing willows and button-bushes, the half-shorn meadows, the higher water on their edges, with wool-grass stand-ing over it, with the notes of flitting bobolinks and red-wings of *this year*, in rustling flocks, all tell of the fall.

[1] *Vide* Sept. 8.   [2] *Vide* Sept. 5.

I hear two or three times behind me the loud *creaking* note of a wood duck which I have scared up, which goes to settle in a new place.

Some deciduous trees are now at least as dark as evergreens, the alders are darker than white pines, and as dark as pitch, as I now see them.

I try the temperature of the river at Bittern Cliff, the deep place. The air over river at 4.30 is 81°; the water at the top, 78°; poured from a bottle (into a dipper) which I let lie on the bottom half an hour, 73°, — or 5° difference. When I merely sunk the thermometer and pulled it up rapidly it stood 73½, though not in exactly the same place, — say two rods off.

When I used to pick the berries for dinner on the East Quarter hills I did not eat one till I had done, for going a-berrying implies more things than eating the berries. They at home got only the pudding: I got the forenoon out of doors, and the appetite for the pudding.

It is true, as is said, that we have as good a right to make berries private property as to make grass and trees such; but what I chiefly regret is the, in effect, dog-in-the-manger result, for at the same time that we exclude mankind from gathering berries in our field, we exclude them from gathering health and happiness and inspiration and a hundred other far finer and nobler fruits than berries, which yet we shall not gather ourselves there, nor even carry to market. We strike only one more blow at a simple and wholesome relation to nature. As long as the berries are free to all comers they are beautiful, though they may be few and small, but tell me that is a blueberry swamp which somebody has hired, and I shall not want even to look at it. In laying claim for the first time to the spontaneous fruit of our pastures we are, accordingly, aware of a little meanness inevitably, and the gay berry party whom we turn away naturally look down on and despise us. If it were left to the berries to say who should have them, is it not likely that they would prefer to be gathered by the party of children in the hay-rigging, who have come to have a good time merely?

I do not see clearly that these successive losses are ever quite made up to us. This is one of the taxes which we pay for having a railroad. Almost all our improvements, so called, tend to convert the country into the town.

This suggests what origin and foundation many of our laws and institutions have, and I do not say this by way of complaining of this particular custom. Not that I love Cæsar less, but Rome more.

Yes, and a potato-field is a rich sight to me, even when the vines are half decayed and blackened and their decaying scent fills the air, though unsightly to many; for it speaks then more loudly and distinctly of potatoes than ever. I see their weather-beaten brows peeping out of the hills here and there, for the earth cannot contain them, when the creak of the cricket and the shrilling of the locust prevail more and more, in the sunny end of summer. There the confident husbandman lets them lie for the present, even as if he knew not of them, or as if that property were insured, so carelessly rich he is. He relaxes now his labors somewhat, seeing to their successful end, and takes long mornings, perchance, stretched in the shade of his ancestral elms.

Returning down the river, when I get to Clamshell I see great flocks of the young red-wings and some crow blackbirds on the trees and the ground. They are not very shy, but only timid, as inexperienced birds are. I do not know what they find to eat on this half bare, half grassy bank, but there they hop about by hundreds, while as many more are perched on the neighboring trees; and from time to time they all rise from the earth and wheel and withdraw to the trees, but soon return to the ground again. The red-wings are almost reddish about the throat. The crow blackbirds have some notes now just like the first croaks of the wood frog in the spring.

Sorghum nutans well out (behind the birch); how long? Paspalum ditto.

The recent heavy rains have washed away the bank here considerably, and it looks and smells more mouldy with human relics than ever. I therefore find myself inevitably exploring it. On the edge of the ravine whose beginning I witnessed, one foot beneath the surface and just over a layer some three inches thick of pure shells and ashes, — a gray-white line on the face of the cliff. — I find several pieces of Indian pottery with a rude orna-ment on it, not much more red than the earth itself. Looking farther, I find more fragments, which have been washed down the sandy slope in a stream, as far as ten feet. I find in all thirty-one pieces, averaging an inch in diameter and about a third of an inch thick. Several of them made part of the upper edge of the vessel, and have a rude ornament encircling them in three rows, as if pricked with a stick in the soft clay, and also another line on the narrow edge itself. At first I thought to match the pieces again, like a geographical puzzle, but I did not find that any I [got] belonged together. The vessel must have been quite large, and I have not got nearly all of it. It appears to have been an impure clay with much sand and gravel in it, and I think a little pounded shell. It is [of] very unequal thickness, some of the unadorned pieces (probably the bottom) being half an inch thick, while near the edge it is not more than a quarter of an inch thick. There was under this spot and under the layer of shells a manifest hollowness in the ground, not yet filled up. I find many small pieces of bone in the soil of this bank, probably of animals the Indians ate.

In another bank, in the larger heap of been exposed, delicate stone form and size: stone. It is very on each side the middle is an eighth of an suspect that this open clams with.

It is curious pected to find and in this very I reached it (I Indeed, I never

part of the midst of a much shells which has I found a tool of this of a soft slate- thin and sharp edge, and in not more than inch thick. I was used to

that I had ex- as much as this, spot too, before mean the pot). find a remarkable Indian relic — and I find a good many — but I have first divined its existence, and planned the discovery of it. Frequently I have told myself distinctly what it was to be before I found it.

The river is fifteen and three quarters inches above summer level.[1]

Aug. 24. This and yesterday very foggy, dogdayish days. Yesterday the fog lasted till nine or ten, and to-day, in the afternoon, it amounts to a considerable drizzling rain.

P. M. — To Walden to get its temperature. The air is only 66 (in the mizzling rain the 23d it was 78); the water at top, 75° (the 23d also 75). What I had sunk to the bottom in the middle, where a hundred feet deep by my line, left there half an hour, then pulled up and poured into a quart dipper, stood at 53°.[2] I tried the same experiment yesterday, but then in my haste was uncertain whether it was not 51°; certain that a little later it was 54°. So 53° it must be for the present. I may have been two or more minutes pulling up the line so as to prevent its snarling. Therefore I think the water must have acquired a temperature two or three degrees higher than it had at the bottom by the time I tried it. So it appears that the bottom of Walden has, in fact, the temperature of a genuine and cold spring, or probably is of the same temperature with the average mean temperature of the earth, and, I *suspect*, the same all the year. This shows that springs need not come from a very great depth in order to be cold. What various tem-

[1] And about the same the 25th.   [2] *Vide* 28th.

peratures, then, the fishes of this pond can enjoy! They require no other refrigerator than their deeps afford. They can in a few moments sink to winter or rise to summer. Walden, then, must be included among the springs, but it is one which has no outlet, — is a well rather. It reaches down to where the temperature of the earth is unchanging. It is not a superficial pond, — not in the mere skin of the earth. It goes deeper. How much this varied temperature must have to do with the distribution of the fishes in it! The few trout must oftenest go down below in summer.

At the bottom of the deep cove I see much black birch and red maple just sprung up, and their seeds have evidently been drifted to this shore. The little birches are already fragrant.

Aug. 25. 2 P. M. — To Clamshell.

See a large hen-hawk sailing over Hubbard's meadow and Clamshell, soaring at last very high and toward the north. At last it returns southward, at that height impelling itself steadily and swiftly forward with its wings set in this wise: *i. e.* more curved, or, as it were, trailing behind, without apparent motion. It thus moves half a mile directly.

The front-rank polygonum is apparently in prime; low, solid, of a pinkish rose-color. Notice the small botrychium's leaf.

As I row by, see a green bittern near by standing erect on Monroe's boat. Finding that it is observed, it draws in its head and stoops to conceal itself. When it flies it seems to have no tail. It allowed me to approach so

near, apparently being deceived by some tame ducks
there.

Aug. 26. 2 p. m. — To White Pond.

The leersia or cut-grass in the old pad ditch by path
beyond Hubbard's Grove.

As I cross the upland sprout-land south of Ledum
Swamp, I see that the fine sedge there is half withered
and brown, and it is too late for that cheerful yellow
gleam.

Thread my way through the blueberry swamp in front
of Martial Miles's. The high blueberries far above your
head in the shade of the swamp retain their freshness
and coolness a long time. Little blue sacks full of swampy
nectar and ambrosia commingled, like schnapps or
what-not, that you break with your teeth. Is not this
the origin of the German name as given by Gerard? But
there is far the greatest show of choke-berries there, rich
to see. I wade and press my way through endless thickets of these untasted berries, their lower leaves now fast
reddening. Yet they have an agreeable juice, — though
the pulp may be rejected, — and perhaps they might be
made into wine.

The shrilling of the alder locust is the solder that welds
these autumn days together. All bushes (*arbusta*)
resound with their song, and you wade up to your ears
in it. Methinks the burden of their song is the countless
harvests of the year, — berries, grain, and other fruits.

I am interested by the little ridge or cliff of foam
which the breeze has raised along the White Pond shore,
the westerly breeze causing the wavelets to lapse on the

shore and mix the water with the air gradually. Though this is named *White* Pond from the whiteness of its sandy shore, the line of foam is infinitely whiter, far whiter than any sand. This reminds me how far a white pond-shore, *i. e.* the sand, may be seen. I saw from Monadnock the north shore of a large pond in Nelson which was some eight miles north by the map, very distinct to every one who looked that way. Perhaps in such cases a stronger light is reflected from the water on to the shore. The highest ridge of foam is where it is held or retained and so built up gradually behind some brush or log on the shore, by additions below, into a little cliff, like a sponge. In other places it is rolled like a muff. It is all light and trembling in the air.

Thus we are amused with foam, a hybrid between two elements. A breeze comes and gradually mingles some of the water with the air. It is, as it were, the aspiration of the pond to soar into the air. The debatable ground between two oceans, the earth, or shore, being only the point of resistance, where they are held to mingle.

See nowadays the pretty little Castile-soap galls on the shrub oaks. Their figure is like the Indian girdle of triangular points. Also other galls, yellowish and red on dif- ferent sides.

The pussy clover heads were most interesting, large, and puffy, say ten days ago.

I notice milkweed in a hollow in the field by the cove at White Pond, as if the seed had settled there, owing to the lull of the wind.

It is remarkable how commonly you see the thistle-down sailing just over water (as I do after this — the 2d of September — at Walden). I see there, *i. e.* at Walden, at 5 p. m., September 2d, many seedless thistle-downs sailing about a foot above the water, and some in it, as if there was a current just above the surface which prevented their falling or rising. They are probably wafted to the water because there is more air over water.

Aug. 27. P. M. — To Ministerial Swamp.

Clear weather within a day or two after the thick dog-days. The nights have been cooler of late, but the heat of the sun by day has been more local and palpable, as it were. It is as if the sun touched your shoulder with a hot hand while there are cool veins in the air. That is, I am from time to time surprised and oppressed by a melting heat on my back in the sun, though I am sure of a greater general coolness. The heat is less like that of an apartment equably warmed, and more like that [of] a red-hot iron carried about and which you occasionally come near.

See one of the shrilling green alder locusts on the under side of a grape leaf. Its body is about three quarters of an inch or less in length; antennæ and all, two inches. Its wings are at first perpendicular above its shoulders, it apparently having just ceased shrilling. Transparent, with lines crossing them.

Notice now that sour-tasting white (creamy, for consistence) incrustation between and on the berries of the smooth sumach, like frostwork. Is it not an exudation? or produced by the bite of an insect?

Calamagrostis coarctata grass by Harrington's Pool, Ministerial Swamp, say one week (not in prime).

Muhlenbergia glomerata, same place, say ten days, or past prime.

Gather some of those large and late low blackberries (as at Thrush Alley) which run over the thin herbage, green moss, etc., in open pitch pine woods.

Aug. 28. About 6.20 P. M. paddled on Walden. Near the shore I see at least one little skater to a foot, further off one to a yard, and in middle not more than one to a rod; but I see no gyrinus at all here to-night. At first the sky was completely overcast, but, just before setting, the sun came out into a clear space in the horizon and fell on the east end of the pond and the hillside, and this sudden blaze of light on the still very fresh green leaves was a wonderful contrast with the previous and still surrounding darkness. Indeed, the bright sunlight was at this angle reflected from the water at the east end — while I in the middle was in the shade of the east woods — up under the verdure of the bushes and trees on the shore and on Pine Hill, especially to the tender under sides and to the lower leaves not often lit up. Thus a double amount of light fell on them, and the most vivid and varied shades of green were revealed. I never saw such a green *glow* before. The outline of each shrub and tree was a more or less distinct downy or silvery crescent, where the light was reflected from the under side of the most downy, or newest, leaves, — as I should not have seen it at midday, — either because the light fell more on the under sides of the leaves, being so horizontal and also reflected upward, or because the leaves stood more erect at this hour and after a cloudy day, or for both reasons. The lit water at the east end was invisible to me, or no more than a line, but the shore itself was a very distinct whitish line. When the sun fell lower, and the sunlight no longer fell on the pond, the green blaze of the hillside was at once very much diminished, because the light was no longer reflected upward to it.

At sunset the air over the pond is 62 + ; the water at the top, 74°; poured from a stoppled bottle which lay at the bottom where one hundred feet deep, twenty or thirty minutes, 55° (and the same when drawn up in an open bottle which lay five minutes at the bottom); in an open bottle drawn up from about fifty feet depth (*there*) or more, after staying there five minutes, 63°. This about half the whole difference between the top and bottom, so that the temperature seems to fall regularly as you descend, at the rate of about one degree to five feet. When I let the stoppled bottle down *quickly*, the cork was forced out before it got to the bottom, when [?] the water drawn up stood at 66°. Hence it seemed to be owing to the rising of the warmer water and air in the bottle. Five minutes with the open bottle at the bottom was as good as twenty with it stoppled.

I found it 2° warmer than the 24th, though the air was then 4° warmer than now. Possibly, comparing one day with the next, it is warmer at the bottom in a cold day and colder in a warm day, because when the surface is cooled it mixes more with the bottom, while the average temperature is very slightly changed.

The *Lycopodium inundatum* common by Harrington's mud-hole, Ministerial Swamp.

Hear the night-warbler and whip-poor-will.

There was no prolonged melody of birds on the summit of Monadnock. They for the most part emitted sounds there more in harmony with the silent rocks, — a faint chipping or *chink*ing, often somewhat as of two stones struck together.

Aug. 30. Surveying Minott's land.

Am surprised to find on his hard land, where he once raised potatoes, the hairy huckleberry, which before I had seen in swamps only. Here, too, they are more edible, not so insipid, yet not quite edible generally. They are improved, you would say, by the firmer ground. The berries are in longer racemes or clusters than any of our huckleberries. They are the prevailing berry all over this field. They are oblong and black, and the thick, shaggy-feeling coats left in the mouth are far from agreeable to the palate. Are now in prime.

Also find, in one of his ditches where peat was dug (or mud), the *Lemna polyrhiza;* not found in Concord before, and said not to blossom in this country. I found it at Pushaw. Also the *Muhlenbergia glomerata* near the lemna, or southeast of it.

The hairy huckleberry and muhlenbergia, I think, grow here still because Minott is an old-fashioned man and has not scrubbed up and improved his land as many, or most, have. It is in a wilder and more primitive condition. The very huckleberries are shaggy there. There was only one straight side to his land, and that I cut through a dense swamp. The fences are all meandering, just as they were at least in 1746, when it was described.

The lemna reminds me strongly of that greenish or yellowish scum which I see mantling some barn-yard pools. It makes the same impression on the eye at a little distance. You would say it was the next higher stage of vegetation. The smallest of *pads*, one sixth of an inch in diameter and, like the white lily pad, crimson beneath. It completely covers two or three ditches under the edge of the wood there, except where a frog has jumped in and revealed the dark water, — and maybe there rests, his green snout concealed amid it; but it soon closes over him again when he has dived. These minute green scales completely cover some ditches, except where a careless frog has leapt in or swam across, and rent the veil.

There is also, floating in little masses, a small ranunculus-like plant, flattish-stemmed with small forks, some of it made into minute caddis-cases. Perhaps it was cut up by some creature at the bottom. *Vide* press.

II

SEPTEMBER, 1860

(ÆT. 43)

Sept. 1. P. M. — To Walden.

Saw a fish hawk yesterday up the Assabet. In one position it flew just like a swallow; of the same form as it flew.

We could not judge correctly of distances on the mountain, but greatly exaggerated them. That surface was so novel, — suggested so many thoughts, — and also so uneven, a few steps sufficing to conceal the least ground, as if it were half a mile away, that we would have an impression as if we had travelled a mile when we had come only forty rods. We no longer thought and reasoned as in the plain.

Now see many birds about E. Hubbard's elder hedge, — bobolinks, kingbirds, pigeon woodpeckers, — and not elsewhere.

Many pine stipules fallen yesterday. Also see them on Walden to-day.

Hear that F. Hayden saw and heard geese a fortnight ago!

I see within an oak stump on the shore of Walden tomato plants six or eight inches high, as I found them formerly about this pond in a different place. Since they do not bear fruit the seed must be annually brought here by birds, yet I do not see them pecking the tomatoes in our gardens, and this is a mile and a half from the village and half a mile from the nearest house in Lincoln.

River about eight inches above summer level yesterday.

We are so accustomed to see another forest spring up immediately as a matter of course, whether from the stump or from the seed, when a forest is cut down, never troubling about the succession, that we hardly associate the seed with the tree, and do not anticipate the time when this regular succession will cease and we shall be obliged to plant, as they do in all old countries. The planters of Europe must have a very different, a much correcter, notion of the value of the seed of forest trees than we. To speak generally, they know that the forest trees spring from seeds, as we do of apples and pears, but we know only that they come out of the earth.

See how artfully the seed of a cherry is placed in order that a bird may be compelled to transport it. It is placed in the very midst of a tempting pericarp, so that the creature that would devour a cherry must take a stone into its mouth. The bird is bribed with the pericarp to take the stone with it and do this little service for Nature. Cherries are especially birds' food, and many kinds are called birds' cherry, and unless we plant the seeds occasionally, I shall think the birds have the best right to them. Thus a bird's wing is added to the cherry-stone which was wingless, and it does not wait for winds to transport it. If you ever ate a cherry, and did not make two bites of it, you must have perceived it. There it is, right in the midst of the luscious morsel,

an earthy residuum left on the tongue. And some wild
men and children instinctively swallow it, like the birds,
as the shortest way to get rid of it. And the consequence is that cherries not only grow here but there, and
I know of some handsome young English cherries
growing naturally in our woods, which I think of trans-
planting back again to my garden. If the seed had been
placed in a leaf, or at the root, it would not have got
transported thus. Consider how many seeds of plants
we take into our mouths. Even stones as big as peas, a
dozen at once.

The treatment of forests is a very different question
to us and to the English. There is a great difference
between replanting the cleared land from the super-
abundance of seed which is produced in the forest around
it, which will soon be done by nature alone if we do not
interfere, and the planting of land the greater part of
which has been cleared for more than a thousand years.

Sept. 2. P. M. — To Annursnack.

Solidago nemoralis apparently in prime, and *S. stricta.*
The former covers A. Hosmer's secluded turtle field
near the bridge, together with johnswort, now merely
lingering.

Sept. 3. P. M. — To Bateman's Pond.

2 P. M. — River six and seven eighths above [sum-
mer level].

Here is a beautiful, and perhaps *first* decidedly
autumnal, day, — a cloudless sky, a clear air, with,

[1] [*Excursions*, p. 188; Riv. 230, 231.]

maybe, veins of coolness. As you look toward the sun, the [*sic*] shines more than in the spring. The dense fresh green grass which has sprung up since it was mowed, on most ground, reflects a blaze of light, as if it were morning all the day. The meads and slopes are enamelled with it, for there has been no drought nor withering. We see the smokes of burnings on various sides. The farmers are thus clearing up their pastures, — some, it may be, in preparation for plowing. Though it is warm enough, I notice again the swarms of fuzzy gnats dancing in the cooler air, which also is decidedly autumnal.

See on the two pear trees by the Boze cellar ripe pears, some ripe several days. Most are bitter, others mealy, but one was quite sweet and good, of middling size, and prettier than most cultivated ones. It had a few faint streaks of red and was exceeding wax-like.

Sept. 4. P. M. — To Conantum.

At my Swamp Brook crossing at Willow Bay, I see where a great many little red maples have sprung up in a potato-field, apparently since the last plowing or cultivating this year. They extend more or less thickly as much as eleven rods in a northwest direction from a small tree, the only red maple in that neighborhood. And it is evidently owing to the land having been cultivated this year that the seed vegetated there; otherwise there would now be no evidence that any such seeds had fallen here. Last year and for many years it has been a pasture. It is evident that land may be kept as a pasture and covered with grass any number of years, and though there are maples adjacent to it, none of the seed will catch in it; but at last it is plowed, and this year the seed which falls on it germinates, and if it chances not to be plowed again, and cattle are kept out, you soon have a maple wood there. So of other light-seeded trees.

It is cooler these days and nights, and I move into an eastern chamber in the morning, that I may sit in the sun. The water, too, is cooler when I bathe in it, and I am reminded that this recreation has its period. I feel like a melon or other fruit laid in the sun to ripen. I grow, not gray, but yellow.

Saw flocks of pigeons the 2d and 3d. I see and hear on Conantum an upland plover. The goldfinch is very busy pulling the thistle to pieces.

What I have called *Muhlenbergia sobolifera* is in prime (say a week); the *M. Mexicana* not quite (say in two or three days).

Sept. 5. P. M. — To Ball's Hill.

The brink of the river [1] is still quite interesting in some respects, and to some eyes more interesting than ever. Though the willows and button-bushes have already assumed an autumnal hue, and the pontederia is extensively crisped and blackened, the dense masses of mikania, now, it may be, paler than before, are perhaps more remarkable than ever. I see some masses of it, overhanging the deep water and completely conceal-ing the bush that supports them, which are as rich a sight as any flower we have, — little terraces of contigu-ous corymbs, like mignonette (?). Also the dodder is

[1] *Vide* Aug. 22d.

more revealed, also draping the brink over the water. The mikania is sometimes looped seven or eight feet high to a tree above the bushes, — a manifest vine, with its light-colored corymbs at intervals.

See the little dippers back. Did I not see a marsh hawk in imperfect plumage? Quite brown, with some white midway the wings, and tips of wings black?

What further adds to the beauty of the bank is the hibiscus, in prime, and the great bidens.

Having walked through a quantity of desmodium under Ball's Hill, by the shore there (*Marilandicum* or *rigidum*), we found our pants covered with its seeds to a remarkable and amusing degree. These green scales closely covering and greening my legs reminded me of the lemna on a ditch. It amounted to a kind of coat of mail. It was the event of our walk, and we were proud to wear this badge, as if he were the most distinguished who had the most on his clothes. My companion expressed a certain superstitious feeling about it, for he said he thought it would not be right to walk intentionally amid the desmodium so as to get more of the ticks on us, nor yet to pick them off, but they must be carried about till they are rubbed off accidentally. I saw that Nature's design was furthered even by his superstition.

Sept. 6. The willows and button-bushes have very rapidly yellowed since I noticed them August 22d. I think it was the 25th of August that I found the lower or older leaves of the willow twigs decidedly and rapidly yellowing and decaying on a near inspection. Now the change is conspicuous at a distance.

Sept. 7. P. M. — To Cardinal Shore.

I see many seedling shrub oaks springing up in
Potter's field by the swamp-side, some (of last year) in
the open pasture, but many more in the birch wood half a
dozen rods west from the shrub oaks by the path. The
former were dropped by the way. They plant in birch
woods as in pines. This small birch wood has been a
retreat for squirrels and birds. When I examine the
little oaks in the *open* land there is always an effete acorn
with them.

Common rose hips as handsome as ever.

Sept. 8. To Lowell *via* Boston.

Rainy day.

Pursh's [*sic*] [1] *Brassica Napus* is "radice caulescente
fusiformi, fol. laevibus, superioribus cordato-lanceolatis
amplexicaulibus, inferioribus lyratis dentatis." Frequently found wild. The lower leaves of mine are considerably bristly. Sowerby's Botany at Cambridge says
of *B. campestris*, "Pods upright, cylindrical, or very
obscurely quadrangular, veiny, the seeds slightly projecting, the beak awl-shaped, striated, square at its
base." *B. Napus*, — "Pod on a slender stalk, spreading, round, beaded, with an angular point." Mine is
apparently *B. Napus*, judging from pods, for the lower
leaves are all eaten. *Vide* young plants in spring. [2]

Sept. 9. In Lowell. — My host says that the thermometer was at 80° yesterday morning, and this morning is at 52°. Sudden coolness.

[1] [The quotation is from Persoon's *Synopsis Plantarum.*]

[2] *Vide* back, Aug. 19th.

Clears up in afternoon, and I walk down the Merrimack on the north bank. I see very large plants of the lanceolate thistle, four feet high and very branching. Also *Aster cordata* with the *corymbosus*.

Concord River has a high and hard bank at its mouth, maybe thirty feet high on the east side; and my host thinks it was originally about as high on the west side, where now it is much lower and flat, having been dug down. There is a small isle in the middle of the mouth. There are rips in the Merrimack just below the mouth of the Concord. There is a fall and dam in the Concord at what was Hurd's factory, — the principal fall on the Concord, in Lowell, — one at a bleachery above, and at Whipple's, — three in all below Billerica dam.

Sept. 10. Lowell to Boston and Concord.

There was a frost this morning, as my host, who keeps a market, informed me.

Leaving Lowell at 7 A. M. in the cars, I observed and admired the dew on a fine grass in the meadows, which was almost as white and silvery as frost when the rays of the newly risen sun fell on it. Some of it *was* probably the frost of the morning melted. I saw that this phenomenon was confined to one species of grass, which grew in narrow curving lines and small patches along the edges of the meadows or lowest ground, — a grass with very fine stems and branches, which held the dew; in short, that it was what I had falsely called *Eragrostis capillaris*, but which is probably the *Sporobolus serotinus*, almost the only, if not the only, grass there in its prime. And thus this plant has its day. Owing to the number of its very fine branches, now in their prime, it holds the dew like a cobweb, — a clear drop at the end and lesser drops or beads all along the fine branches and stems. It grows on the higher parts of the meadows, where other herbage is thin, and is the less apt to be cut; and, seen toward the sun not long after sunrise, it is very conspicuous and bright a quarter of a mile off, like frostwork. Call it dew-grass. I find its *hyaline* seed.[1]

Almost every plant, however humble, has thus its day, and sooner or later becomes the characteristic feature of some part of the landscape or other.

Almost all other grasses are now either cut or withering, and are, beside, so coarse comparatively that they can never present this phenomenon. It is only a grass that is in its full vigor, as well as fine-branched (capillary), that can thus attract and uphold the dew. This is noticed about the time the first frosts come.

If you sit at an open attic window almost anywhere, about the 20th of September, you will see many a milkweed down go sailing by on a level with you, — though commonly it has lost its freight, — notwithstanding that you may not know of any of these plants growing in your neighborhood.

My host, yesterday, told me that he was accustomed once to chase a *black* fox [2] from Lowell over this way and lost him at Chelmsford. Had heard of him within about six years. A Carlisle man also tells me since that this fox used to turn off and run northwest from Chelmsford, but that he would soon after return.

---

[1] Also saw it the 16th.

[2] Like the silver, made a variety of the red by Baird.

Sept. 11. George Melvin came to tell me this fore-noon that a strange animal was killed on Sunday, the 9th, near the north line of the town, and it was not known certainly what it was. From his description I judged it to be a Canada lynx. In the afternoon I went to see it. It was killed on Sunday morning by John Quincy Adams, who lives in Carlisle about half a mile (or less) from the Concord line, on the Carlisle road.

Some weeks ago a little girl named Buttrick, who was huckleberrying near where the lynx was killed, was frightened by a wild animal leaping out of the bushes near her — *over* her, as she said — and bounding off. But no one then regarded her story. Also a Mr. Grimes, who lives in Concord just on the line, tells me that some month ago he heard from his house the loud cry of an animal in the woods northward, and told his wife that if he were in Canada he should say it was a bob-tailed cat. He had lived seven years in Canada and seen a number of this kind of animal. Also a neighbor of his, riding home in the night, had heard a similar cry. Jacob Farmer saw a strange animal at Bateman's Pond a year ago, which he thinks was this.

Adams had lost some of his hens, and had referred it to a fox or the like. He being out, his son told me that on Sunday he went out with his gun to look after the depredator, and some forty or fifty rods from his house northwesterly [1] (on Dr. Jones's lot, which I surveyed) in the woods, this animal suddenly dropped within two feet of him, so near that he could not fire. He had heard a loud hiss, but did not mind it. He accordingly struck

[1] *Vide* forward.

it with the butt of his gun, and it then bounded off
fifteen feet [1] or more, turned about, and faced him,
whereupon he fired directly into its eyes, putting them
out. His gun was loaded with small shot, No. 9. The
creature then bounded out of sight, and he had a chance
to reload, by which time it appeared again, crawling
toward him on its belly, fiercely seeking him. He fired
again, and, it still facing him, he fired a third time also,
and finally finished it with the butt of his gun.

It was now skinned and the skin stuffed with hay, and
the skull had been boiled, in order to be put into the
head.

I measured the stuffed skin carefully. From the forehead (the nose pointing down) to end of tail, 3 feet 4½
[inches]. Tail stout and black at the abrupt end,
5 inches. Extreme length from fore paws to hind paws,
4 feet 8 inches, when stretched out, the skin being *stiff*.
(They said it measured 5 feet before it was skinned,
which is quite likely.) Forehead to extremity of hind
feet, 50½ inches. It stood, as nearly as I could measure,
holding it up, 19 to 20 inches high from ground to
shoulder. From midway between the legs beneath, the
hind legs measured 19 inches, within; the fore legs, 16
inches, within. From skull to end of tuft on ear, 4½
inches; tuft on ear (black and thin), 1½ inches. The
width of fore paw gently pressed was 3½ inches; would
have made a track perhaps four inches wide in snow.
There was a small *bare* brown tubercle of flesh to each toe,
and also a larger one for the sole, amid the grayish-white

---

[1] Another says he told him thirty feet and that they went and
measured it. *Vide* forward.

hair. A principal claw was ¾ inch long measured directly, but it was very curving.

For color: It was, above, brownish-gray, with a dark-brown or black line down the middle of the back. Sides gray, with small dark-brown spots, more or less within the hair. Beneath, lighter, *hoary*, and long-haired. Legs gray, like the sides, but more reddish-brown behind, especially the hind legs, and these, like the belly and sides, were indistinctly spotted with dark brown, having the effect more of a dark-brown tinge at a little distance than of spots. General aspect brownish-hoary. Tail, above, more reddish than rest of back, much, and conspicuously black at end. Did not notice any white at tip. Throat pretty white. Ears, without, broadly edged with black half an inch or more wide, the rest being a triangular white. There was but a small muffler, chiefly a triangular whitish and blackish tuft on the sides of the face or neck, not noticeably under the chin.

It weighed, by their account, nineteen pounds. This was a female, and Farmer judged from his examination of the mammæ — two or more of them being enlarged, and the hair worn off around them — that it had suckled young this year. The fur was good for nothing now.

I cannot doubt that this is a Canada lynx; yet I am somewhat puzzled by the descriptions of the two lynxes. Emmons says of the Canada lynx that it has " no naked spots or tubercles [on the soles of its feet] like the other species of the feline race;" and Audubon says, "Soles, hairy;" but of the *Lynx rufus*, "Soles . . . naked." It is Audubon's *L. rufus* in the naked soles, also in "ears, outer surface, a triangular spot of dull white, . . . bordered with brownish-black," not described in his *Canadensis*. It is his *L. Canadensis* in size, in color generally, in length of ear-tuft (his *L. rufus* tufts being only half an inch), in "upper surface of the tail, to within an inch of the tip, and exterior portion of the thighs, rufous," in tail being stout, not "slender" like *rufus*. Audubon says that the *L. rufus* is easily distinguished from small specimens of the female *L. Canadensis* by "the larger feet and more tufted ears of the latter, . . . as well as its grayer color." This is four inches longer than his smaller Canada lynx and exactly as long as his larger one, — both his being males. Emmons's one is also just 37 inches, or the same length. Emmons's largest *L. rufus* is, thus measured, only 29 inches long and Audubon's "fine specimen" only 30 inches.

Grimes, who had lived seven years in Canada, called this a "bob-tailed cat," and said that the Canada lynx was as dark as his dog, which would be called a black dog, though somewhat brownish.

They told me there that a boy had seen another, supposed to be its mate,[1] this morning, and that they were going out to hunt it toward night.[2]

The water is cold to-day, and bathing begins to be questionable.

[1] Only a stone.　　　　[2] *Vide* next page.

The turtles, painted and sternothærus, are certainly less timid than in the spring. I see a row of half a dozen or more painted turtles on a slanting black willow, so close together that two or three of them actually have their fore feet on the shells of their predecessors, somewhat like a row of bricks that is falling. The scales of some are curled up and just falling.

Sept. 12. Very heavy rain to-day (equinoctial), raising the river suddenly. I have said, within a week, that the river would rise this fall because it did not at all in the spring, and now it rises. A very dark and stormy night (after it); shops but half open. Where the fence is not painted white I can see nothing, and go whistling for fear I run against some one, though there is little danger that any one will be out. I come against a stone post and bruise my knees; then stumble over a bridge, — being in the gutter. You walk with your hands out to feel the fences and trees. There is no vehicle in the street to-night.

The thermometer at 4 p. m. was 54°.

There was pretty high wind in the night.

Sept. 13. I go early to pick up my windfalls. Some of them are half buried in the soil, the rain having spattered the dirt over them.

The river this morning, about 7 a. m., is already twenty-eight and a half inches above summer level, and more than twenty inches of this is owing to the rain of yesterday and last night!! By 1.30 p. m., when it has risen two or three inches more, I can just cross the meadow in a straight line to the Rock. I see a snake swimming on the middle of the tide, far from shore, washed out of the meadow, and myriads of grasshoppers and beetles, etc., are wrecked or clinging to the weeds and stubble that rises above the flood. At evening the river is five inches higher than in the morning.

There is very little current at my boat's place this evening, yet a chip floats down (and next morning, the 14th, I see that a large limb has been carried up-stream during the night, from where it lay at evening, some twenty rods above the junction, to a place thirty rods above the junction). Yet, when I try the current (in the evening of the 13th) with a chip, it goes down at Heron Rock, but the limb was large and irregular, and sank very deep in the water; so I think that the Assabet water was running up beneath while the Musketaquid flowed down over it slowly.

A Carlisle man tells me of a coon he killed in Carlisle which weighed twenty-three and a half pounds and dressed fourteen pounds. He frequently sees and hears them at present.

On the 13th I go to J. Q. Adams's again to see the lynx. Farmer said that if the skin was tainted the hair would come off.

The tail is black at extremity for one inch, and no white at tip; the rest of it above is rust-color (beneath it is white), with the slightest possible suggestion of white rings, i. e. a few white hairs noticed. When stretched or spread the fore foot measured just 5 inches in width, the hind foot scarcely less than 6 inches. The black border on the ear was broadest on the inner (*i. e.* toward the other ear) and forward side, — ½ inch and more. The tufts on the ears only about ⅛ + inch wide.

Adams went to show me the carcass. It was quite sweet still (13th, in afternoon), only a little fly-blown. No quadruped or bird had touched it. Remarkably long and slender, made for jumping. The muscles of the thigh were proportionately very large. I thought the thigh would measure *now* 9 inches in circumference. I had heard that there was nothing in its stomach, but we opened the paunch and found it full of rabbits' fur. I cut off a fore leg.

He said that he had lost two or three hens only, and apparently did not think much of that. The first he knew the animal was within three feet of him, so that he could hardly turn his gun to strike him. He did not know where he came from, — whether from over the wall, to which he was near, or from a chestnut, for he was in the midst of the woods of Jones's lot, *not cut.* He felt somewhat frightened. Struck him with the butt of his gun, but did not hurt him much, he was so quick. He jumped at once *thirty feet,* turned round, and faced him. He then fired, about thirty feet, at his eyes, and destroyed one, — perhaps put out the other, too. He then bounded out of sight. When he had loaded he found him crawling toward him on his belly as if to spring upon him; fired again, and thinks he mortally wounded him then. After loading, approached, and the lynx faced him, all alive. He then fired, and the lynx leapt up fifteen feet, fell, and died. Either at the second or last shot leapt within ten feet of him. He was much impressed by his eyes and the ruff standing out on the sides of his neck.

This was about one hundred and thirty rods easterly from his house.

The skinned tail measured 5 inches. I boiled the leg on the 14th (five days after it was killed) for the bone. It smelled and looked like very good meat, like mutton.

Vide Salem lynxes, September 23d, 1858.[1]

It is remarkable how slow people are to believe that there are any wild animals in their neighborhood. They who have seen this generally suppose that it got out of a menagerie; others that it strayed down from far north. At most they call it *Canada* lynx. In Willey's White Mountain book the same animal is spoken of as a terror to the hunter and called the "Siberian Lynx." What they call it I know not.

I do not think it necessary even to suppose it a straggler, but only very rare hereabouts. I have seen two lynxes that were killed between here and Salem since '27. Have heard of another killed in or near Andover. There may have been many more killed as near within thirty years and I not have heard of it, for they who kill one commonly do not know what it is. They are nocturnal in their habits, and therefore are the more rarely seen, yet a strange animal is seen in this town by somebody about every year, or its track. I have heard of two or three such within a year, and of half a dozen within fifteen years. Such an animal might range fifteen to twenty miles back and forth from Acton to Tewksbury

[1] *Vide* extract from Richardson, Nov. 10, 1860.

and find more woodland than in the southern part of New Hampshire generally.

Farmer says that a farmer in Tewksbury told him two or three years ago that he had seen deer lately on the pine plain thereabouts.

Adams got a neighbor to help him skin the lynx, a middle-aged man; but he was "so nervous" and un-willing to touch even the dead beast, when he came to see it, that he gave him but little assistance.

Dr. Reynolds tells me of a lynx killed in Andover, in a swamp near Haggerty's Pond, one winter when he kept school in Tewksbury, about 1820. At first it was seen crossing the Merrimack into Tewksbury, and there was accordingly a story of an animal about that was ten feet long. They turned out, all the hunters of the neighbor-hood, and tracked it in the snow, across Tewksbury to the swamp in Andover and back again to Tewksbury. One old hunter bet something that they could not show him a track which he did not know, but when they showed him this he gave up. Finally they tracked it to the Andover swamp, and a boy shot it on a tree, though it leapt and fell within a few feet of him when shot.

Rice tells of a common wildcat killed in Sudbury some forty years ago, resting on some ice as it was crossing the Sudbury meadows amid ice and water.

Mr. Boutwell of Groton tells me that a lynx was killed in Dunstable within two or three years. Thinks it is in the State Museum.[1]

This makes five that I have heard of (and seen three)

[1] *Vide* "New England's Prospect" near beginning of Indian Book No. 9.

killed within some fifteen or eighteen miles of Concord
within thirty years past, and no doubt there have been
three times as many of them killed here.[1]

Sept. 14. A. M. — River still rising; at 4 P. M. one
and an eighth inches higher than in morning.

Sept. 15. In morning river is three feet two and a half
plus inches above summer level. 6 P. M., river is slightly
higher than in morning, or at height. Thus it reached
its height the third day after the rain ; had risen on the
morning of the third day about thirty inches on account
of the rain of one day (the 12th).

Joe Smith's man brings me this forenoon a fish hawk
which was shot on George Brooks's pigeon-stand last
evening. It is evidently a female of this year, full grown.
Length 23 inches; alar extent 5 feet 6½ inches. It probably lit there merely for a perch.

Looked at Mr. Davis's museum. Miss Lydia Hosmer
(the surviving maiden lady) has given him some relics
which belonged to her (the Hosmer) family. A small
lead or pewter sun-dial, which she told him was brought
over by her ancestors and which has the date 1626
scratched on it. Also some *stone* weights in an ancient

---

[1] *Vide* Sept. 29, 1856. Walcott [?] saw a lynx of some kind which
was killed in (his father's ?) barn in Bolton [?] some twenty-five years
ago; not so big as mine. Bradford says the Essex Institute have another killed in that neighborhood more recently.

Oct. 15. — Channing reads in papers that within a few days a wildcat was killed in Northampton weighing twenty-two pounds and
another in Tyringham, Berkshire County, of thirty-six pounds (of
course *L. Canadensis* both).

linen bag, said to have been brought from England.
They were oval stones or pebbles from the shore, — or
might have been picked up at Walden. There was a
pound, a half-pound, a quarter, a two-ounce, and several
one-ounce weights, now all rather dark and ancient to
look at, like the bag. This was to me the most interesting
relic in his collection. I love to see anything that implies
a simpler mode of life and greater nearness to the
earth.

Sept. 16. 7 A. M. — River fallen one and a half inches.
Is three feet and seven eighths of an inch above summer
level, *i. e.* at notch on tree. I mark a willow eight feet
above summer level.

See no zizania seed ripe, or black, yet, but almost all
is fallen.

Sept. 17. 6.30 A. M. — River thirty-four and an
eighth above summer level, or fallen about four inches
since evening of 15th. It flows now (a sunk bottle) one
hundred feet in two minutes at boat's place, there being
no wind.

P. M. — Up river.

Pontederia seeds falling.

See a flock of eight or ten wood ducks on the Grind-
stone Meadow, with glass, some twenty-five rods off, —
several drakes very handsome. They utter a creaking
scream as they sail there, — being alarmed, — from
time to time, shrill and loud, very unlike the black duck.
At last one sails off, calling the others by a short creaking
note.

Sept. 18. According to all accounts, very little corn is fit to grind before October 1st (though I have one kind ripe and fit to grind September 1st). It becomes hard and dry enough in the husk in the field by that time, much of it. But long before this, or say by the 1st of September, it begins to glaze (or harden on the surface), when it begins to be too hard to boil.

P. M. — To beeches.

This is a beautiful day, warm but not too warm, a harvest day (I am going down the railroad causeway), the first unquestionable and conspicuous autumnal day, when the willows and button-bushes are a yellowed bower in parallel lines along the swollen and shining stream. The first autumnal tints (of red maples) are now generally noticed. The shrilling of the alder locust fills the air. A brightness as of spring is reflected from the green shorn fields. Both sky and earth are bright. The first clear blue and shining white (of clouds). Corn-stalk-tops are stacked about the fields; potatoes are being dug; smokes are seen in the horizon. It is the season of agricultural fairs. If you are not happy to-day you will hardly be so to-morrow.

Leaving Lowell on the morning of the 10th, after the rain of the day before, I passed some heaps of brush in an opening in the woods, — a pasture surrounded by woods, — to which the owner was just setting fire, wet as they were, it being the safest time to burn them. Hence they make so much smoke sometimes. Some farmer, perhaps, wishes to plow this fall there, and sow rye perchance, or merely to keep his pasture clear. Hence the smokes in the horizon at this season. The

rattle-pod (in Deep Cut) has begun to turn black and
rattle for three or four days.

Notice some green pods of lady's-slipper still, full of
chaffy seed.

The beechnut burs are browned but not falling. They
open directly in my chamber. The nuts are all empty.

White pine cones (a small crop), and all open that I
see.[1]

The toadstools in wood-paths are perforated (almost
like pepper-boxes) by flattish slippery insects, bronze
and black, which are beneath and within it. Or you
see their heads projecting and the dust (or exuviæ) they
make like a curb about the holes.

Smooth sumach berries are about past their beauty
and the white creamy incrustation mostly dried up.

I see in the Walden road two dead shrews and some
fox-dung by them. They look as if bitten and flatted by
the fox. Were they not dropped there by him? Perhaps
they will not eat one.[2]

Sept. 19. 4 P. M. — River fallen about one foot.

Sept. 20. Cattle-Show.
Rainy in forenoon.

Sept. 21. Hard rain last night. About one and seven
eighths inches fallen since yesterday morning, and river
rising again.

See, at Reynolds's, Hungarian millet raised by

[1] Are they not last year's?
[2] *Vide* 24th.

Everett. It is smaller and more purple than what is commonly raised here.

P. M. — To Easterbrooks Country.

The fever-bush berries have begun some time, — say one week; are not yet in prime. Taste almost exactly like lemon-peel. But few bushes bear any.

The bayberries are perhaps ripe, but not so light a gray and so rough, or wrinkled, as they will be.

The pods of the broom are nearly half of them open. I perceive that one, just ready to open, opens with a slight spring on being touched, and the pods at once twist and curl a little. I suspect that such seeds as these, which the winds do not transport, will turn out to be more sought after by birds, etc., and so transported by them than those lighter ones which are furnished with a pappus and are accordingly transported by the wind; *i. e.*, that those which the wind takes are less generally the food of birds and quadrupeds than the heavier and wingless seeds.

Muhlenbergia Mexicana by wall between E. Hosmer and Simon Brown, some time. Some large thorn bushes quite bare.

Sept. 22. P. M. — To Clamshell by boat.

Find more pieces of that Indian pot. Have now thirty-eight in all.

Evidently the recent rise of the river has caused the lower leaves of the button-bush to fall. A perfectly level line on these bushes marks the height to which the water rose, many or most of the leaves so high having fallen.

The clematis yesterday was but just beginning to be feathered, but its feathers make no show. Feathers out next day in house.

See a large flock of crows.

The sweet-gale fruit is yet quite green, but perhaps it is ripe. The button-bush balls are hardly reddened.

Moreover the beach plum appears to prefer a sandy place, however far inland, and one of our patches grows on the only desert which we have.

Some of the early botanists, like Gerard, were prompted and compelled to *describe* their plants, but most nowadays only measure them, as it were. The former is affected by what he sees and so inspired to portray it; the latter merely fills out a schedule prepared for him, — makes a description *pour servir*. I am constantly assisted by the books in identifying a particular plant and learning some of its humbler uses, but I rarely read a sentence in a botany which reminds me of flowers or living plants. Very few indeed write as if they had seen the thing which they pretend to describe.

Sept. 23. P. M. — To Cliffs.

Some small botrychium ripe.

I see on the top of the Cliffs to-day the dung of a fox, consisting of fur, with part of the jaw and one of the long rodent teeth of a woodchuck in it, and the rest of it huckleberry seeds with some whole berries. I saw exactly the same beyond Goose Pond a few days ago, on a rock, — except that the tooth (a curved rodent) was much smaller, probably of a mouse. It is evident, then, that the fox eats huckleberries and so contributes very much to the dispersion of this shrub, for there were a number of entire berries in its dung, — in both the last two I chanced to notice. To spread these seeds, Nature employs not only a great many birds but this restless ranger the fox. Like ourselves, he likes two courses, rabbit and huckleberries.

I see everywhere in the shady yew wood those pretty round-eyed fungus-spots on the upper leaves of the blue-stemmed goldenrod (*vide* press), contrasting with the few bright-yellow flowers above them, — yellowish-white rings (with a slate-colored centre), surrounded by green and then dark.

Red pine-sap by north side of Yew Path some ten rods east of yew, not long done. The root of the freshest has a decided checkerberry scent, and for a long time — a week after — in my chamber, the bruised plant has a very pleasant earthy sweetness.

I hear that a large owl, probably a cat owl, killed and carried off a full-grown turkey in Carlisle a few days ago.

Sept. 24. P. M. — To Flint's Pond *via* Smith's chestnut grove.

See a dead shrew in road on Turnpike Hill. (Had hard rain the night of the 20th.) *Vide* back, 18th.

It is remarkable how persistently Nature endeavors to keep the earth clothed with wood of some kind, — how much vitality there is in the stumps and roots of some trees, though small and young. For example, examined the little hickories on the bare slope of Smith's

Hill. I have observed them endeavoring to cover that slope for a dozen years past, and have wondered how the seed came there, planted on a bare pasture hillside, but I now see that the nuts were probably planted just before the pine wood (the stumps of which remain) was cut down, and, having sprung up about that time, have since been repeatedly cut down to keep the pasture clear, till now they are quite feeble or dying, though many are six feet high. When a part of the hill has been plowed and cultivated I examine the roots which have been turned out, and find that they are two inches thick at the ground though only one to three feet high above. I *judge* that it is fifteen years since the pine wood was cut, and if the hickories had not been cut down and cattle been kept out, there would have been a dense hickory wood there now fifteen to twenty feet high at least. You see on an otherwise perfectly bare hillside or pasture where pines were cut, say fifteen years before, remote from any hickories, countless little hickories a foot high or little more springing up every few feet, and you wonder how they came there, but the fact that they preserve their vitality, though cut down so often and so long, accounts for them.

This shows how heedlessly wood-lots are managed at present, and suggests that when one is cut (if not before) a provident husbandman will carefully examine the ground and ascertain what kind of wood is about to take the place of the old and how abundantly, in order that he may act understandingly and determine if it is best to clear the land or not. I have seen many a field perfectly barren for fifteen or twenty years, which, if

properly managed, or only let alone, would naturally have yielded a crop of birch trees within that
time.

In Wood Thrush Path at Flint's Pond, a great many
of the geiropodium fungus now shed their dust. When
closed it is [a] roundish or conical orange-colored fungus
three quarters of an inch in diameter, covered with a
mucilaginous matter. The thick outer skin of many (it
is pink-red inside) had already curled back (it splits into
segments and curls parallel to the axis of the plant) and
revealed the pinkish fawn-colored puffball capped with
a red dimple or crown. This is a hollow bag, which,
when you touch it, spurts forth a yellowish-white
powder three or four inches through its orifice.

See two very handsome butterflies on the Flint's Pond
road in the woods at Gourgas lot, which C. had not seen
before. I find that they are quite like the *Vanessa Ata-
lanta*, or red admiral, of England.

2 p. m. — The river risen about thirty-three inches
above summer level.

Sept. 25. Hard, gusty rain (with thunder and lightning) in afternoon. About seven eighths of an inch
falls.

Sept. 26. P. M. — Round Walden and Pleasant
Meadow.

Small oaks in hollows (as under Emerson Cliff) have
fairly begun to change.

The taller grass and sedge is now generally withered
and brown, and reveals the little pines in it.

I see that acorns — white oak, etc. — have fallen after the rain and wind, just as leaves and fruit have.

I see, just up, the large light-orange toad-stools with white spots, — at first : then:

Sept. 27. A. M. — Sawing up my raft by river.

River about thirty-five inches above summer level, and goes no higher this time.

Monroe's tame ducks sail along and feed close to me as I am working there. Looking up, I see a little dipper, about one half their size, in the middle of the river, evidently attracted by these tame ducks, as to a place of security. I sit down and watch it. The tame ducks have paddled four or five rods down-stream along the shore. They soon detect the dipper three or four rods off, and betray alarm by a tittering note, especially when it dives, as it does continually. At last, when it is two or three rods off and approaching them by diving, they all rush to the shore and come out on it in their fear, but the dipper shows itself close to the shore, and when they enter the water again joins them within two feet, still diving from time to time and threatening to come up in their midst. They return up-stream, more or less alarmed, and pursued in this wise by the dipper, who does not know what to make of their fears, and soon the dipper is thus tolled along to within twenty feet of where I sit, and I can watch it at my leisure. It has a dark bill and considerable white on the sides of the head or neck, with black between it, no tufts, and no observable white on back or tail. When at last disturbed by me, it suddenly sinks low (all its body) in the water without diving.

Thus it can float at various heights. (So on the 30th I saw one suddenly dash along the surface from the meadow ten rods before me to the middle of the river, and then dive, and though I watched fifteen minutes and examined the tufts of grass, I could see no more of it).

Sept. 28. Butternuts still on tree and falling, as all September.

This morning we had a very severe frost, the first to kill our vines, etc., in garden; what you may call a black frost, — making things look black. Also ice under pump.

Sept. 29. Another hard frost and a very cold day.

Sept. 30. Frost and ice.

III

OCTOBER, 1860

(ÆT. 43)

Oct. 1. Remarkable frost and ice this morning; quite a wintry prospect. The leaves of trees stiff and white at 7 A. M. I hear it was 21° this morning early. I do not remember such cold at this season. This is about the full of the moon (it fulled at 9 P. M. the 29th) in clear, bright moonlight nights. We have fine and bright but cold days after it. One man tells me that he regretted that he had not taken his mittens with him when he went to his morning's work, — mowing in a meadow, — and when he went to a spring at 11 A. M., found the dipper with two inches of ice in it frozen solid.

P. M. — Rain again.

Button-bush balls were fairly reddened yesterday, and the *Andropogon scoparius* looked silvery in sun. Gossamer was pretty thick on the meadows, and noticed the round green leafy buds of the utricularia in the clear, cold, smooth water. Water was prepared for ice, and C. saw the first *Vanessa Antiopa* since spring.

Oct. 3. See *Vanessa Antiopa*.

The hard frost of September 28th, 29th, and 30th, and especially of October 1st, has suddenly killed, crisped, and caused to fall a great many leaves of ash, hickory, etc., etc. These (and the locusts, *generally*) look shrivelled and hoary, and of course they will not ripen or be bright. They are killed and withered green, — all the more tender leaves. Has killed all the burdock flowers and no doubt many others.

Sam Barrett says that last May he waded across the Assabet River on the old dam in front of his house without going over his india-rubber boots, which are sixteen and a half inches high. I do not believe you could have done better than this a hundred years ago, or before the canal dam was built.

Bay-wings about.

I have seen and heard sparrows in *flocks*, more as if flitting by, within a week, or since the frosts began.

Gathered to-day my apples at the Texas house. I set out the trees, fourteen of them fourteen years ago and five of them several years later, and I now get between ten and eleven barrels of apples from them.

Oct. 5. Rain, more or less, yesterday afternoon and this forenoon.

P. M. — To Walden.

The frosts have this year killed all of Stow's artichokes before one of them had blossomed, but those in Alcott's garden had bloomed probably a fortnight ago. This suggests that this plant could not have grown much further north than this. I see a great many young hickories fifteen feet high killed, turned brown, almost black, and withering in the woods, as I do not remember to have seen them before. Indeed, the woods have a strong decaying scent in consequence. Also much indigo-weed is killed and turned black and broken off, as well as ferns generally. The butternut is also killed, turned dark-brown, and the leaves mostly fallen, — not turning yellow at all. The maples generally are what Gerard would have called an " over-worn " scarlet color.

About 4 P. M. it is fast clearing up, the clouds withdrawing, with a little dusky scud beyond their western edges against the blue. We came out on the east shore of Walden. The water is tolerably smooth. The smooth parts are dark and dimpled by many rising fishes. Where it is rippled it is light-colored, and the surface thus presents three or four alternate light and dark bars. I see a fish hawk, skimming low over it, suddenly dive or stoop for one of those little fishes that rise to the surface so abundantly at this season. He then sits on a bare limb over the water, ready to swoop down again on his finny prey, presenting, as he sits erect, a long white breast and belly and a white head. No doubt he well knows the habits of these little fishes which dimple the surface of Walden at this season, and I doubt if there is any better fishing-ground for him to resort to. He can easily find a perch overlooking the lake and discern his prey in the clear water.

The sporobolus grass in the meadows is now full of rain (as erst of dew) and would wet you through if you walked there.

Apparently all the celtis and horse-chestnut leaves are killed, turned dark-brown and withering, before changing or ripening, so severe has been the frost, and, looking from hills over huckleberry-fields, the sweet-fern patches are turned a dark brown, almost black (mulberry black) amid the crimson blueberry and huckleberry, so that the surface is parded black and scarlet from the same cause.

Oct. 6. P. M. — Over hill to Woodis Park.

I see not one hemlock cone of this year at the Hemlocks, but very many of last year holding on. Apparently they bore so abundantly last year that they do not bear at all this year.

I hear that the late cold of September 29 and 30 and October 1 froze all Bull's grapes (papers say some fifty bushels), the thermometer going down to 20°.

As I go over the hill, I see a large flock of crows on the dead white oak and on the ground under the living one. I find the ground strewn with white oak acorns, and many of these have just been broken in two, and their broken shells are strewn about, so that I suppose the crows have been eating them. Some are merely scratched, as if they had been pecked at without being pierced; also there are two of the large swamp white oak acorncups joined together dropped under this oak, perhaps by a crow, maybe a quarter of a mile from its tree, and that probably across the river. Probably a crow had transported one or more swamp white oak acorns this distance. They must have been too heavy for a jay.

The crow, methinks, is our only large bird that hovers and circles about in flocks in an irregular and straggling manner, filling the air over your head and sporting in it as if at home here. They often burst up above the woods where they were perching, like the black fragments of a powder-mill just exploded.

One crow lingers on a limb of the dead oak till I am

within a dozen rods. There is strong and blustering northwest wind, and when it launches off to follow its comrades it is blown up and backward still nearer to me, and it is obliged to tack four or five times just like a vessel, a dozen rods or more each way, very deliberately, first to the right, then to the left, before it can get off; for as often as it tries to fly directly forward against the wind, it is blown upward and backward within gunshot, and it only advances directly forward at last by stooping very low within a few feet of the ground where the trees keep off the wind. Yet the wind is not remarkably strong.

Horace Mann tells me that he saw a painted turtle in this town eating a unio, in our river, in the shell, it evidently having just caught and opened it. He has been collecting shells in Ohio recently, and was obliged to wade at least knee-deep into the streams for mussels, the hogs, which run at large there, having got them all in the shallower water.

Oct. 7. P. M. — To Hubbard's Bath and Grove.

Now and for a week the chip-birds in flocks; the withered grass and weeds, etc., alive with them.

Rice says that when a boy, playing with darts with his brother Israel, one of them sent up his dart when a flock of crows was going over. One of the crows followed it down to the earth, picked it up, and flew off with it a quarter of a mile before it dropped it. He has observed that young wood ducks swim faster than the old, which is a fortunate provision, for they can thus retreat and hide in the weeds while their parents fly off. He says that you must shoot the little dipper as soon as it comes up, — before the water is fairly off its eyes, — else it will dive at the flash.

I see one small but spreading white oak full of acorns just falling and ready to fall. When I strike a limb, great numbers fall to the ground. They are a very dark hazel, looking black amid the still green leaves, — a singular contrast. Some that have fallen have already split and sprouted, an eighth of an inch. This when, on *some* trees, far the greater part have not yet fallen.

Probably the blueberry and huckleberry, ame-lanchier, and other bushes which spring up immediately when the woods are cut have been already planted and started annually, as the little oaks have. Nature thus keeps a supply of these plants in her nursery (*i. e.* under the larger wood), always ready for casualties, as fires, windfalls, and clearings by man. Birds and foxes, etc., are annually conveying the seed into the woods.

Rice reminds me that when the maples in a blueberry swamp have got up high, the blueberries die, and you have at length a maple wood clear of underwood.

Remarking to old Mr. B—— the other day on the abundance of the apples, "Yes," says he, "and fair as dollars too." That 's the kind of beauty they see in apples.

Looked over Hayden's farm and granary. He now takes pleasure in his field of corn just ready for harvest-ing, — the rather small ears fully filled out and rounded at the end, setting low and many on one stalk. He loves to estimate the number of bushels he will have; has already calculated the number of hills, — some forty thousand in this field, — and he shows some one the ear in his granary. Also his rye in barrels and his seed-corn tucked into the mow as he was husking, — the larger and fuller ears picked out, with the husk on. But all this corn will be given to his pigs and other stock. Three great hogs weighing twelve hundredweight lie asleep under his barn already sold. Hears of one man who sold his fat hog for $75.00. He has two high and very spreading apple trees, looking like one, they are so close together, from which he gathered one year twenty-one barrels of sound Hubbardston's nonesuch and five barrels of windfalls, grafted on to it within a few years.

If we have not attended to the subject, we may think that the activity of the animals is not enough to account for the annual planting of such extensive tracts; just as we wonder where all the flies and other insects come from in the spring, because we have not followed them into their winter quarters and counted them there. Yet nature does preserve and multiply the race of flies while we are inattentive and sleeping.

Many people have a foolish way of talking about small things, and apologize for themselves or another having attended to a small thing, having neglected their ordinary business and amused or instructed themselves by attending to a small thing; when, if the truth were known, their ordinary business was the small thing, and almost their whole lives were misspent, but they were such fools as not to know it.

Oct. 8. P. M. — To Damon's wood-lot, part of the burnt district of the spring.

Am surprised to see how green the forest floor and the sprout-land north of Damon's lot are already again, though it was a very severe burn. In the wood-lot the trees are *apparently* killed for twenty feet up, especially the smaller, then six or ten feet of green top, while very vigorous sprouts have shot up from the base below the influence of the fire. This shows that they will die, I think. The top has merely lived for the season while the growth has been in their sprouts around the base. This is the case with oaks, maples, cherry, etc. Also the blue-berry (*Vaccinium vacillans*) has sent up very abundant and vigorous shoots all over the wood from the now more open and cleaned ground. These are evidently from stocks which were comparatively puny before. The adjacent oak sprout-land has already sprung up so high that it makes on me about the same impression that it did before, though it [was] from six to ten feet high and was generally killed to the ground. The fresh shoots from the roots are very abundant and three to five feet high, or half as high as before. So vivacious are the roots and so rapidly does Nature recover herself. You see myriads of little shrub oaks and others in the woods which look as if they had just sprung from the seed, but on pulling one up you find it to spring from a long horizontal root which has survived perhaps several burnings or cuttings. Thus the stumps and roots of young oak, chestnut, hickory, maple, and many other trees retain their vitality a very long time and after many accidents, and produce thrifty trees at last.

In the midst of the wood, I noticed in some places, where the brush had been more completely burned and the ground laid bare, some fire-weed (*Senecio*), golden-rods, and ferns.

Standing by a pigeon-place on the north edge [of] Damon's lot, I saw on the dead top of a white pine four or five rods off — which had been stripped for fifteen feet downward that it might die and afford with its branches a perch for the pigeons about the place, like the more artificial ones that were set up — two wood-peckers that were new to me. They uttered a peculiar sharp *kek kek* on alighting (not so sharp as that of the hairy or downy woodpecker) and appeared to be about the size of the hairy woodpecker, or between that and the golden-winged. I had a good view of them with my glass as long as I desired. With the back to me, they were clear black all above, as well as their feet and bills, and each had a yellow or orange (or possibly orange-scarlet?) front (the anterior part of the head at the base of the upper mandible). A long white line along the side of the head to the neck, with a black one below it. The breast, as near as I could see, was gray specked with white, and the under side of the wing expanded was also gray, with small white spots. The throat white and vent also white or whitish. Is this the arctic three-toed? [1] Probably many trees dying on this large burnt tract will attract many woodpeckers to it.

I find a great many white oak acorns already sprouted, although they are but half fallen, and can easily believe that they sometimes sprout before they fall. It is a good year for them. It is remarkable how soon and unac-

[1] *Not* of Nuttall. [The birds must have been arctic three-toed woodpeckers, though Thoreau misplaces the yellow crown-patch.]

countably they decay. Many which I cut open, though they look sound without, are discolored and decaying on one side or throughout within, though there is no worm in them. Perhaps they are very sensitive to moisture. Those which I see to-day are merely hazel and not nearly so black as what I saw yesterday. Trees that stand by themselves without the wood bear the most.

The sugar maple seeds are now browned — the seed end as well as wing — and are ripe. The severe frosts about the first of the month ripened them.

Oct. 9. P. M. — Up Assabet.

See one crow chasing two marsh hawks over E. Hosmer's meadow. Occasionally a hawk dives at the crow, but the crow perseveres in pestering them. Can it *now* have anything to do with the hawk's habit of catching young birds? In like manner smaller birds pursue crows. The crow is at length joined by another.

See several squirrels' nests of leaves formed in the maples lately.

Though the red maples have not their common brilliancy on account of the very severe frost about the end of September, some are very interesting. You cannot judge a tree by seeing it from one side only. As you go round or away from it, it may overcome you with its mass of glowing scarlet or yellow light. You need to stand where the greatest number of leaves will transmit or reflect to you most favorably. The tree which looked comparatively lifeless, cold, and merely parti-colored, seen in a more favorable light as you are floating away from it, may affect you wonderfully as a warm, glowing drapery. I now see one small red maple which is all a pure yellow within and a bright red scarlet on its outer surface and prominences. It is a remarkably distinct painting of scarlet on a yellow ground. It is an indescribably beautiful contrast of scarlet and yellow. Another is yellow and green where this was scarlet and yellow, and in this case the bright and liquid green, now getting to be rare, is by contrast as charming a color as the scarlet.

I met in the street afterward a young lady who rowed up the river after me, and I could tell exactly where she plucked the maple twig which she held in her hand. It was the one so conspicuous for a quarter of a mile in one reach of the river.

I wonder that the very cows and the dogs in the street do not manifest a recognition of the bright tints about and above them. I saw a terrier dog glance up and down the painted street before he turned in at his master's gate, and I wondered what he thought of those lit trees, — if they did not touch his philosophy or spirits, — but I fear he had only his common doggish thoughts after all. He trotted down the yard as if it were a matter of course after all, or else as if he deserved it all.

Wood ducks are about now, amid the painted leaves.

For two or more nights past we have had remarkable glittering golden sunsets as I came home from the post-office, it being cold and cloudy just above the horizon. There was the most intensely bright golden light in the west end of the street, extending under the elms, and the very dust a quarter of a mile off was like gold-dust. I wondered how a child could stand quietly in that light, as if it had been a furnace.

This haste to kill a bird or quadruped and make a skeleton of it, which many young men and some old ones exhibit, reminds me of the fable of the man who killed the hen that laid golden eggs, and so got no more gold. It is a perfectly parallel case. Such is the knowledge which you may get from the anatomy as compared with the knowledge you get from the living creature. Every fowl lays golden eggs for him who can find them, or can detect alloy and base metal.

Oct. 10. In August, '55, I levelled for the artificial pond at Sleepy Hollow. They dug gradually for three or four years and completed the pond last year, '59. It is now about a dozen rods long by five or six wide and two or three deep, and is supplied by copious springs in the meadow. There is a long ditch leading into it, in which no water now flows, nor has since winter at least, and a short ditch leading out of it into the brook. It is about sixty rods from the very source of the brook. Well, in this pond thus dug in the midst of a meadow a year or two ago and supplied by springs in the meadow, I find to-day several small patches of the large yellow and the kalmiana lily already established. Thus in the midst of death we are in life. The water is otherwise apparently clear of weeds. The river, where these abound, is about half a mile distant down the little brook near which this pond lies, though there *may* be a few pads in the ditched part of it at half that distance. How, then, did the seed get here? I learned last winter (*vide* December 23, 1859) that many small pouts and some sizable pickerel had been caught here, though the connection with the brook is a very slight and shallow ditch. I think, therefore, that the lily seeds have been conveyed into this pond from the river immediately, or perchance from the meadow between, either by fishes, reptiles, or birds which fed on them, and that the seeds were not lying dormant in the mud. You have only to dig a pond anywhere in the fields hereabouts, and you will soon have not only water-fowl, reptiles, and fishes in it, but also the usual water-plants, as lilies, etc. You will no sooner have got your pond dug than nature will begin to stock it. I suspect that turtles eat these seeds, for I often see them eating the decayed lily leaves. If there is any water communication, perhaps fishes arrive first, and then the water-plants for their food and shelter.

Horace Mann shows me the skeleton of a blue heron. The neck is remarkably strong, and the bill. The latter is 5 + inches long to the feathers above and $6\frac{1}{2}$ to the gape. A stake-driver which he has, freshly killed, has a bill 3 inches long above and $4\frac{1}{8}$ to the gape and between $\frac{5}{8}$ and $\frac{6}{8}$ deep vertically at the base. This bird weighs a little over two pounds, being quite large and fat. Its nails are longer and less curved than those of the heron. The sharp bill of the heron, like a stout pick, wielded by that long and stout neck, would be a very dangerous weapon to encounter. He has made a skeleton of the fish hawk which was brought to me within a month. I remark the great eye-sockets, and the claws, and perhaps the deep, sharp breast-bone. Including its strong hooked bill it is clawed at both ends, harpy-like.

P. M. — Went to a fire — or smoke — at Mrs. Hoar's. There is a slight blaze and more smoke. Two or three hundred men rush to the house, cut large holes in the roof, throw many hogsheads of water into it, — when a few pails full well directed would suffice, — and then they run off again, leaving your attic three inches deep with water, which is rapidly descending through the ceiling to the basement and spoiling all that can be spoiled, while a torrent is running down the stairways. They were very forward to put out the [fire], but they take no pains to put out the water, which does far more damage. The first was amusement; the last would be mere work and utility. Why is there not a little machine invented to throw the water out of a house?

They are hopelessly cockneys everywhere who learn to swim with a machine. They take neither disease nor health, nay, nor life itself, the natural way. I see dumb-bells in the minister's study, and some of their dumbness gets into his sermons. Some travellers carry them round the world in their carpetbags. Can he be said to travel who requires still this exercise? A party of school-children had a picnic at the Easterbrooks Country the other [day], and they carried bags of beans from their gymnasium to exercise with there. I cannot be interested in these extremely artificial amusements. The traveller is no longer a wayfarer, with his staff and pack and dusty coat. He is not a pilgrim, but he travels in a saloon, and carries dumb-bells to exercise with in the intervals of his journey.

Oct. (10 *and*) 11. P. M. — To Sleepy Hollow and north of M. Pratt's.

There is a remarkably abundant crop of white oak acorns this fall, also a fair crop of red oak acorns; but not of scarlet and black, very few of them. Which is as well for the squirrel. The acorns are now in the very midst of their fall. The white oak acorn is about the prettiest of ours. They are a glossy hazel (while the red and black are more or less downy at first) and of various forms, — some nearly spherical but commonly oblong and pointed, some more *slender* oval or elliptical; and of various shades of brown, — some almost black, but generally a wholesome hazel. Those which have fallen longest, and been exposed to the severe frosts on the ground, are partly bleached there. The white oak acorns are found chiefly on trees growing in the open or on the edge of the wood, and on the most exposed side of these trees. They grow either singly or in twos and threes.

This afternoon (11th) the strong wind which arose at noon has strewn the ground with them. I could gather many bushels in a short time. This year is as good for white oak acorns as for apples and pears. What pleasant picking on the firm, green pasture sod which is browned with this glossy fruit! The worms are already at work in them, — sometimes three or four in one, — and some are already decayed and decaying on the tree without a worm. The fibery [*sic*] inner bark of the nut appears to retain moisture and hasten rot, especially when the fruit has once been swollen by the wet. The best time to gather these nuts is now, when a strong wind has arisen suddenly in the day, before the squirrels have preceded you; and so of chestnuts.

Of red oak acorns, some are short and broad, others

longer. I see some pretty shrub oak acorns longitudinally striped. Chestnuts also are frequently striped, but before they have been exposed to the light, and are completely ripe.

The season is as favorable for pears as for apples. R. W. E.'s garden is strewn with them. They are not so handsome as apples, — are of more earthy and homely colors, — yet they are of a wholesome color enough. Many, inclining to a rough russet or even ferruginous, both to touch (rusty) and eye, look as if they were proof against frost. After all, the few varieties of wild pears here have more color and are handsomer than the many celebrated varieties that are cultivated. The cultivated are commonly of so dull a color that it is hard to distinguish them from the leaves, and if there are but two or three left you do not see them revealing themselves distinctly at a distance amid the leaves, as apples do, but I see that the gatherer has overlooked half a dozen large ones on this small tree, which were concealed by their perfect resemblance to the leaves, — a yellowish green, spotted with darker-green rust or fungi (?). Yet some have a fair cheek, and, generally, in their form they are true pendants, as if shaped expressly to hang from the trees.

They are a more aristocratic fruit. How much more attention they get from the proprietor! The hired man gathers the apples and barrels them. The proprietor plucks the pears at odd hours for a pastime, and his daughter wraps them each in its paper. They are, perchance, put up in the midst of a barrel of Baldwins as if something more precious than these. They are spread on the floor of the best room. They are a gift to the most distinguished guest. Judges and ex-judges and honorables are connoisseurs of pears, and discourse of them at length between sessions. I hold in my hand a Bonne Louise which is covered with minute brown specks or dots one twelfth to one sixteenth [of an inch] apart, largest and most developed on the sunny side, quite regular and handsome, as if they were the termination or operculum of pores which had burst in the very thin pellicle of the fruit, producing a slight roughness to the touch. Each of these little ruptures, so to call them, is in form a perfect star with five rays; so that, if the apple is higher-colored, reflecting the sun, on the duller surface of this pear the whole firmament with its stars shines forth. They whisper of the happy stars under whose influence they have grown and matured. It is not the case with all of them, but only the more perfect specimens.

Pears, it is truly said, are less poetic than apples. They have neither the beauty nor the fragrance of apples, but their excellence is in their flavor, which speaks to a grosser sense. They are *glouts-morceaux*. Hence, while children dream of apples, ex-judges realize pears. They are named after emperors and kings and queens and dukes and duchesses. I fear I shall have to wait till we get to pears with American names, which a republican can swallow.

Looking through a more powerful glass, those little brown dots are stars with from four to six rays, — commonly five, — where a little wart-like prominence (perhaps the end of a pore or a thread) appears to have

burst through the very thin pellicle and burst it into so
many rays.

Oct. 13. P. M. — Up river.

I find no new cones on Monroe's larch by the river,
but many old ones (the same was the case with the hemlocks on Assabet), unless those imperfect ones with a
twig growing from their extremity were this year's, —
but I think they were last year's. Last year both white
pine, hemlock, and larches bore abundantly and there
were very few white oak acorns. This year, so far as I
observe, there are scarcely any white pine cones (were
there any?) or hemlock or larch, and a great abundance
of white oak acorns in all parts of the town. So far as I
have observed, if pines or oaks bear abundantly one
year they bear little or nothing the next year. This is a
white oak year, not a pine year. It is also an apple and a
potato year. I should think that there might be a bushel
or two of acorns on and under some single trees. There
are but few in the woods. Those spreading trees that
stand in open pastures fully exposed to the light and air
are the most fertile ones. I rejoice when the white oaks
bear an abundant crop. I speak of it to many whom I
meet, but I find few to sympathize with me. They seem
to care much more for potatoes. The Indians say that
many acorns are a sign of a cold winter. It is a cold fall
at any rate.

The shore at Clamshell is greened with pontederia
seed which has floated up and been left there, with some
button-bush seed and some of those slender bulbs of the
lysimachia and those round green leaf-buds of the

Utricularia vulgaris. Thus, probably, are all these dispersed. I also see large masses of the last-named weed lodged against the bridges, etc., with the conspicuous greener leaf-buds attached. I find no yellow lily seeds, only a few white lily seed-pods. These are full of seeds the color of apple seeds and but a quarter as big. They sink in water as soon as the slimy matter which invests them is washed off. I see a white lily stem coiled up with many whorls like a wire spring. They are almost only white lily pads that are left now.

There is some of the fresh-water sponge in this the main stream too.

The *F. hyemalis* back, and I think I see and hear the shore larks.

The shrub oaks on J. Hosmer's hillside this side of Hollowell place have already passed the height of their beauty. Is it not early on account of frost?

At Holden Swamp. — Now, as soon as the frost strips the maples, and their leaves strew the swamp floor and conceal the pools, the note of the chickadee sounds cheerfully wintryish.

I see many pine and oak tree tops in the woods that were blown off last spring. They lie many rods from their trunks, so that I have to look a little while to tell where they came from. Moreover, the butt of the piece over which I stand looks so large compared with the broken shaft up there so high that I at first feel sure it did not come from there, — which [?] it did, — and so am puzzled to locate it.

The lentago fruit is quite sweet and reminds me of

dates in their somewhat mealy pulp. It has large flat black seeds, somewhat like watermelon seeds, but not so long.

The scientific differs from the poetic or lively description somewhat as the photographs, which we so weary of viewing, from paintings and sketches, though this comparison is too favorable to science. All science is only a makeshift, a means to an end which is never attained. After all, the truest description, and that by which another living man can most readily recognize a flower, is the unmeasured and eloquent one which the sight of it inspires. No scientific description will supply the want of this, though you should count and measure and analyze every atom that seems to compose it.

Surely poetry and eloquence are a more universal language than that Latin which is confessedly dead. In science, I should say, all description is postponed till we know the whole, but then science itself will be cast aside. But unconsidered expressions of our delight which any natural object draws from us are something complete and final in themselves, since all nature is to be regarded as it concerns man; and who knows how near to absolute truth such unconscious affirmations may come? Which are the truest, the sublime conceptions of Hebrew poets and *seers*, or the guarded statements of modern geologists, which we must modify or unlearn so fast?

As they who were present early at the discovery of gold in California, and observed the sudden fall in its value, have most truly described that state of things, so it is commonly the old naturalists who first received Amer-

ican plants that describe them best. A scientific description is such as you would get if you should send out the
scholars of the polytechnic school with all sorts of metres
made and patented to take the measures for you of any
natural object. In a sense you have got nothing new
thus, for every object that we see mechanically is mechanically daguerreotyped on our eyes, but a true
description growing out [of] the perception and appreciation of it is itself a new fact, never to be daguerreotyped, indicating the highest quality of the plant, — its
relation to man, — of far more importance than any
merely medicinal quality that it may possess, or be
thought to-day to possess. There is a certainty and
permanence about this kind of observation, too, that
does not belong to the other, for every flower and weed
has its day in the medical pharmacopœia, but the beauty
of flowers is perennial in the taste of men.

Truly this is a world of vain delights. We think that
men have a substratum of common sense but sometimes are peculiarly frivolous. But consider what a
value is seriously and permanently attached to gold and
so-called precious stones almost universally. Day and
night, summer and winter, sick or well, in war and in
peace, men speak of and believe in gold as a great trea-
sure. By a thousand comparisons they prove their devo-
tion to it. If wise men or true philosophers bore any
considerable proportion to the whole number of men,
gold would be treated with no such distinction. Men
seriously and, if possible, religiously believe in and wor-
ship gold. They hope to earn golden opinions, to celebrate their golden wedding. They dream of the golden

age. Now it is not its intrinsic beauty or value, but its rarity and arbitrarily attached value, that distinguishes gold. You would think it was the reign of shams.

The one description interests those chiefly who have not seen the thing; the other chiefly interests those who have seen it and are most familiar with it, and brings it home to the reader. We like to read a good description of no thing so well as of that which we already know the best, as our friend, or ourselves even. In proportion as we get and are near to our object, we do without the measured or scientific account, which is like the measure they take, or the description they write, of a man when he leaves his country, and insert in his passport for the use of the detective police of other countries. The men of science merely look at the object with sinister eye, to see if [it] corresponds with the passport, and merely visé or make some trifling additional mark on its passport and let it go; but the real acquaintances and friends which it may have in foreign parts do not ask to see nor think of its passport.

Gerard has not only heard of and seen and raised a plant, but felt and smelled and tasted it, applying all his senses to it. You are not distracted from the thing to the system or arrangement. In the true natural order the order or system is not insisted on. Each is first, and each last. That which presents itself to us this moment occupies the whole of the present and rests on the very topmost point of the sphere, under the zenith. The species and individuals of all the natural kingdoms ask our attention and admiration in a round robin. We make straight lines, putting a captain at their head and a lieutenant at their tails, with sergeants and corporals all along the line and a flourish of trumpets near the beginning, insisting on a particular uniformity where Nature has made curves to which belongs their own sphere-music. It is indispensable for us to square her circles, and we offer our rewards to him who will do it.

Who [sic] describes the most familiar object with a zest and vividness of imagery as if he saw it for the first time, the novelty consisting not in the strangeness of the object, but in the new and clearer perception of it.

Oct. 14. This year, on account of the very severe frosts, the trees change and fall early, or fall before fairly changing. The willows have the bleached look of November. Consider how many leaves there are to fall each year and how much they must add to the soil. Coultas (in " What may be Learned from a Tree ") finds that a single beech twig twenty-seven inches and three lines long and six years old was " the leaf-labor of one hundred and fifty-five leaves," and quotes from Asa Gray's " First Lessons in Botany " that " the Washington Elm at Cambridge — a tree of no extraordinary size — was some years ago estimated to produce a crop of seven millions of leaves, exposing a surface of 200,000 square feet, or about five acres, of foliage." Supposing this to be true, and that the horizontal spread of this (like other the largest elms) is one hundred feet, then, if all its leaves should be spread evenly on the ground directly under it, there would be about twenty-five thicknesses. An ordinary forest would probably cover the ground as thickly as this tree would. Supposing a

leaf to be of the same thickness with an ordinary sheet
of letter-paper, and that the mass is compressed as much
as paper packed in a ream, the twenty-five would be
about one sixteenth of an inch thick. This is a rude
calculation.

We have had a remarkably fertile year. Let us see
now if we have a cold winter after it.

P. M. — Up Groton Turnpike.

If you examine a wood-lot after numerous fires and
cuttings, you will be surprised to find how extremely
vivacious are the roots of oaks, chestnuts, hickories,
birches, cherries, etc. The little trees which look like
seedlings of the year will be found commonly to spring
from an older root or horizontal shoot or a stump. Those
layers which you may have selected to transplant will
be found to have too much of old stump and root underground to be removed. They have commonly met with
accidents and seen a good deal of the world already.
They have learned to endure and bide their time. When
you see an oak fully grown and of fair proportions, you
little suspect what difficulties it may have encountered in
its early youth, what sores it has overgrown, how for
years it was a feeble layer lurking under the leaves and
scarcely daring to show its head above them, burnt and
cut, and browsed by rabbits. Driven back to earth again
twenty times, — as often as it aspires to the heavens.
The soil of the forest is crowded with a mass of these
old and tough fibres, annually sending up their shoots
here and there. The underground part survives and
holds its own, though the top meets with countless accidents; so that, although seeds were not to be supplied

for many years, there would still spring up shoots enough to stock it. So with the old and feeble huckleberry roots. Nay, even the sedge (*Carex Pennsylvanica*) is already rooted in most woods, and at once begins to spread and prevail when the wood is cut, especially if a frost or fire keeps down the new wood.

I examine the John Hosmer wood-lot (sprout-land) cut off last winter on the north side at Colburn Hill. Next to the conspicuous sprouts from the large stumps (of which the white birch have here grown the most, — commonly four or five feet) you notice an increased growth of weeds, as goldenrods (especially *S. puberula*), the two fire-weeds, asters, everlasting (fragrant), hawk-weeds, yarrow, low blackberry, cinquefoil, etc. All of these, I believe, except the erechthites, are perennials, and those which blossomed this year (with this exception) must have sprung up before the wood was cut. The others were probably planted last fall or in the winter, unless their seed endures in the soil. I see, for example, what I consider seedling goldenrods, everlasting, and yarrow, *i. e.* mere radical leaves without any stem, which will bloom next year. The seedling trees of this year, of course, will be scarcely noticed among the sprouts and weeds. I chance to see none. I see, however, many young black cherry trees, three to six inches high, which are just three years old, with roots partly coiled up (as if they had met with difficulties in their upward growth) and much larger than their stems. These, then, were planted in the midst of this pine and oak and birch wood at least two years before it was cut, though the tree they came from is so far off that I know not where it is, and they have not effectually risen above the surface till this year. If you look through a sprout-land you will find no tree, not strictly speaking a forest tree, and which at the same time did not attain to its growth there before, so common as these little black cherries, the birds having conveyed the stones into the midst of the woods and dropped them there; *i. e.* they are planted chiefly before the wood is cut. *These* cherry trees are, however, short-lived. They live a few years and bear large and pleasant-tasted fruit, but when the forest trees have grown up around them they die.

I see that a great part of the club-moss (*Lycopodium complanatum*) which was so abundant in the lower part of this wood has already been killed, and is completely withered and bleached white, probably by the cold last winter, if not also by exposure to the light and heat of the summer.

This lot is thickly covered with the rubbish or tops. I suspect that it is, on the whole, better to leave this than to clear the ground, — that when it is not too thick (as masses of pine-tops) it is an important protection to the seedling trees (gardeners find that seedling pines require shade in their nurseries), and of course the soil is enriched by its decay.

Under one white oak where, on the 8th, the ground was strewn with acorns, I find but a single sound one left to-day, and under another, though many acorns are left, all of them are decayed, so rapidly are they gathered by the squirrels. I take them from the tree already decayed without a worm in them. Far the greater part that you find destroyed (this does not include those eaten by animals) have thus decayed, and I think that the cause was the severe frost of about October 1st, which especially injured those on the ground. It is surprising that any escape the winter. I am not sure that white oak acorns do (as I am that many scarlet and red oak, etc., do). These are not protected by any downiness, and their shoots and leaves I know are the most tender in the spring. Probably almost all the white oak acorns would be destroyed by frost if left on the surface in pastures, and so it may be that more escape because the squirrels carry them off and bury them, or leave them under the shelter of the woods and leaves, though they consume so many, than would if they were not disturbed. Also I find many full-grown worms in them, and the acorn all powder, on the tree.

Do I not see yellow-crowned warblers? Much yellow on shoulders or sides, and white in wings when they fly.[1]

Acorns that fall in open pastures decay so fast that you might wonder how any survived the winter, but the fact is that they are not suffered to lie long, but are picked up and carried off by animals, and either deposited in holes or buried under the leaves in the forest, or consumed; and so, probably, more of these survive than would if they were not carried off.

Oct. 16. P. M. — To White Pond and neighborhood. As a consequence of the different manner in which trees which have winged seeds and those which have not are planted, — the [former] being blown together in one direction by the wind, the latter being dispersed ir-

[1] Yes. They fly up against the windows the next day.

regularly by animals, — I observe that the former, as pines (which (the white) are said in the primitive wood to grow in communities), white birches, red maples, alders, etc., often grow in more or less regular rounded or oval or conical patches, as the seeds fell, while oaks, chestnuts, hickories, etc., simply form woods of greater or less extent whether by themselves or mixed; *i. e.*, they do not naturally spring up in an oval form (or elliptical) unless they derive it from the pines under which they were planted.

For example, take this young white pine wood half a dozen years old, which has sprung up in a pasture adjacent to a wood of oaks and pines mixed. It has the form of a broad crescent, or half-moon, with its diameter resting on the old wood near where a large white pine stood. It is true most such groves are early squared by our plows and fences, for we square these circles every day in our rude practice. And in the same manner often they fall in a sprout-land amid oaks, and I, looking from a hilltop, can distinguish in distant old woods still, of pine and oak mixed, these more exclusive and regular communities of pine, a dozen or more rods wide, while it is the oak commonly that fills up the irregular crevices, beside occupying extensive spaces itself. So it happens that, as the pines themselves and their fruit have a more regularly conical outline than deciduous trees, the groves they form also have.

Our wood-lots, of course, have a history, and we may often recover it for a hundred years back, though we *do* not. A small pine lot may be a side of such an oval, or a half, or a square in the inside with all the curving sides cut off by fences. Yet if we attended more to the history of our lots we should manage them more wisely.

Looking round, I observe at a distance an oak wood-lot some twenty years old, with a dense narrow edging of pitch pines about a rod and a half wide and twenty-five or thirty years old along its whole southern side, which is straight and thirty or forty rods long, and, next to it, an open field or pasture. It presents a very singular appearance, because the oak wood is broad and has no pines within it, while the narrow edging is perfectly straight and dense, and pure pine. It is the more re-markable at this season because the oak is all red and yel-low and the pine all green. I understand it and read its history easily before I get to it. I find, as I expected, a fence separating the pines from the oaks, or that they be-long to different owners. I also find, as I expected, that eighteen or twenty years ago a pitch pine wood had stood where the oaks are, and was then cut down, for there are their old stumps. But before they were cut, their seeds were blown into the neighbor's field, and the little pines came up all along its edge, and they grew so thickly and so fast that that neighbor refrained at last from plowing them up or cutting them off, for just this rod and a half in width, where they were thickest, and moreover, though there are no sizable oaks mixed with these pines, the whole surface even of this narrow strip is as usual completely stocked with little seedling oaks less than a foot high. But I ask, if the neighbor so often lets this narrow edging grow up, why not often, by the same rule, let them spread over the whole of his field? When at length he sees how they have grown, does he not often regret that he did not do so? Or why be dependent, even to this extent, on these windfalls from our neighbors' trees, or an accident? Why not control our own woods and destiny more? (This was north from the lane beyond Conant's handsome wood.) There are many such problems in forest geometry to be solved.

Again, I read still further back a more varied story. Take the line between Rice and Conant (?) or Garfield (?). Here is a green strip of dense pitch and white pine some thirty or forty rods long by four wide and thirty years old. On the east side is a large red and yellow [*sic*] oak wood-lot, the nearest part of it some dozen or more years old, and on the west a strip three rods wide of little white and pitch pines four to ten feet high that have sprung up in the open land, and next to these is an open field occasionally cultivated. Given these facts, to find the wall. If you think a moment you will know without my telling you that it is between the pine wood and the oak. Some dozen or more years ago there was a large pine wood extending up to the wall on the west, and then an open field belonging to another man. But, as before, the pine seed had blown over the wall and taken so well that for four rods in width it was suffered to grow, or rather may be said to have defended itself and crowded the farmer back (no thanks to him). But when, some fifteen years ago, the old pine wood was cut by its owner, the other was not ready to cut his younger one. This is now about thirty years old and for many years it has been endeavoring to spread into the open land by its side, as its parents did, but for a long time the proprietor, not taking the hint, blind to his own interests, plowed quite up to the edge of the wood, as I noticed, — and got a few beans for his pains. But the pines (which he did not plant) grew while he slept, and at length, one spring, he gave up the contest and concluded at last to plow only within three rods of the wood, the little pines were so thick and promising. He concluded not to cut his own fingers any more, *i. e.* not further than up to the last joint, and hence this second row of little pines. They would have covered the half or perhaps the whole of his barren field before this if he had let them.

I examined these pine lots. The strip of little pines contained also a little white birch, much sweet-fern, and thin open sod, but scarcely one oak, and that very small. The strip of large pines contained countless oaks of various kinds, — white, red, black, and shrub oak, — which had come from the young oak lot, many little pines of both kinds, and *little* wild cherry, — white [*sic*], — and some hazel and high blueberry. (It was rather elevated as well as dry soil.)

I dug up some of the little oaks to see how old they were and how they had fared. The largest in the lot were about one foot high. First, a red or scarlet oak, apparently four years old. The acorn was about one inch below the surface of the pine leaves. It rose five inches above the leaves, and the root extended about one foot below the surface. It had died down once.

The second was a black oak which rose six inches above the leaves (or eight, measured along the stem). It was apparently four years old. It was much branched, and its tops had been cut off by rabbits last year. The root ran straight down about one inch, then nearly horizontally five or six inches, and when I pulled it up it broke off where less than one eighth inch thick, at sixteen inches below the surface. This tree was one fourth of an inch in diameter at the surface and nearly three fourths of an inch in diameter at five inches below (along the root). At the same height above the surface it was hardly one fifth of an inch in diameter.

The third was a white oak ten inches high, apparently seven years old. It also had been browsed by a rabbit and put out a new shoot accordingly. Two years' growth was buried in the leaves. The root was very similar, both in direction and form, to the last, only not quite so thick.

Fourth, a shrub oak also quite similar, though less thick still and with two or more shoots from one stock.

In all these cases, or especially the first three [?], there was one main and an unexpectedly great, fusiform root, altogether out of proportion to the top, you would say, tapering both ways, but of course largest and sharpest downward, with many fine stringy fibres extending on every side from it perhaps a foot. Just as a biennial plant devotes its energies the first year to producing a stock on which it can feed the next, so these little oaks in their earliest years are forming great fusiform vigorous roots on which they can draw when they are suddenly left to seek their fortunes in a sprout-land.

Thus this double forest was advancing to conquer new (or old) land, sending forward their children on the wings of the wind, while already the oak seedlings from the oak wood behind had established themselves beneath the old pines ready to supplant them. The pines were the vanguard. They stood up to fire with their children before them, while the little oaks kneeled behind and between them. The pine is the pioneer, the oak the more permanent settler who lays out his improvements. Pines are by some considered lower in the scale of trees — in the order of development — than oaks.

While the pines were blowing into the pasture from this narrow edging, the animals were planting the acorns under the pines. Even the small pine woods are thus perfectly equipped.

There was even under these dark, dense pines, thirty years old, a pretty thick bed of blueberry and huckleberry bushes next the wall, ten feet wide, the relics of a still denser and higher one that grew there when it was an open field. The former had thus been driven back three times, first by the blueberry hedge, then by the pines of thirty years ago, and lastly by the young pines that sprang from them. Thus a wood-lot had been forced upon him, and yet perhaps he will talk of it as a creation of his own.

I have come up here this afternoon to see ——'s dense white pine lot beyond the pond, that was cut off last winter, to know how the little oaks look in it. To my surprise and chagrin, I find that the fellow who calls himself its owner has burned it all over and sowed winter-rye here. He, no doubt, means to let it grow up again in a year or two, but he thought it would be clear gain if he could extract a little rye from it in the meanwhile. What a fool! Here nature had got everything ready for this emergency, and kept them ready for many years, — oaks half a dozen years old or more, with fusiform roots full charged and tops already pointing skyward, only waiting to be touched off by the sun, — and he thought he knew better, and would get a little rye out of it first, which he could feel at once between his fingers, and so he burned it, and dragged his harrow over it. As if oaks would bide *his* time or come at his bidding. Or as if he preferred to have a pine or a birch wood here possibly half a century hence — for the land is "pine sick" — rather than an oak wood at once. So he trifles with nature. I am chagrined for him. That he should call himself an agriculturalist! He needs to have a guardian placed over him. A forest-warden should be appointed by the town. Overseers of poor husbandmen.

He has got his dollars for the pine timber, and now he wishes to get his bushels of grain and finger the dollars that they will bring; and then, Nature, you may have your way again. Let us purchase a mass for his soul. A greediness that defeats its own ends.

I examined a little lot of his about a dozen rods square just this side, cut off last winter, apparently two thirds white pine and one third white oak. Last year the white pine seed was very abundant, but there was little or no white oak seed. Accordingly I noticed twenty or more seedling white pines of this year on the barest spots, but not a single seedling oak. This suggests how much the species of the succeeding forest may depend on whether the trees were fertile the year before they were cut, or not.

I see a very large white oak acorn which has a double meat with a skin between. There is a very young grub in it.

They appear to be last year's hemlock and larch cones that still hold on in great numbers!

As time elapses, and the resources from which our forests have been supplied fail, we shall of necessity be more and more convinced of the significance of the seed.

I see in a thick pitch pine wood half a dozen stout pine twigs five eighths of an inch thick that have been gnawed off with their plumes. Why?

Hear the alder locust still. Robins apparently more numerous than a month ago. See grackles in corn-fields in two places to-day.

It chanced that here were two proprietors within half a mile who had done exactly the same, *i. e.*, accepted part of a wood-lot that was forced on them, and I have no doubt that there are several more exactly similar cases within that half-mile diameter.

The history of a wood-lot is often, if not commonly, *here*, a history of cross-purposes, — of steady and con-sistent endeavor on the part of Nature, of interference and blundering with a glimmering of intelligence at the eleventh hour on the part of the proprietor. The pro-prietor of wood-lots commonly treats Nature as an Irishman drives a horse, — by standing before him and beating him in the face all the way across a field.

If I find any starved pasture in the midst of our woods, — and I remember many such, and they are the least valuable tracts we have, — I know that it has commonly had such a history as this wood-lot (above). It was burned over when cut, and perhaps cultivated a year or two, often because the owner thought it was what the soil needed in order that it might produce trees. In some cases there may be sense in such a course if he can afford to wait a century instead of a third of that time for a crop. It depends on what the trees are, the local-ity, etc. But commonly the owner who adopts this course makes a move in the dark and in ninety-nine cases in a hundred [an indecipherable word] his own fingers.

The time will soon come, if it has not already, when we shall have to take special pains to secure and encour-age the growth of white oaks, as we already must that of chestnuts for the most part. These oaks will become so scattered that there will be not seed enough to seed the ground rapidly and completely.

Horace Mann tells me that he found in the crop or inside of the stake-driver killed the other day one grass-hopper, several thousand-legs one to one and a half inches long, and not much else.

It commonly happens in settled countries like this that the new community of pines, sprung from seeds blown off from an older one, is very youthful compared with the trees it sprang from because many successive crops of trees or seeds have been plowed up or cut before the owner allowed Nature to take her course. Naturally the pines spread more steadily and with no such abrupt descents. In the wildwood at least there are commonly only fires and insects or blight, and not the axe and plow and the cattle, to interrupt the regular progress of things.

Oct. 17. P. M. — To Walden Woods.

The trees which *with us* grow in masses, *i. e.* not merely scattering, are: —

    1, 2. White and pitch pine
       3. Oaks
       4. White birch
       5. Red maple
       6. Chestnut
       7. Hickory
          Alder
          Hemlock, spruce, and larch
          Cedar (white and red)
          Willow
          Locust
          Apple
          Red cherry (in neighboring towns) W. [*sic*]
          Sugar maple (rare)

Of these only white and pitch pine, oaks, white birch, and red maple are *now* both important and abundant. (Chestnut and hickory have become rare.)

It is an interesting inquiry what determines which species of these shall grow on a given tract. It is evident that the soil determines this to some extent, as of the oaks only the swamp white stands in our meadows, and, so far as these seven trees are concerned, swamps will be composed only of red maples, swamp white oaks, white birch, and white pine. By removing to upland we get rid of the swamp white oak and red maples in *masses*, and are reduced to white and pitch pine, oaks, and white birch only, *i. e.* of those that are abundant and important.

Secondly, ownership, and a corresponding difference

of treatment of the land as to time of cutting, etc., decides the species.

Third, age, as, if the trees are one hundred years old, they may be chestnut, but if sprout-land are less likely to be; etc., etc., etc.

The noblest trees and those which it took the longest to produce, and which are the longest-lived, as chestnuts, hickories (?), oaks, are the first to become extinct under our present system and the hardest to reproduce, and their place is taken by pines and birches, of feebler growth than the primitive pines and birches, for want of a change of soil.

There is many a tract now bearing a poor and decaying crop of birches, or perhaps of oaks, dying when a quarter grown and covered with fungi and excrescences, where two hundred years ago grew oaks or chestnuts of the largest size.

I look through a lot of young oaks twenty or twenty-five years old (Warren's, east of the Deep Cut, exclusively oak, the eastern part). There are plenty of little oaks from a few inches to a foot in height, but on examination I find fewer seedlings in proportion to the whole (i. e. manifestly seedlings) and they have much older and larger and poorer or more decayed roots than the oaks in dense pine woods. Oftenest they are shoots from the end of a horizontal twig running several feet under the leaves and leading to an old stump [?] under the surface. But I must examine again and further.

Looking through this wood and seeking very carefully for oak seedlings and anything else of the kind, I am surprised to see where the wood was chiefly oak a

cluster of little chestnuts six inches high and close together. Working my hand underneath, I easily lift them
up with all their roots, — four little chestnuts two years
old, which partially died down the first year, — and to
my surprise I find still attached four great chestnuts
from which they sprang and four acorns which have
also sent up puny little trees beneath the chestnuts.
These eight nuts all lay within a diameter of two inches
about an inch and a half beneath the present leafy
surface, in a very loose soil of but [?] half decayed
leaves in the midst of this young oak wood. If I had not
been looking for something of the kind, I should never
have seen either the oaks or the chestnuts. Such is the
difference between looking for a thing and waiting for it
to attract your attention. In the last case you will
probably never see it [at] all. They were evidently
planted there two or three years ago by a squirrel or
mouse. I was surprised at the sight of these chestnuts,
for there are not *to my knowledge* any chestnut trees —
none, at least, nearly large enough to bear nuts — within
about half a mile of that spot, and I should about as soon
have expected to find chestnuts in the artificial pine grove
in my yard. The chestnut trees old enough to bear fruit
are near the Lincoln line about half a mile east of this
through the woods and over hill and dale. No one acquainted with these woods — not the proprietor — would
have believed that a chestnut lay under the leaves in
that wood or within a quarter of a mile of it, and yet
from what I saw then and afterward I have no doubt
that there were hundreds, which were placed there by
quadrupeds and birds. This wood lies on the south of

the village, separated from it by a mile of open fields and meadows. It is the northern part of an extensive pine and oak forest which half a mile eastward, near the Lincoln line, begins to contain a few chestnuts. These little chestnuts were growing well, but the oaks appeared to be dead and dying.[1]

It is well known that the chestnut timber of this vicinity has rapidly disappeared within fifteen years, having been used for railroad sleepers, for rails, and for planks, so that there is danger that this part of our forest will become extinct.

The last chestnut tracts of any size were on the side of Lincoln. As I advanced further through the woods toward Lincoln, I was surprised to see how many little chestnuts there were, mostly two or three years old and some even ten feet high, scattered through them and also under the dense pines, as oaks are. I should say there was one every half-dozen rods, made more distinct by their yellow leaves on the brown ground, which surprised me because I had not attended to the spread of the chestnut, and it is certain that every one of these came from a chestnut placed there by a quadruped or bird which had brought it from further east, where alone it grew.

You would say that the squirrels, etc., went further for chestnuts than for acorns in proportion as they were a greater rarity. I suspect that a squirrel may convey them sometimes a quarter or a half a mile even, and no doubt as soon as a young chestnut fifteen or twenty feet

[1] I dug up three or four more a few days after, and found that they had not the very large roots that young oaks have.

high, far advanced beyond the chestnut woods, bears a single bur, which no man discovers, a squirrel or bird is almost sure to gather it and plant it in that neighbor-hood or still further forward. A squirrel goes a-chest-nutting perhaps as far as the boys do, and when he gets there he does not have to shake or club the tree or wait for frost to open the burs; he walks [?] up to the bur and cuts it off, and strews the ground with them before they have opened. And the fewer they are in the wood the more certain it is that he will appropriate every one, for it is no transient afternoon's picnic with him, but the pursuit of his life, a harvest that he gets as surely as the farmer his corn.

Now it is important that the owners of these wood-lots should know what is going on here and treat them and the squirrels accordingly. They little dream of what the squirrels are about; know only that they get their seed-corn in the adjacent fields, and encourage their boys to shoot them every day, supplying them with powder and shot for this purpose. In newer parts of the country they have squirrel-hunts on a large scale and kill many thousands in a few hours, and all the neighborhood re-joices.

Thus it appears that by a judicious letting Nature alone merely we might recover our chestnut wood in the course of a century.

This also suggests that you cannot raise one kind of wood alone in a country unless you are willing to plant it yourself. If no oaks grow within miles of your pines, the ground under the pines will not be filled with little oaks, and you will have to plant them. Better have your wood of different kinds in narrow lots of fifty acres, and not one kind covering a township.

I took up a red oak seedling of this year five inches high. In this case the top is larger, putting length and breadth together, than the root, and the great acorn is still perfectly sound, lying on its side, and the plant this first year evidently derives a great part of its nourishment from it. The root is abruptly curved back under the acorn, and I find that seedling or young oaks generally have roots which slant off more or less horizontally from where the acorn lay two to five or six inches, and then, having acquired their greatest thickness, descend straight downward. To this irregularity is sometimes added a half-turn or spiral in the upper part of the root: or, looking down on it: The acorn is still so sound that I think it must continue to furnish nourishment to the plant a part of next year.

Apparently the pine woods are a natural nursery of oaks, from whence we might easily transplant them to our grounds, and thus save some of those which annually decay, while we let the pines stand. Experience has proved, at any rate, that these oaks will bear exposure to the light. It is remarkable that for the most part there are no seedling oaks in the open grassy fields and pastures. The acorns are little likely to succeed if dropped there. Those springing up in such places appear to have been dropped or buried by animals when on their way with them to another covert.

I examine under the pitch pines by Thrush Alley to see how long the oaks live under dense pines. The oldest oaks there are about eight or ten years old. I see none older under these and other dense pines, even when the pines are thirty or more years old, though I have no doubt that oaks began to grow there more than twenty years ago. Hence they must have died, and I suppose I could find their great roots in the soil if I should dig for them. I should say that they survived under a very dense pine wood only from six to ten years. This corresponds exactly with the experience of the English planters, who begin to shred the branches of the nursing pines when the oaks are six or seven years old and to remove the pines altogether when the oaks are eight to ten years old.

But in openings amid the pines, though only a rod in diameter, or where the pines are thin, and also on their edges, the oaks shoot up higher and become trees, and this shows how mixed woods of pine and oak are produced. If the pines are quite small or grow but thinly, fewer acorns will be planted amid them, it is true, but more will come to trees, and so you have a mixed wood. Or when you thin out a pine wood, the oaks spring up here and there; or when you thin an oak wood, the pines plant themselves and grow up in like manner.

It is surprising how many accidents these seedling oaks will survive. We have seen [?] that they commonly survive six to ten years under the thickest pines and acquire stout and succulent roots. Not only they bear the sudden exposure to the light when the pines are cut,

but, in case of a more natural succession, when a fire
runs over the lot and kills pines and birches and maples,
and oaks twenty feet high, these little oaks are scarcely
injured at all, and they will still be just as high the
next year, if not in the fall of the same year if the fire
happens early in the spring. Or if in the natural course
of events a fire does not occur nor a hurricane, the soil
may at last be exhausted for pines, but there are always
the oaks ready to take advantage of the least feebleness
and yielding of the pines.

Hereabouts a pine wood, or even a birch wood, is no
sooner established than the squirrels and birds begin to
plant acorns in it. First the pines, then the oaks; and
coniferous trees, geologists tell us, are older, as they
are lower in the order of development, — were created
before oaks.

I observe to-day a great many pitch pine plumes cut
off by squirrels and strewn under the trees, as I did
yesterday.[1]

I count the rings of a great white pine sawed off in
Laurel Glen a few years ago, —about one hundred and
thirty. This, probably, was really of the second growth,
at least, but probably now even the second growth is all
gone in this town. We may presume that any forest tree
here a hundred and thirty years old belongs to the
second growth, at least. We may say that all pines and
oaks of this age or *growth* are now extinct in this town,

---

[1] The next day (18th) I see twenty pine twigs, some three-plumed,
at Beck Stow's, recently gnawed off and lying under one tree. This
is to be seen now on all sides of the town. Why so? Saw the same
last fall and before.

and the present generation are not acquainted with large trees of these species.

A month ago I saw the smoke of many burnings in the horizon (even now see one occasionally), and now in my walks I occasionally come to a field of winter-rye already greening the ground in the woods where such a fire was then kindled.

If any one presumes that, after all, there cannot be so many nuts planted as we see oaks spring up at once when the pines are cut, he must consider that *according to the above calculation* (two pages back) there are some ten years for the animals to plant the oak wood in; so that, if the tract is ten rods square or contains one hundred square rods, it would only be necessary that they should plant ten acorns in a year which should not be disturbed, in order that there might be one oak to every square rod at the end of ten years.[1] This, or anything like this, does not imply any very great activity among the squirrels. A striped squirrel could carry enough in his cheeks at one trip.

While the man that killed my lynx (and many others) thinks it came out of a menagerie, and the naturalists call it the Canada lynx, and at the White Mountains they call it the Siberian lynx,—in each case forgetting, or ignoring, that it belongs here,—I call it the Concord lynx.

Oct. 18. P. M. — To Merriam's white pine grove.

I often see amid or beside a pitch or white pine grove, though thirty years old, a few yet larger and older trees,

[1] But some English planters plant only an acorn to two or three rods, others four or five times as many.

from which they came, rising above them, like patri-
archs surrounded by their children.

Early cinquefoil again.

I find fair-looking white oak acorns, which abound
on the trees near Beck Stow's, to be decayed on the tree.
Wishing to see what proportion were decayed I pull
down a bough, and pluck forty-one acorns, which I cut
open successively with my knife. Every one is soft and
spoiled, turned black or dark-brown within, though
there is not a single worm in them. Indeed, abundant
and beautiful as the crop is, they are all decayed on
that and the neighboring trees, and I only find one sound
one after long search. This is probably the reason why
they hold on still so numerously, and beside the squirrels do not disturb them. I suspect that they were killed
by the severe frost of about October 1st. Abundant as
the crop is, perhaps half of them have already been
destroyed thus. Those that were touched first and most
severely are paler-brown on one or both sides. Here, or
on *these* trees, is a whole crop destroyed before it fell,
though remarkably abundant. How many thousand
bushels there must be in this state in this town!

See how an acorn is planted by a squirrel, just under
a loose covering of moist leaves where it is shaded and
concealed, and lies on its side on the soil, ready to send
down its radicle next year.

If there are not so many oak seedlings in a deciduous
wood as in a pine one, it may be because both oaks (and
acorns) and squirrels love warmth. The ground does
not freeze nearly so hard under dense pines as in a
deciduous wood.

Look through an oak wood, say twenty-five or thirty years old, north of the Sherman grove on the road. It appeared to me that there were fewer seedling oaks under this than under pines, and the roots of the other little ones that looked like seedlings were old and decaying, and the shoots slender, feeble, and more or less prostrate under the leaves. You will find seedling oaks under oaks, it is true, but I think that you will not find a great many of them. You will not find, as under pines, a great many of these little oaks one to eight or ten years old, with great fat, or fusiform, roots, all ready to spring up when the pines are cut.

If it were true that the little oaks under oaks steadily grew and came to trees there, then even that would be a reason why the soil would not be so well stocked with them when the wood was cut as when a pine wood is cut, for there would be only ten trees in the first case to one hundred in the last (according to our calculation before).

Most of the little oaks here were little or dwarfed, apparently because they were shoots from poor and diseased rootstocks, which were common in the ground.

But I think that neither pines nor oaks do well under older trees.

Methinks you do not see numerous oaks of all ages and sizes in an old oak wood, but commonly large trees of about the same age and little ones like huckleberry bushes under your feet; and so commonly with pine woods. In either case, if the woods are well grown and dense, all the trees in them appear to have been planted at the same time.

For aught that I know, I would much rather have a young oak wood which has succeeded to pines than one that has succeeded to oaks, for they will make better trees, not only because the soil is new to them, but because they are all seedlings, while in the other case far the greater part are sprouts; just as I would prefer apple trees five or six years from the seed for my orchard to suckers from those which have come to maturity or decayed. Otherwise your young oaks will soon, when half grown, have the diseases of old trees, — warts and decay.

I find that Merriam's white pine grove is on the site of an oak wood, the old oak stumps being still very common. The pines appear to be some forty years old. The soil of pine leaves is an inch to an inch and a half thick. The oldest little oaks here are five years old and six inches high.

Am surprised to see that the pasture west of this, where the little pitch pines were cut down last year, is now even more generally green with pines than two years ago.

What shall we say to that management that halts between two courses, — does neither this nor that, but botches both ? I see many a pasture on which the pitch or white pines are spreading, where the bush-whack is from time to time used with a show of vigor, and I despair of my trees, — I say mine, for the farmer evidently does not mean they shall be his, — and yet this questionable work is so poorly done that those very fields grow steadily greener and more forest-like from year to year in spite of cows and bush-whack, till at length the farmer gives up the contest from sheer weariness, and finds himself the owner of a wood-lot. Now whether wood-lots or pastures are most profitable for him I will not undertake to say, but I am certain that a wood-lot and pasture combined is not profitable.

I see spatter-dock pads and pontederia in that little pool at south end of Beck Stow's. How did they get there? There is no stream in this case? It was perhaps rather reptiles and birds than fishes, then. Indeed we might as well ask how they got anywhere, for all the pools and fields have been stocked thus, and we are not to suppose as many new creations as pools. This suggests to inquire how any plant came where it is, — how, for instance, the pools which were stocked with lilies before we were born or this town was settled, and ages ago, were so stocked, as well as those which we dug. I think that we are warranted only in supposing that the former was stocked in the same way as the latter, and that there was not a sudden new creation, — at least since the first; yet I have no doubt that peculiarities more or less considerable have thus been gradually produced in the lilies thus planted in various pools, in consequence of their various conditions, though they all came originally from one seed.

We find ourselves in a world that is already planted, but is also still being planted as at first. We say of some plants that they grow in wet places and of others that they grow in desert places. The truth is that their seeds are scattered almost everywhere, but here only do they succeed. Unless you can show me the pool where the lily was created, I shall believe that the oldest fossil lilies which the geologist has detected (if this is found fossil) originated in that locality in a similar manner to these of Beck Stow's. We see thus how the fossil lilies which the geologist has detected are dispersed, as well as these which we carry in our hands to church.

The development theory implies a greater vital force in nature, because it is more flexible and accommodating, and equivalent to a sort of constant *new* creation.

Mr. Alcott tells me that the red squirrels which live in his elms go off to the woods (pitch pines behind his house) about June, and return in September, when the butternuts, etc., are ripe. Do they not go off for hazelnuts and pine seed? No doubt they are to be found where their food is.

Young oaks, especially white oaks, in open woodland hollows and on plains [are] almost annually killed down by frost, they are so tender. Large tracts in this town are bare for this reason. Hence it is very important that the little oaks, when they are tenderest, should have the shelter of pines and other trees as long as they can bear it, or perhaps till they get above the level of the frosts. I know of extensive open areas in the woods where it would be of no use to sow acorns or to set seedling oaks, for every one would be killed by the frost, as they have already been; but if you were to plant pines thinly there, or thickly at first and then thin them out, you could easily raise oaks, for often you have only got to protect them till they are five or six feet high, that they may be out of the way of ordinary frosts, whose surface is as level as that of a lake.

According to Loudon (*vide* Emerson on oaks), the

best authorities say plant some two hundred and fifty acorns to an acre (*i. e.* some from three hundred to five hundred, others from sixty to one hundred), or about one and one half acorns to a rod, or two hundred and forty to an acre.

In my walk in Walden Woods yesterday I found that the seedling oaks and chestnuts were most common under the fullest and densest white pines, as that of Brister Spring.

Oct. 19. P. M. — To Conantum.

Indian-summer-like and gossamer.

That white oak in Hubbard Grove which on the 7th was full of those glossy black acorns is still hanging full, to my surprise. Suspecting the cause, I proceed to cut them open, and find that they are all decayed or decaying. Even if not black within, they are already sour and softened. Yet Rice told me that he collected from this tree about a week ago some thousands of acorns and planted them in Sudbury. I can tell him that probably not more than half a dozen of them were alive, though they may then have looked well, as they do now externally. First, then, I was surprised at the abundance of the crop this year. Secondly, by the time I had got accustomed to that fact I was surprised at the vast proportion that were killed, apparently by frost. The squirrels are wiser than to gather these, but I see where they have gathered many black oak acorns, the ground beneath being strewn with their cups, which have each a piece bitten out in order to get out the acorn. I suspect that black and red oak acorns are not so easily injured by frost. Indeed, I find this to be the case as far as I look.

Sophia tells me that the large swamp white oak acorns in their cups, which she gathered a fortnight ago, are now all mouldy about the cups, or base of the acorn.

It is a remarkable fact, and looks like a glaring imperfection in Nature, that the labor of the oaks for the year should be lost to this extent. The softening or freezing of cranberries, the rotting of potatoes, etc., etc., seem trifling in comparison. The pigeons, jays, squirrels, and woodlands are thus impoverished. It is hard to say what great purpose is served by this seeming waste.

I frequently see an old and tall pine wood standing in the midst of a younger but more extensive oak wood, it being merely a remnant of an extensive pine wood which once occupied the whole tract, but, having a different owner, or for some other reason, it has not been cut. Sometimes, also, I see these pines of the same age reappear at half a mile distant, the intermediate pines having been cut for thirty or forty years, and oaks having taken their place. Or the distant second growth of pines, especially if they stand on the land of another than he who owns the oaks, may, as we have seen, be a generation smaller and have sprung from the pines that stood where the oaks do. Two or three pines will run swiftly forward a quarter of a mile into a plain, which is their favorite field of battle, taking advantage of the least shelter, as a rock, or fence, that may be there, and intrench themselves behind it, and if you look sharp, you may see their plumes waving there. Or, as I have said, they will cross a broad river without a bridge, and as swiftly climb and permanently occupy a steep hill beyond.

At this season of the year, when each leaf acquires its peculiar color, Nature prints this history distinctly, as it were an illuminated edition. Every oak and hickory and birch and aspen sprinkled amid the pines tells its tale a mile off, and you have not to go laboriously through the wood examining the bark and leaves. These facts would be best illustrated by colors, — green, yellow, red, etc.

Pines take the first and longest strides. Oaks march deliberately in the rear.

The pines are the light infantry, *voltigeurs*, supplying the scouts and skirmishers; the oaks are the grenadiers, heavy-paced and strong, that form the solid phalanx.

It is evident to any who attend to the matter that pines are here the natural nurses of the oaks, and therefore they grow together. By the way, how nearly identical is the range of our pines with the range of our oaks? Perhaps oaks extend beyond them southward, where there is less danger of frost.

The *new* woodlands, *i. e.*, forests that spring up where there were no trees before, are pine (or birch or maple), and accordingly you may see spaces of bare pasture sod between the trees for many years. But oaks, in masses, are not seen springing up thus with old sod between them. They form a sprout-land, or stand amid the stumps of a recent pine lot.

It will be worth the while to compare seedling oaks with sprout-lands, to see which thrive best.

I see, on the side of Fair Haven Hill, pines which

have spread, apparently from the north, one hundred rods, and the hillside begins to wear the appearance of woodland, though there are many cows feeding amid the pines. The custom with us is to let the pines spread thus into the pasture, and at the same time to let the cattle wander there and contend with the former for the possession of the ground, from time to time coming to the aid of the cattle with a bush-whack. But when, after some fifteen or twenty years, the pines have fairly prevailed over us both, though they have suffered terribly and the ground is strewn with their dead, we then suddenly turn about, coming to the aid of the pines with a whip, and drive the cattle out. They shall no longer be allowed to scratch their heads on them, and we fence them in. This is the actual history of a great many of our wood-lots. While the English have taken great pains to learn how to create forests, this is peculiarly our mode. It is plain that we have thus both poor pastures and poor forests.

I examine that oak lot of Rice's next to the pine strip of the 16th. The oaks (at the southern end) are about a dozen [1] years old. As I expected, I find the stumps of the pines which stood there before quite fresh and distinct, not much decayed, and I find by their rings that they were about forty years old when cut, while the pines which sprang from [them] are now about twenty-five or thirty. But further, and unexpectedly, I find the stumps, in great numbers, now much decayed, of an oak wood which stood there more than sixty years ago. They are mostly shells, the sap-wood rotted off and the inside

[1] Oct. 31, count ten rings on one sprout.

turned to mould. Thus I distinguished four successions of trees.

Thus I can easily find in countless numbers in our forests, frequently in the third succession, the stumps of the oaks which were cut near the end of the last century. Perhaps I can recover thus generally the oak woods of the beginning of the last century, if the land has remained woodland. I have an advantage over the geologist, for I can not only detect the order of events but the time during which they elapsed, by counting the rings on the stumps. Thus you can unroll the rotten papyrus on which the history of the Concord forest is written.

It is easier far to recover the history of the trees which stood here a century or more ago than it is to recover the history of the men who walked beneath them. How much do we know — how little more can we know — of these two centuries of Concord life?

Go into a young oak wood, and commonly, if the oaks are not sprouts, then they were preceded by pines.

Of course, the gradual manner in which many wood-lots are cut — often only thinned out — must affect the truth of my statements in numerous instances. The regularity of the succession will be interfered with, and what is true of one end of a lot will not be true of the other.

If the ground chances to be broken or burned over or cleared the same year that a good crop of pine seed falls, then expect pines; not otherwise.

I examined the huckleberry bushes next the wall in that same dense pitch and white pine strip. I found

that the oldest bushes were about two feet high and
some eight or ten years old, and digging with spade
and hands, I found that their roots did not go deep, but
that they spread by a vigorous shoot which forked
several times, running just under the leaves or in the
surface soil, so that they could be easily pulled up. One
ran seven feet before it broke, and was probably ten
feet or more in length. And three or four bushes stood
on this shoot, and though these bushes after a few years
did not grow more than an inch in a year, these subterranean shoots had grown six to twelve inches at the end,
and there seemed to be all the vigor of the plant. The
largest bushes preserved still a trace of their origin from
a subterranean shoot, the limbs being one-sided and the
brash aslant. It is very likely, then, if not certain, that
these roots are as old as the pine wood which over-
shadows them; or it is so long since the seedling huckleberry came up there. The pines were thirty years old,
but some of the separate huckleberry bushes were ten,
and were sending up new vigorous shoots still. The
same was the case with the *Vaccinium vacillans* and the
Pennsylvanicum, the last one, of course, on a smaller
scale. You could see the *V. vacillans* growing in rows
for several feet above the subterranean shoots, indicating
where it was. The shoot turns up to make a bush thus:

Thus the roots of huckleberries may survive till the
woods are cut again. They certainly will here. A huckleberry bush is apparently in its prime at five to seven

years, and the oldest are ten to twelve years. Plants of this order (*Ericaceæ*) are said to be among the earlier ones among fossil plants, and they are likely to be among the last.

The oldest oak, fairly speaking, in this wood was a black, thirteen years old. Its root, as usual, ran not straight down but with a half-turn or twist (as well as to one side), which would make it harder to pull up at any rate.

The white oak acorn has very little bitterness and is quite agreeable to eat. When chestnuts are away I am inclined to think them as good as they. At any rate it braces my thought more, and does me more good to eat them, than it does to eat chestnuts. I feel the stronger even before I have swallowed one. It gives me heart and back of oak.

I found that the squirrels, or *possibly* mice, which have their holes about those old oak stumps ran along in various directions through the roots, whose insides are rotted away, leaving a wall of thin bark which prevents the earth falling in. Such are their highways underground. The holes above led to them.

On the monuments of the old settlers of this town, if they can be found, are recorded their names and ages and the time of their death, and so much can be read on these monuments of the oaks, with some additional reliable information, as where they lived, and how healthily, and what trees succeeded them, etc., etc.

Looking at Sophia's large collection of acorns from Sleepy Hollow and elsewhere, I cannot find a sound white oak one (*i. e.* not decayed and blackened), but

the black and shrub oaks at least are sound. This suggests that the very fertile shrub oaks are more sure of
succeeding and spreading, while the noblest oak of all
may fail.

First, by examining the twigs (*vide* Coultas) you tell
the age and the number of shoots and the leaves and the
various accidents of the tree for half a dozen years
past, — can read its history very minutely; and at
length, when it is cut down, you read its ancient and
general history on its stump.

If you would know the age of a young oak lot, look
round for a sprout, — for there will commonly be some
to be found even in a seedling wood, — cut, and count
the rings. But if you have to count the rings of a seedling, begin about six inches from the ground, for it was
probably so high when the previous wood was cut.

Oct. 20. E. Hosmer tells me to-day that while digging
mud at the Pokelogan the other day he found several
fresh acorns planted an inch or two deep under the
grass just outside the oaks and bushes there. Almost
every observant farmer finds one such deposit each
year.

If that Merriam lot is fifteen rods square, then, instead
of there being no oaks in it, there are some twenty-five
hundred oaks in it, or far more oaks than pines, — say
five times as many, for there are probably not nearly
five hundred pines in the lot. This is only one of the
thousand cases in which the proprietor and woodchopper
tell you that there is not a single oak in the lot. So the
tables were turned, and, so far as numbers were con-

cerned, it would have been truer to say that this was an exclusively oak wood and that there were no pines in it. Truly appearances are deceptive.

P. M. — To Walden Woods to examine old stumps.

In Trillium Wood the trees are chiefly pine, and I judge them to be forty to fifty years old, though there are not a few oaks, etc. Beneath them I find some old pitch pine stumps and one white pine. They would not be seen by a careless observer; they are indistinct mounds and preserve no form nor marks of the axe. This is low ground. Part of the cores, etc., of the stumps are, nevertheless, preserved by fat.

I then look at Farrar's [?] hill lot east of the Deep Cut. This is oak, cut, as I remember, some twenty-five years ago, the trees say five to eight inches [in] diameter. I find beneath the oaks innumerable pitch pine stumps, well preserved, or rather, distinct, some of them two feet and more in diameter, with .bark nearly three inches thick at the ground, but generally fifteen inches in diameter. Though apparently thoroughly rotten and of a rough (crumbly) conical form and more or less covered with fine moss (hypnum), they were firm within on account of the fat in flakes on the whole core, and frequently showed the trace of the axe in the middle. I could get cartloads of fat pine there now, often lifting out with my hands the whole core, a clear mass of yellow fat. When the stump was almost a mere mound mossed over, breaking off an inch or two deep of the crust, with the moss, I could still trace on one side the straight edge made by the axe. There were also, especially on the lower, or northern, side, some large oak stumps, no doubt of the same age.

These were much better preserved than the pines, — at least the part above ground. The whole shape and almost every stroke of the axe apparent sometimes, as in a fresh stump. I counted from seventy to seventy-five rings on one. The present wood appears to be chiefly from the seed, with some sprouts. The latter two or more close together, with the old stump more or less overgrown. The sprouts, I think, were from small trees. (Methinks you do not see trees which have sprouted from old or large stumps two or three feet in diameter. I doubt if a very old wood, like E. Hubbard's, would send up sprouts from the stump.) I saw one large oak stump so much decayed that it may have belonged to a generation further back.

I next examined Ebby Hubbard's old oak and pine wood. The trees may be a hundred years old. The older or decaying trees have been cut out from time to time, neglecting these more recent stumps. The very oldest evidences of a tree were a hollow three or four feet across, in which you often slumped, — a hollow place in which squirrels have their holes covered with many layers of leaves, and perhaps with young oaks springing up in it, for the acorns rolled into it. But if you dug there, from under the moss (there was commonly a little green moss around it) and leaves and soil, in the midst of the virgin mould which the tree had turned to, you pulled up flakes and shoulder-blades of wood that might still be recognized for oak, portions preserved by some quality which they concentrated, like the fat leaves or veins of the pine, — the oak of oak. But for the most part it was but the mould and mildew of the grave, — the grave of a tree which was cut or died eighty or a hundred years ago there. It is with the graves of trees as with those of men, — at first an upright stump (for a monument), in course of time a mere mound, and finally, when the corpse has decayed and shrunk, a depression in the soil. In such a hollow it is better to plant a pine than an oak. The only other ancient traces of trees were perhaps the semiconical mounds which had been heaved up by trees which fell in some hurricane.

I saw where Ebby had tried a pitch pine with his axe, though there was not a green twig on it, and the wood-peckers had bored it from top to bottom, — effectually proved it, if he had not been blind.

Looked at that pitch and white pine wood just east of Close at Brister Spring, which I remember as pas-ture some thirty years ago. The pasture is still betrayed under the pines by the firmer, sward-like surface, there being fewer leaves and less of leafy mould formed, — less virgin soil, — and by the patches of green (*pine*) moss and white cladonia peeping out here and there.

Young chestnuts (I dig up three or four) have not the large roots that oaks have.

I see the acorn after the tree is five or six years old.

Brassica Napus, or rape, a second crop, is blooming now, especially where grain has been cut and the field laid down to grass and clover. It has there little slender plants; rough, or bristly, lower leaves.

1st. There is the primitive wood, woodland which was woodland when the township was settled, and which has not been cut at all. Of this I know of none in Concord. Where is the nearest? There is, perhaps, a large tract in Winchendon.

2d. Second growth, the woodland which has been cut but once, — true second growth. This country has been so recently settled that a large part of the older States is covered now with this second growth, and the same name is occasionally still applied, though falsely, to those wood-lots which have been cut twice or many more times. Of this second growth I think that we have considerable left, and I remember much more. These are our forests which contain the largest and oldest trees, — shingle pines (very few indeed left) and oak timber.

3d. Primitive woodland, *i. e.*, which has always been woodland, never cultivated or converted into pasture or grain-field, nor burned over intentionally. Of two kinds, first, that which has only been thinned from time to time, and secondly, that which has been cut clean many times over. A larger *copsewood*.

4th. Woodland which has been cleared one or more times, enough to raise a crop of grain on it, burned over and perhaps harrowed or even plowed, and suffered to grow up again in a year or two. Call this "interrupted woodland" or "tamed."

5th. *New woods*, or which have sprung up *de novo* on land which has been cultivated or cleared long enough to kill all the roots in it. (The 3d, 4th, and 5th are a kind of copsewood.)

6th. Artificial woods, or those which have been set out or raised from the seed, artificially.

It happens that we have not begun to set out and plant till all the primitive wood is gone. All the *new woods* (or

5th kind) whose beginning I can (now) remember are
pine or birch (maple, etc., I have not noticed enough).
I suspect that the greater part (?) of our woodland is the
3d kind, or primitive woodland, never burned over intentionally nor plowed, though much of it is the 4th
kind. Probably almost all the large wood cut ten or
fifteen years ago (and since) here was second growth,
and most that we had left was cut then.

Of the new woods I remember the beginning of
E. Hubbard's east of Brister Spring; Bear Garden,
pitch pine; Wheeler's pigeon-place, pitch pine; also
his blackberry-field, pitch pine and a few white; West
Fair Haven Spring woods, pitch pine and white; E.
Hubbard's Close Mound, pitch pine; Conantum-top,
pitch pine; Mason's pasture (?), white pine; behind
Baker's (?), pitch pine; my field at Walden, pitch pine;
Kettle Hill, pitch pine; Moore's corn-hill, pitch pine,
cut say '59; behind Moore's house (??), pitch pine
(was it new?); front of Sleepy Hollow, poplars, pitch
pine; E. Wood's, front of Colburn place (??), pitch
pine, not new wood; John Hosmer's, beyond house (?),
pitch pine; Fair Haven Hill-side, white pine, just
begun; Merriam's pasture, beyond Beck Stow's, just
begun, pitch pine; old coast behind Heywood's, pitch
pine; Conant's white pine crescent in front of W.
Wheeler's; J. P. Brown pasture, white pine; at Hemlocks, pitch pine; northwest of Assabet stone bridge,
pitch pine; Tarbell's pitch pines; Baker's, above
beech, pitch pine; Henry Shattuck's, pitch pine;
northwest of Farmer's, pitch pine; William Brown's,
pitch pine; north of H. Shattuck's, pitch pine; white

and pitch pine south of Rice's lot; pitch pine northwest of old Corner schoolhouse, pitch pine southeast of new Corner schoolhouse; large pitch pine hill behind Hagar's in Lincoln.

In several of these new woods — pitch pine and birches — can see the old corn-hills still.

The woods within my recollection have gradually withdrawn further from the village, and woody capes which jutted from the forest toward the town are now cut off and separated by cleared land behind. The Irish have also made irruptions into our woods in several places, and cleared land.

Edmund Hosmer tells me of a gray squirrel which he kept in his old (Everett) house; that he would go off to the woods every summer, and in the winter come back and into his cage, where he whirled the wire cylinder. He would be surprised to see it take a whole and large ear of corn and run out a broken window and up over the roof of the corn-barn with it, and also up the elms.

We have a kitten a third grown which often carries its tail almost flat on its back like a squirrel.

Oct. 22. P. M. — To Walden Woods.

See in the yard many chip-birds, but methinks the chestnut crown is not so distinct as in the spring, — has a pale line in middle of it, — and many, maybe females or young, have no chestnut at all. I do not find them so described.

Are not maples inclined to die in a white pine wood? There was the one in Merriam's grove and the sickly ones in our grove in the yard.

I notice that the first shrubs and trees to spring up in the sand on railroad cuts in the woods are sweet-fern, birches, willows, and aspens, and pines, white and pitch; but all but the last two chiefly disappear in the thick wood that follows. The former are the pioneers. Such sandy places, the edges of meadows, and sprout-lands are almost the only localities of willows with us.

In the Deep Cut big wood (Stow's), pines and oaks, there are thousands of little white pines as well as many oaks. After a mixed wood like this you may have a mixed wood, but after dense pines, commonly oak chiefly, yet not always; for, to my surprise, I find that in the pretty dense pitch pine wood of Wheeler's blackberry-field, where there are only several white pines old enough to bear, and accordingly more than a thousand pitch pine seeds to one white pine one, yet there are countless white pines springing up under the pitch pines (as well as many oaks), and very few or scarcely any little pitch pines, and they sickly, or a thousand white pine seedlings to one pitch pine, — the same proportion reversed (in inverse proportion). It is the same in the pigeon-place lot east of this. So if you should cut these pitch pines you would have next a white pine wood with some oaks in it, the pines taking the lead. Indeed, these white pines bid fair to supplant the pitch pines at last, for they grow well and steadily. This reminds me that, though I often see little white pines under pines and under oaks, I rarely if ever (unless I am mistaken) see many young pitch pines there. How is it? Do the pitch pines require more light and air?

You may conveniently tell the age of a pine, especially

white pine, by cutting off the lowest branch that is still growing and counting its rings. Then estimate or count the rings of a pine growing near *in an opening*, of the same height as to that branch, and add the two sums together.

I found in the midst of this pitch pine wood a white oak some eight feet high and an inch and a half thick at ground, which had borne a great many — say sixty or a hundred — large oak-balls, and the ground beneath and near by was strewn with the fragments of fifty of them, which some creature, probably a squirrel, — for a bird could hardly have opened the hard nut-like kernel within, — had opened, no doubt for their living contents, and all the inside was gone. They looked like egg-shells strewn about. Opening one, I found within the hard kernel a humpbacked black fly nearly half an inch long, body and wings, with a very large or full shining black abdomen and two small black spots on each wing. The only two that I open have flies in them. Harris says that this fly is the *Cynips confluens*, and that the grub becomes a chrysalis in the autumn and not, commonly, a fly till spring, though he has known this gall-fly to come out in October. It must have been squirrels (or mice) that opened them, for birds could not break into the hard kernel.

Counted the rings of a white pine stump in Hubbard's owl wood by railroad. Ninety-four years. So this was probably second growth.

Swamps are, of course, least changed with us, — are nearest to their primitive state of any woodland. Commonly they have only been cut, not redeemed.

I see how meadows were primitively kept in the state of meadow by the aid of water, — and even fire and wind. For example, Heywood's meadow, though it may have been flowed a hundred years ago by the dam below, has been bare almost ever since in the midst of the wood. Trees have not grown over it. Maples, alders, birches, pitch and white pines are slow to spread into it. I have named them in the order of their slowness. The last are the foremost, — furthest into the meadow, — but they are sickly-looking. You may say that it takes a geological change to make a wood-lot there.

Looked at stumps in J. Hosmer's lot, hillside south of first Heywood meadow, cut eleven (?) years ago. One white pine perfect in shape, forty-one rings; two large oak stumps, each one hundred and nine rings; and a large pitch pine, probably same age. These stumps are all well preserved. The whole outline and the rings can for most part be counted; but they are successive ridges, and the bark is ready to fall off, and they are more or less mossed over with cockscomb moss. The main part of this lot north of this hole is apparently oak sprouts next railroad.

I next look through Emerson's lot (half-burned and cut last spring). The last year's growth (and present) chiefly oak, with a little pine. The stumps are chiefly oak and pitch pine, with apparently some hemlock (?) and chestnut and a little white pine. (So it seems the pitch pine and hemlock did not survive the old cutting; the pitch pine did not come up under itself.) The pitch pine stumps are all decayed but the core and the bark,

and hardly in any instance show a trace of the axe.
They are low rounded mounds, yet the inmost parts are
solid fat, and the bark edge is very plain. The oak
stumps are very much better preserved, — have half
or two thirds their form, and show that proportion of
the cutting, — yet the sap-wood is often gone (with the
bark), and as often the inmost heart. You can partially
count rings even. Yet some of these are as decayed as
the pines, and all flaky, and, turned up, look like
stumps of old teeth with their prongs. They (the oaks)
are all loose to the foot, yet you will see the white bark
lying about a white oak stump when all the rest is about
gone. Most of the old stumps, both oaks and pines,
can easily be found now, but the rings of not one oak
even can be wholly counted, or nearly. I could not be
sure about the hemlock and chestnut, only that there
was *some* of both. There was little moss on these
stumps, either pine or oak; the latter too crumbly.

The southeast part of this lot, beyond the deep
cove, is apparently an oak sprout-land and good part
pine. I see what were sprouts from a scarlet oak stump
eighteen or more inches in diameter and from white
oaks one foot in diameter; yet in the other lot, though
there were so many large oak stumps, I did not notice
that trees had ever sprung from them. You find plenty
of old oak stumps without their trees in the woods,
which (if nothing else) shows that there is an end to
this mode of propagation.

I could tell a white pine here when it was for the most
part a mere rotten mound, by the regularity crosswise
of the long knots a foot from the ground in the top of

the rotten core, representing the peculiarly regular branches of the little white pine and the best preserved as the hardest and pitchiest part.

It is apparent that fires often hasten the destruction of these stumps. They are very apt to be charred.

I dug in the hollow where an oak had been, and though it was so completely decayed that I found not a particle that looked like decayed wood or even bark and my spade met with no resistance, yet there were perfectly open channels raying out from this hollow with the pellicle of the root for a wall still, which for a hundred years the earth had learned to respect. Indeed, these stumps, both of this age and more recent, are the very metropolis of the squirrels and mice. Such are their runways.

Yet what is the character of our gratitude to these squirrels, these planters of forests? We regard them as vermin, and annually shoot and destroy them in great numbers, because — if we have any excuse — they sometimes devour a little of our Indian corn, while, perhaps, they are planting the nobler oak-corn (acorn) in its place. In various parts of the country an army of grown-up boys assembles for a squirrel hunt. They choose sides, and the side that kills the greatest number of thousands enjoys a supper at the expense of the other side, and the whole neighborhood rejoices. Would it [not] be far more civilized and humane, not to say godlike, to recognize once in the year by some significant symbolical ceremony the part which the squirrel plays, the great service it performs, in the economy of the universe?

The Walden side of Emerson's main wood-lot is oak (except a few pines in the oaks at the northwest or railroad end), and the oaks are chiefly sprouts, some thirty years old. Yet, not to mention the pitch pine stumps, there are a great many oak stumps without sprouts, and yet not larger stumps than the others. How does this happen ? They are all of the same age, *i. e.* cut at the same time.

Sometimes, evidently, when you see oak stumps from which no trees have sprung in the midst of a pine or birch wood, it may be because the land was cleared and burned over and cultivated after the oaks were cut.

Oct. 23. Anthony Wright tells me that he cut a pitch pine on Damon's land between the Peter Haynes road and his old farm, about '41, in which he counted two hundred and seventeen rings, which was therefore older than Concord, and one of the primitive forest. He tells me of a noted large and so-called primitive wood, Inches Wood, between the Harvard turnpike and Stow, sometimes called Stow Woods, in Boxboro and Stow. Also speaks of the wood north of Wetherbee's mill near Annursnack and belonging to W., as large and old, if not cut.

Melvin thinks that a fox would not on an average weigh more than ten pounds. Says that he saw a flock of brant yesterday by day. (Rarely seen by day or even by night here.) He says that Hildreth collects moss (probably cladonia) from the rocks for kindling.

There is no such mortality in nobler seeds — seeds of living creatures, as eggs of birds, for instance — as I have noticed in white oak acorns. What if the eggs of any species of bird should be addled to this extent, so that it should be hard to find a sound one? In Egypt, where they hatch eggs artificially in an oven, they can afford to return one chicken for every two eggs they receive (and do so) and yet find it profitable. It is true one third of human infants are said to die before they are five years old, but even this is a far less mortality than that of the acorns. The oak is a scarce bearer, yet it lasts a good while.

More or less rain to-day and yesterday.

Oct. 24. P. M. — To Walden Woods.

See three little checkered adders lying in the sun by a stump on the sandy slope of the Deep Cut; yet sluggish. They are seven or eight inches long. The dark blotches or checkers are not so brown as in large ones. There is a transverse dark mark on the snout and a forked light space on the back part [of] the head.

Examine again Emerson's pond lot, to learn its age by the stumps cut last spring. I judge from them that they were some five (?) years cutting over the part next the water, for I count the rings of many stumps and they vary in number from twenty-four or five to thirty, though twenty-six, seven, and eight are commonest, as near as I can count. It is hard to distinguish the very first ring, and often one or more beside before you reach the circumference. But, these being almost all sprouts, I know that they were pretty large the first year. I repeatedly see beside the new tree (cut last spring) the now well-rotted stump from which it sprang. But I do not see the stump from which the last sprang. I should like to know how long they may continue to spring from the stump. Here are shoots of this year which have sprung vigorously from stumps cut in the spring, which had sprung in like manner some twenty-eight or thirty years ago from a stump which is still very plain by their sides. I see that some of these thirty-year trees are sprouts from a white oak stump twenty inches in diameter, — four from one in one case. Sometimes, when a white pine stump is all crumbling beside, there is a broad shingle-like flake left from the centre to the circumference, the old ridge of the stump, only a quarter of an inch thick, and this betrays the axe in a straight inclined surface.

The southeast part of Emerson's lot, next the pond, is yet more exclusively oak sprouts, or oak from oak, with fewer pine stumps. I examine an oak seedling in this. There are two very slender shoots rising ten or more inches above the ground, which, traced downward, conduct to a little stub, which I mistook for a very old root or part of a larger tree, but, digging it up, I found it to be a true seedling. This seedling had died down to the ground six years ago, and then these two slender shoots, such as you commonly see in oak woods, had started. The root was a regular seedling root (fusiform if *straightened*), at least seven eighths of an inch thick, while the largest shoot was only one eighth of in inch thick, though six years old and ten inches high.

The root was probably ten years old when the seedling first died down, and is now some sixteen years old. Yet, as I say, the oak is only ten inches high. This shows how it endures and gradually pines and dies. As you look down on it, it has two turns, and three as you look from the side, so firmly is it rooted. Any one will be surprised on digging up some of these lusty oaken carrots.

Look at stumps in Heywood's lot, southeast side pond, from Emerson's to the swimming-place. They are white pine, oak, pitch pine, etc. I count rings of three white pine (from sixty to seventy). There are a few quite large white pine stumps; on one, ninety rings. One oak gives one hundred and sixteen rings. A pitch pine some fifteen or sixteen inches over gives about one hundred and thirty-five. All these are very easy, if not easier than ever, to count. The pores of the pines are distinct ridges, and the pitch is worn off. (Many white and pitch pines elsewhere cut this year cannot be counted, they are so covered with pitch.) I remember this as a particularly dense and good-sized wood, mixed pine and oak.

Mrs. Heywood's pitch pines by the shore, judging from some cut two or three years ago, are about eighty-five years old. As far as I have noticed, the pitch pine is the slowest-growing tree (of pines and oaks) and gives the most rings in the smallest diameter.

Then there are the countless downy seeds (thistle-like) of the goldenrods, so fine that we do not notice them in the air. They cover our clothes like dust. No wonder they spread over all fields and far into the woods.

I see those narrow pointed yellow buds now laid bare so thickly along the slender twigs of the *Salix discolor*, which is almost bare of leaves.

Oct. 25. P. M. — To Eb. Hubbard's wood and Sleepy Hollow.

See a little reddish-brown snake (bright-red beneath) in the path; probably *Coluber amœnus*.

Cut one of the largest of the lilacs at the Nutting wall, eighteen inches from the ground. It there measures one and five sixteenths inches and has twenty distinct rings from centre, then about twelve very fine, not thicker than previous three; equals thirty-two in all. It evidently dies down many times, and yet lives and sends up fresh shoots from the root.

Jarvis's hill lot is oak, pitch pine, and some white, and quite old. There are a great many little white pines springing up under it, but I see no pitch. Yet the large pitch are much more common than the large white. Nevertheless the small white have come on much faster and more densely in the hollows just outside the large wood on the south.

E. Hubbard's mound of pitch pines contains not one seed-bearing white pine, yet there are under these pines many little white pines (whose seed must have blown some distance), but scarcely one pitch pine. The latter, however, are seen along its edge and in the larger openings. So at Moore's pitch pine promontory

south of the Foley house, cut off lately by Walcott.
Where the large pines had stood are no little ones,
but in the open pasture northward quite a little grove,
which had spread from them. Yet from a hasty look
at the south end of the Sleepy Hollow Cut pitch pines,
it appeared that small pitch pines were abundant under
them. *Vide* again.

I have seen an abundance of white oak acorns this
year, and, as far as I looked, swamp white oak acorns
were pretty numerous. Red oak acorns are also pretty
common. Black and scarlet oak I find also, but not
very abundant. I have seen but few shrub oak, comparatively. Of the above, only the white oak have
decayed so remarkably. The others are generally
sound, or a few wormy. The red oak, as far as I notice,
are remarkably sound. The scarlet oak I cut this
afternoon are *some* of them decaying, but not like the
white oak. Only the white have sprouted at all, as far
as I perceive.

I find some scarlet oak acorns on the back side
northeast end of Sleepy Hollow which are rounder than
usual, considerably like a filbert out of the shell. They
are indistinctly marked with meridional lines and thus
betray a relation to the black and black shrub oak.[1]

I see an immense quantity of asparagus seed in the
mist of its dead branches, on Moore's great field of it,
near Hawthorne's. There must be a great many bushels
of the seed, and the sight suggested how extensively
the birds must spread it. I saw, accordingly, on Hawthorne's hillside, a dozen rods north of it, many plants

[1] *Vide* swamp white oak, p. [180].

(with their own seed) two or three feet high. It is planted in the remotest swamps in the town.

Saw in E. Hubbard's clintonia swamp a large spider with a great golden-colored abdomen as big as a hazel-nut, on the wet leaves. There was a figure in brown lines on the back, in the form of a pagoda with its stories successively smaller. The legs were pale or whitish, with dark or brown bars.

Find many of those pale-brown roughish fungi (it looks like Loudon's plate of *Scleroderma*, perhaps *verrucosum*), two to three inches in diameter. Those which are ripe are so softened at the top as to admit the rain through the skin (as well as after it opens), and the interior is shaking like a jelly, and if you open it you see what looks like a yellowish gum or jelly amid the dark fuscous dust, but it is this water colored by the dust; yet when they are half full of water they emit dust nevertheless. They are in various states, from a firm, hard and dry unopen[ed] to a half-empty and flabby moist cup.

See the yellow butterfly still and great devil's-needles.

Dug up and brought home last night three English cherry trees from Heywood's Peak by Walden. There are a dozen or more there, and several are as handsome as any that you will find in a nursery. They remind me of some much larger which used to stand above the cliffs. This species too comes up in sprout-lands like the wild rum cherry. The amount of it is that such a tree, whose fruit is a favorite with birds, will spring up far and wide and wherever the earth is bared of trees, but since the forest overpowers and destroys

them, and also cultivation, they are only found young in
sprout-lands or grown up along fences. It looks as if
this species preferred a hilltop. Whether the birds
are more inclined to convey the seeds there or they
find the light and exposure and the soil there which
they prefer. These have each one great root, somewhat like a long straight horn, making a right angle
with the stem and running far off one side close to the
surface.

The thistles which I now see have their heads recurved, which at least saves their down from so great a
soaking. But when I pull out the down, the seed is for
the most part left in the receptacle (?), in regular order
there, like the pricks in a thimble. A slightly convex
surface. The seeds set like cartridges in a circular cartridge-box, in hollow cylinders which look like circles
crowded into more or less of a diamond, pentagonal, or
hexagonal form. The perfectly dry and bristly involucre
which hedges them round, so repulsive externally, is
very neat and attractive within, — as smooth and tender
toward its charge as it is rough and prickly externally
toward the foes that might do it injury. It is a hedge
of imbricated thin and narrow leafets of a light-brown
color, beautifully glossy like silk, a most fit receptacle
for the delicate downy parachutes of the seed, a cradle
lined with silk or satin. The latter are kept dry under
this unsuspected silky or satiny ceiling, whose old and
weather-worn and rough outside alone we see, like a
mossy roof, little suspecting the delicate and glossy
lining. I know of no object more unsightly to a careless glance than an empty thistle-head, yet, if you ex-

amine it closely, it may remind you of the silk-lined cradle in which a prince was rocked. Thus that which seemed a mere brown and worn-out relic of the summer, sinking into the earth by the roadside, turns out to be a precious casket.

I notice in the pitch pine wood behind Moore's the common pinweed (*Lechea major* or the next) growing on the top of a pitch pine stump which is yet quite in shape and firm, one foot from the ground, with its roots firmly set in it, reaching an inch or two deep. Probably the seed was blown there, perhaps over the snow when it was on a level with the stump.

Oct. 26. P. M. — To Baker's old chestnut lot near Flint's Pond.

As I go through what was formerly the dense pitch pine lot on Thrush Alley (G. Hubbard's), I observe that the present growth is scrub oak, birch, oaks of various kinds, white pines, pitch pines, willows, and poplars. Apparently, the birch, oaks, and pitch pines are the oldest of the *trees*. From the number of small white pines in the neighboring pitch pine wood, I should have expected to find larger and also more white pines here. It will finally become a mixed wood of oak and white and pitch pine. There is much cladonia in the lot.

Observed yesterday that the row of white pines set along the fence on the west side of Sleepy Hollow had grown very fast, apparently from about the time they were set out, or the last three years. Several had made about seven feet within the three years. Do they not grow the fastest at just this age, or after they get to be about five feet high?

I see to-day sprouts from chestnut stumps which are two and a half feet in diameter (*i. e.* the stumps). One of these large stumps is cut quite low and hollowing, so as to hold water as well as leaves, and the leaves prevent the water from drying up. It is evident that in such a case the stump rots sooner than if high and roof-like.

I remember that there were a great many hickories with R. W. E.'s pitch pines when I lived there, but now there are but few comparatively, and they appear to have died down several times and come up again from the root. I suppose it is mainly on account of frosts, though perhaps the fires have done part of it. Are not hickories most commonly found on hills? There are a few hickories in the open land which I once cultivated there, and these may have been planted there by birds or squirrels. It must be more than thirty-five years since there was wood there.

I find little white pines under the pitch pines (of E.), near the pond end, and few or no little pitch pines, but between here and the road about as many of one as of the other, but the old pines are much less dense that way, or not dense at all.

This is the season of the fall when the leaves are whirled through the air like flocks of birds, the season of birch spangles, when you see afar a few clear-yellow leaves left on the tops of the birches.

It was a mistake for Britton to treat that Fox Hollow lot as he did. I remember a large old pine and chestnut wood there some twenty years ago. He came and cut it off and burned it over, and ever since it has been good for nothing. I mean that acre at the bottom of the hollow. It is now one of those frosty hollows so common in Walden Woods, where little grows, sheep's fescue grass, sweet-fern, hazelnut bushes, and oak scrubs whose dead tops are two or three feet high, while the still living shoots are not more than half as high at their base. They have lingered so long and died down annually. At length I see a few birches and pines creeping into it, which at this rate in the course of a dozen years more will *suggest* a forest there. Was this wise?

Examined the stumps in the Baker chestnut lot which was cut when I surveyed it in the spring of '52. They were when cut commonly from fifty to sixty years old (some older, some younger). The sprouts from them are from three to six inches thick, and may average — the largest — four inches, and eighteen feet high. The wood is perhaps near half oak sprouts, and these are one and a half to four inches thick, or average two and a half, and not so high as the chestnut. Some of the largest chestnut stumps have sent up no sprout, yet others equally large and very much more decayed have sent up sprouts. Can this be owing to the different time when they were cut? The cutting was after April. The largest sprouts I chanced to notice were from a small stump in low ground. Some hemlock stumps there had a hundred rings.

Was overtaken by a sudden thunder-shower.

Cut a chestnut sprout two years old. It grew about

five and a half feet the first year and three and a half
the next, and was an inch in diameter. The tops of these
sprouts, the last few inches, had died in the winter, so
that a side bud continued them, and this made a slight
curve in the sprout, thus: There was on
a cross-section, of course,   but one ring of
pores within the wood,   just outside the
large pith, the diameter of   the first year's
growth being just half an   inch, radius a
fourth of an inch. The thickness of the second year's
growth was the same, or one fourth, but it was distinctly marked to the naked eye with about seven concentric lighter lines, which, I suppose, marked so many
successive growths or waves of growth, or seasons in its
year. These were not visible through a microscope
of considerable power, but best to the naked eye. Probably you could tell a seedling chestnut from a vigorous
sprout, however old or large, provided the heart were
perfectly sound to the pith, by the much more rapid
growth of the last the first half-dozen years of its existence.

There are scarcely any chestnuts this year near
Britton's, but I find as many as usual east of Flint's
Pond.

Oct. 27. Emerson planted his lot with acorns (chiefly
white oak) pretty generally the other day. There were
a few scarlet oak acorns planted there on the south side
in spring of '59. There is on the Lee farm, west of hill,
a small wood-lot of oak and hickory, the south end
chiefly hickory.

I have come out this afternoon to get ten seedling oaks out of a purely oak wood, and as many out of a purely pine wood, and then compare them. I look for trees one foot or less in height, and convenient to dig up. I could not find one in the last-named wood. I then searched in the large Woodis Park, the most oaken parts of it, wood some twenty-five or thirty years old, but I found only three. There were many shrub oaks and others three or four feet high, but no more of the kind described. Two of these three had singularly old large and irregular roots, mere gnarled oblong knobs, as it were, with slender shoots, having died down many times. After searching here more than half an hour I went into the new pitch and white pine lot just southwest, toward the old Lee cellar, and there were thousands of the seedling oaks only a foot high and less, quite reddening the ground now in some places, and these had perfectly good roots, though not so large as those near the Corner Spring (next to Rice's wall).

Here is a new but quite open pitch and white pine wood (with birches on south) on cladonia ground. It is so open that many pitch pines are springing up.

E. Wood's dense pitch (and white) pine wood in front of Lee house site conforms to the rule of few or no little pitch pines within it, but many white pines (though not many far within), while the pitch pines are springing up with white pines on the edge and even further toward the road.

The white pine wood southeast of this and not far north of railroad, against Wood's open land, is a *new* wood.

As I am coming out of this, looking for seedling oaks, I see a jay, which was screaming at me, fly to a white oak eight or ten rods from the wood in the pasture and directly alight on the ground, pick up an acorn, and fly back into the woods with it. This was one, perhaps the most effectual, way in which this wood was stocked with the numerous little oaks which I saw under that dense white pine grove. Where will you look for a jay sooner than in a dense pine thicket ? It is there they commonly live, and build.

By looking to see what oaks grow in the open land near by or along the edge where the wood is extensively pine, I can tell surely what kinds of oaks I shall find under the pines.

What if the oaks are far off ? Think how quickly a jay can come and go, and how many times in a day! [1]

Swamp white oak acorns are pretty thick on the ground by the bridge, and all sound that I try. They have no more bitterness than the white oak acorns.

I have now examined many dense pine woods, both pitch and white, and several oak woods, in order to see how many and what kind of oak seedlings there were springing up in them, and I do not hesitate to say that seedlings under one foot high are *very* much more abundant under the pines than under the oaks. They prevail and are countless under the pines, while they are hard to find under the oaks, and what you do find have commonly — for whatever reason — very old and decayed roots and feeble shoots from them.

If you expect oaks to succeed a dense and purely oak

[1] *Vide* [p. 188].

wood you must depend almost entirely on sprouts, but they will succeed abundantly to pine where there is not an oak stump for them to sprout from. Notwithstanding that the acorns are produced only by oaks and not by pines, the fact is that there are comparatively few seedling oaks a foot or less in height under the oaks but thousands under the pines. I would not undertake to get a hundred oaks of this size suitable to transplant under a dense and pure oak wood, but I could easily get thousands from under pines. What are the reasons for this? First it is certain that, generally speaking, the soil under old oaks is more exhausted for oaks than under old pines. Second, seedling oaks under oaks would be less protected from frosts in the spring just after leafing, yet the sprouts prevail. Third, squirrels and jays resort to evergreens with their forage, and the oaks may not bear so many acorns but that the squirrels may carry off nearly all the sound ones. These are some of the reasons that occur to me.

To be more minute:—

I dug up three oak seedlings in the Woodis Park oaks, nine in the small open pitch and white pine and adjoining on southwest, and ten in the pitch and white pine of wood between road and railroad.

Woodis Park is oak and pine some twenty-five years old (the oak). I chose the oaken parts, but there was always a pine within a rod or two. I looked here till I was discouraged, finding only three in three quarters of an hour. One was like those in pine woods; the other two had singular gnarled and twisted great roots. You would think you had come upon a dead but buried stump. The largest, for instance, was perhaps a red oak nine inches high by one eighth inch at ground and apparently three years old, a slender shoot. The root broke off at about eighteen inches depth, where it was one eighth inch thick, and at three inches below the surface it was one and three eighths inches thick by one inch (being flattish). Two or three of the side or horizontal fibres had developed into stout roots which ran quite horizontally twenty inches and then broke off, and were apparently as long as the tap-root. One of these at three inches below surface was about half an inch thick and perfectly horizontal. It was thus fixed very firmly in the ground. I counted the dead bases or stubs of shoots (beside the present one) and several two or three times as large as this, which had formerly died down, being now perfectly decayed. If there was but one at a time and they decayed successively after living each three years only, — and they probably lived twice as long, — then the root would be thirty years old. But supposing there were one and a half shoots at a time, it would then be some twenty years old. I think that this root may be as old as the large oaks around, or some twenty-five years, more or less.

My next nine oaks, from the pines southwest, may be put with the ten from the E. Wood pines (leaving out one which was twice the required height). Their average age, *i. e.* of the present shoot, was four years, and average height seven inches. (This includes white oak, shrub oak, black, and apparently red oak.) The roots averaged about ten inches long by three eighths thick at thickest part. Quite a number were shrub oak, which partly accounts for their slenderness. But the rest were not so thick as those near Rice's wall. Of all the above roots, or the whole twenty-two, none ran directly and perpendicularly downward, but they turned to one side (just under the acorn) and ran more or less horizontally or aslant one to five inches, or say three inches on an average.

Of the last nineteen, more than half had died down once at least, so that they were really considerably older than at first appeared. There are, in all cases, at the surface of the ground or head of the root, a ring of dormant buds, ready to shoot up when an injury happens to the original shoot. One shoot at least had been cut off, and so killed, by a rabbit.

See a very large flock of crows.

To speak from recollection of pines and oaks, I should say that our woods were chiefly pine and oak mixed, but we have also (to speak of the large growth, or trees) pure pine and pure oak woods. How are these three produced ? Are not the pure pine woods commonly new woods, i. e. pioneers ? After oaks have once got established, it must be hard to get them out without clearing the land. A pure oak wood may be obtained by cutting off at once and clean a pure and dense pine wood, and again sometimes by cutting the same oak wood. But pines are continually stealing into oaks, and oaks into pines, where respectively they are not too dense, as where they are burned or otherwise thinned, and so mixed woods may arise.

Oct. 28. In a pine wood are the little oak seedlings

which I have described, also, in the more open parts,
little oaks three to six feet high, but unnoticed, and
perhaps some other hardwood trees. The pines are cut,
and the oaks, etc., soon fill the space, for there is nothing
else ready to grow there.

Are not the most exclusively pine woods new woods,
i. e., those which have recently sprung up in open land,
where oaks do not begin a forest? It may be that where
evergreens most prevail in *our* woods, there at the date of
their springing up the earth was most bare.

P. M. — To Lincoln.

Do I not see tree sparrows?

I see little larches two to six feet high in the meadow
on the north side the Turnpike, six to twelve rods from
Everett's seed-bearing ones. The seed was evidently
blown from these.

There is quite a dense birch wood in the field north of
the Cut on the Turnpike hill.

See much cat-tail whose down has recently burst and
shows white on the south side of the heads. The *Polygonum aviculare* is in bloom as freshly and abundantly
in some places as ever I saw it. Those great tufts of
sedge in the meadows are quite brown and withered. I
suppose they have been so since the beginning of the
month.

Smith's black walnuts are about half of them fallen.

Measure the chestnut stump near the brook northeast
of the old Brooks Tavern on Asa White's land. Its
height from the ground will average but twenty inches.
Measured one way, its diameter is six feet nine inches,
and at right angles with this, eight feet five inches. Its

average diameter seven feet seven inches. You might add three to four feet more for the whole stump above ground. Beginning at the outside, I count one hundred and two rings distinctly and am then fifteen inches from the apparent centre of the tree, for the middle is mostly rotted and gone. Measuring back fifteen inches and counting the rings, I get thirty-nine, which, added to one hundred and two, equals one hundred and forty-one for the probable age of the tree. This tree had grown very fast till the last fifty years of its existence, but since comparatively slowly. It had grown nine inches in the last forty-nine years, or one seventh [*sic*] of an inch in a year, but fifteen inches in the previous forty, or three eighths of an inch in a year. There may possibly have been two shoots or trees grown together, yet I think not. I measured this June 1st, 1852, and it had then been cut, as I remember, but a short time, — a winter, perhaps two winters, before. This would carry its origin back to about 1710. Probably chestnuts did not grow so large in the primitive woods, and this was a forest tree, which, as it stood near the edge of the meadow, was left standing. Another much smaller was cut apparently at the same time near by. Having light and air and room, it grew larger than it would have done if its neighbors had not been cut.

I also measured the stumps of the two great chestnuts which were cut on Weston's land south of the pond some five or six years ago.

They are cut low, some eight or nine inches above ground. The southeasternmost one measures four feet in diameter and has about eighty rings only (I estimate

the first five or six, the heart or core being gone). The
other is four and five twelfths feet in diameter and has
seventy-three rings only. Or, putting both together,
you have an average growth of about a third of an inch
in a year. These were as large as any I know standing
hereabouts except the Strawberry Hill one, and yet it
seems they [were] only some eighty years old. Another,
half a mile east of there, cut perhaps some dozen years
ago, was twenty-three inches in diameter and had sixty-
three rings, and I saw one which had grown faster than
any of the above. Yet another stump near the last on the
high woodland near the pond was but just two feet in
diameter and had one hundred and one rings distinct
to the very core, and so fine there I think it was a seedling.
From this sprouts had grown some fifteen years ago
and [had been] cut last winter on account of a fire, and
fresh shoots several feet high had put out from the last.
The one that had grown slowly was soundest at the
core. None of the three largest stumps described had
sprouts from them. Is not the very rapid growth and the
hollow or rotten core one sign of a sprout? We make a
great noise going through the fallen leaves in the woods
and wood-paths now, so that we cannot hear other
sounds, as of birds or other people. It reminds me of
the tumult of the waves dashing against each other or
your boat. This is the dash we hear as we sail the woods.

Cut a limb of a cedar (near the Irishman's shanty-
site at Flint's Pond) some two inches thick and three
and a half feet from the ground. It had about forty-one
rings. Adding ten, you have say fifty years for the age
of the tree. It was one foot in diameter at one foot

above ground and twenty or more feet high, standing
in the young wood. A little cedar five feet high near it
had some fifteen to seventeen rings. See a great many
chestnut sprouts full six feet high and more and an inch
or more thick the first year.

Aaron's-rod has minute chaffy seeds, now ripe, which
by their very lightness could be blown along the high-
ways.

Oct. 29. P. M. — To Eb. Hubbard's old black birch
hill.

Henry Shattuck's is a *new* pitch pine wood, say thirty
years old. The western, or greater, part contains not a
single seed-bearing white pine. It is a remarkable
proof of my theory, for it contains thousands of little
white pines but scarcely one little pitch pine. It is also
well stocked with minute oak seedlings. It is a dense
wood, say a dozen rods wide by three or four times as
long, running east and west, with an oak wood on the
north, from which the squirrels brought the acorns.
A strip of nearly the same width of the pitch pine was
cut apparently within a year on the south (a part of the
above), and has just been harrowed and sown with rye,
and still it is all dotted over with the little oak seedlings
between the [stumps], which are perhaps unnoticed by
Shattuck, but if he would keep his plow and fire out he
would still have a pretty green patch there by next fall.
A thousand little red flags (changed oak leaves) already
wave over the green rye amid the stumps. The farmer
stumbles over these in his walk, and sweats while he
endeavors to clear the land of them, and yet wonders

how oaks ever succeed to pines, as if he did not consider what *these* are. Where these pines are dense they are slender and tall. On the edge or in open land they are more stout and spreading.

Again, as day before yesterday, sitting on the edge of a pine wood, I see a jay fly to a white oak half a dozen rods off in the pasture, and, gathering an acorn from the ground, hammer away at it under its foot on a limb of the oak, with an awkward and rapid seesaw or teetering motion, it has to lift its head so high to acquire the requisite momentum. The jays scold about almost every white oak tree, since we hinder their coming to it.

At some of the white oaks visited on the 11th, where the acorns were so thick on the ground and trees, I now find them perhaps nearly half picked up, yet perhaps little more than two thirds spoiled. The good appear to be all sprouted now. There are certainly many more sound ones here than at Beck Stow's and Hubbard's Grove, and it looks as if the injury had been done by frost, but perhaps some of it was done by the very heavy rains of September alone.

Yesterday and to-day I have walked rapidly through extensive chestnut woods without seeing what I thought was a seedling chestnut, yet I can soon find them in our Concord pines a quarter or half a mile from the chestnut woods. Several have expressed their surprise to me that they cannot find a seedling chestnut to transplant. I think that [it] is with them precisely as with the oaks; not only a seedling is more difficult to distinguish in a chestnut wood, but it is really far more rare there than in the adjacent pine, mixed, and oak woods. After considerable experience in searching for these and seedling oaks, I have learned to neglect the chestnut and oak woods and go only to the neighboring woods of a different species for them. Only that course will pay.

On the side of E. Hubbard's hill I see an old chestnut stump some two feet in diameter and nearly two feet high, and its outside and form well kept, yet all the inside gone; and from this shot up four sprouts in a square around it, which were cut down seven or eight years ago. Their rings number forty-six, and they are quite sound, so that the old stump was cut some fifty-three years ago. This is the oldest stump of whose age I am certain. Hence I have no doubt that there are many stumps left in this town which were cut in the last century. I am surprised to find on this hill (cut some seven or eight years ago) many remarkably old stumps wonderfully preserved, especially on the north side the hill, — walnuts, white oak and other oaks, and black birch. One white oak is eighteen and a half inches in diameter and has one hundred and forty-three rings. This is very one-sided in its growth, the centre being just four inches from the north side, or thirty-six rings to an inch. Of course I counted the other side. Another, close by, gave one hundred and forty-one rings, another white oak fifteen and a half inches in diameter had one hundred and fifty-five rings. It has so smooth (sawed off) and solid, almost a polished or marble-like, surface that I could not at first tell what kind of wood it was.[1] Another white oak the same as last in rings, i. e. one hundred and fifty-five, twenty-four inches [in]

[1] Was it not a walnut?

diameter. All these were sound to the very core, so that
I could see the first circles, and I suspect that they were
seedlings.

The smaller, but oldest ones had grown very slowly
at first, and yet more slowly at last, but after some sixty-
five years they had then grown much faster for about
fifteen years, and then grew slower and slower to the
last. The rings were exceedingly close together near
the outside, yet not proportionably difficult to count.
For aught that appeared, they might have continued
to grow a century longer. The stumps are far apart,
so that this formed an open grove, and that probably
made the wood sounder and more durable. On the
south slope many white pines had been cut about forty-
six years ago, or when the chestnut was, amid the oaks.
I suppose that these were seedlings, and perhaps the
hill was cleared soon after the settlement of the town,
and after a while pines sprang up in the open land, and
seedling oaks under the pines, and, the latter being cut
near the end of the seventeenth century, those oaks
sprang up, with or without pines, but all but these were
cut down when they were about sixty years old.

If these are seedlings, then seedlings make much the
best timber. I should say that the pasture oaks *generally* must be seedlings on account of their age, being
part of the primitive wood.

I suspect that sprouts, like the chestnut, for example,
may grow very rapidly, and make large trees in comparatively few years, but they will be decaying [?] as
fast at the core as they are growing at the circumference.
The stumps of chestnuts, especially sprouts, are very

shaky. It is with men as with trees; you must grow
slowly to last long. The oldest of these oaks began
their existence about 1697.

I doubt if there were any as old trees in our primitive
wood as stood in this town fifty years ago. The health-
iest of the primitive wood, having at length more room,
light, and air, probably grew larger than its ancestors.

Some of the black birch stumps gave about one
hundred rings.

The pasture oak which Sted Buttrick cut some seven
or eight years ago, northeast of this, was, as near as
I could tell, — one third was calculation, — some one
hundred years old only, though larger than any of these.

The fine chips which are left on the centre of a large
stump preserve it moist there, and rapidly hasten its
decay.

The site of the last-named pasture oak was easily
discovered, by a very large open grass-sward where no
sweet-fern, lambkill, huckleberry, and brakes grew,
as they did almost everywhere else. This may be because of the cattle assembling under the oak, and so
killing the bushes and at the same time manuring the
ground for grass.

There is more chestnut in the northern part of the
town than I was aware of. The first large wood north
of Ponkawtasset is oak and chestnut. East of my house.

Oct. 30. P. M. — To Tarbell pitch pines, etc.

Quite a sultry, cloudy afternoon, — hot walking in
woods and lowland where there is no air.

J. Hosmer cut off the northernmost part of his

pitch pine between roads, *i. e.* next the factory road, last winter. Here was a remarkable example of little white pines under pitch pines with scarcely any little pitch pines. He has accordingly cut off all the pitch pines — and they are some thirty-five years old — and left the white pines, now on an average five to eight feet high and forming already a pretty dense wood (E. Wood is doing the same thing now opposite the Colburn place), a valuable and salable woodland, while a great many little oaks, birches, black cherries, etc., are springing up in their midst; so that it may finally be a mixed wood, if the pines do not overshadow it too quickly. Yet there were only three or four seed-bearing white pines in the grove, — or as big as the pitch pines were. The white pines left are as thick as the pitch pines were under which they sprang up; quite dense enough to grow. I am more and more struck by the commonness of this phenomenon of seedling white pines under older pitch pines and the rareness with which pitch pines spring up under older pitch pines. Yet, going to the open land on east side of the wood, I find that it is mainly the little pitch pines that are spreading into the field there and extending the wood, some a dozen rods from its edge in 'the grass; and their relative proportion is reversed, *i. e.*, there are fifty to one hundred little pitch pines here to one white pine. He had also cut off some, a few, birches, and their sprouts had come up, as well as seedlings.

The oak seedlings between the young pitch pines were manifestly springing up with new vigor, though many may finally be choked by the white pines. Omitting such as were of the character of sprouts, though not cut (*i. e.*, had shot up from old roots to three feet high merely on account of the influx of light and air), I measured this year's growth of the first four which were under a foot high, here where the pitch pines had been cut, and found it to average five and a half inches. The growth of [the] first four in the adjacent pitch pine wood not cut averaged seven and a half. As may be seen, this was not nearly fair enough to the partially cleared part, for I should have included the higher shoots.

The higher parts of this lot are cladonia land. I measured the diameter of several of the pitch pine stumps and counted the rings, with this result: —

Diameter (exclusive of bark)	Rings
7¼ inches	29
7½	33
6	40
6½	33
6	40
8½	35
7	30
7)48¾	7)240
7	34

That is, they averaged seven inches in diameter (or eight with bark) and were thirty-four years old. Had grown (68)7.0(.10) about one tenth of an inch a year from the centre.

White pines will find their way up between pitch pines if they are not very large and exceedingly dense, but pitch pines will not grow up under pitch pines.

I see nowadays in the pitch pine woods countless

white toadstools which have recently been devoured
and broken in pieces and left on the ground and occasionally on the branches or forks of trees, no doubt
by the squirrels. They appear to make a considerable
part of their food at this season.

See a small copper butterfly.

In what I have called the Loring lot, next west of
Hosmer's pitch pine on the back road, though far the
greater part numerically is still shrub oak, there is now
a considerable growth of young oaks rising above the
shrub oaks. These oaks, as far as I observe, are almost,
if not quite, all sprouts from small stumps which were
unnoticed at first, and there are also a very few seedling white and other oaks no higher than the shrub
oaks; *i. e.*, though you may think his oak sprout-land all
shrub oak, it probably is not, as will appear when the
other kinds rise above the shrubs. Probably the shrub
oaks can bear exposure when young better than the
nobler oaks, and if the squirrels plant other acorns
under them, — which may be doubted, — then it will
turn out that they serve as nurses to the others.

I measure amid these young oaks a white pine stump.

Diameter (exclusive of bark)	Rings
13½ inches	35
Another 28	52
24	46
3)65½	133
22	44

Average growth one half inch a year at the level at
which stumps are sawed.

This lot is now as exclusively oak as it was pines

before. You must search to find a few little white pines scattered in it. But why, if there are so many little white pines under the adjacent pitch pines, which are left when the pitch pines are cut, were there no more to be left under the pitch pine part (along the road) of this lot? I think of no reason, unless the pitch pines on this lot were too old and dense. Again, I notice that Hosmer's pitch pines have not spread west at all into this clearing, but only east into the grass ground.

Into this Loring lot years ago the squirrels brought acorns, and hence the oaks which now cover it. Also the wind blew its own seeds into an open strip across the road, and a dense pitch and white pine wood sprang up there. Already, the Loring lot having been cut seven or eight years, the squirrels are carrying the shrub oak acorns from it into that pine strip, and the pine seed from the most forward of that strip is blowing back into the shrub oak land.

Another advantage the shrub oak has over other oaks [is] that it gets to fruit so quickly — certainly in three or four years after the pines are cut — and then bears so profusely.

See a great flock of blackbirds, probably grackles.

Examine Tarbell's pitch pine grove. This is all of one age and very dense. The largest trees on the north side, as estimated by sawing a branch, are twenty-eight to thirty years old. Tarbell says this grove came up in 1826 on land which had been burnt over, — in fact open land. It is so dense that, though it has been thoroughly trimmed up and is only a dozen or fifteen rods wide, you cannot see through it in some directions.

About as dense a pitch pine grove as I know. It is twenty rods from the nearest wood on one side and five times as far from any other, and yet it is well planted with seedling oaks. Looking hastily to where they are most numerous, I counted ten within fifteen square feet, but only five pitch pines within any equal area; *i. e.* there were twice as many oaks as large pines there.

This wood also proves my theory of little white pines in large pitch pines. There is not a seed-bearing white pine, or one six feet high, in the wood, nor less than twenty rods from it, and yet there is a thriving little white pine some two feet high at every rod or two within this wood, and though not *very* numerous, they are conspicuously more numerous and thriving than the pitch pines, yet on the edge the little pitch pines were as much more numerous than the white.

Having seen this fall a great many pitch pine twigs which had been cut off and dropped under the trees by squirrels, I tried the other night while in bed to account for it. I began by referring it to their necessities, and, remembering my own experience, I said then it was done either for food, shelter, clothing, or fuel, but throwing out the last two, which they do not use, it was either for food or shelter. But I never see these twigs used in their nests. Hence I presume it was for food, and as all that I know them to eat on the pitch pine is its seeds, my swift conclusion was that they cut off these twigs in order to come at the cones and also to make them more portable. I am to-day convinced of this, — for I have been looking after it for a day or two. As usual, the ground under this grove is quite strewn with the twigs, but here is one eleven inches long and nearly half an inch thick cut off close below two closed cones, one cone-stem also being partly cut. Also, three or four rods west from this grove, in open land, I see three twigs which have been dropped close together. One is just two feet long and cut off where half an inch thick and more than one foot below three cones (two on one branch and one on another), and the cones are left. Another is still larger, and the other smaller, but their cones are gone. The greater part of the twigs have been cut off above the cones, — mere plumes.

So even the squirrels carry and spread the pine seed far over the fields. I suspect that they bury these cones like nuts. I have seen the cones collected ready to be carried off, where they did not live. It is remarkable to consider how rudely they strip and spoil the trees. It is remarkable how they carried some of these great twigs with their burden of cones.[1]

The fact that the lower limbs of pines growing within a wood always die shows how much they depend on light and air. They are only a green spiring top.

Measure one of Tarbell's black birch stumps: 23 inches [in] diameter (exclusive of bark), 60 rings. A log from a different one: 21 inches, 71 (?) rings. A white oak stump near by: 15 inches, 90 rings (on brow of bank). A black (?) oak stump: 32 inches [in] diameter, 84 rings.

Examine a dozen white pines in a field, and conclude from these that they begin to grow faster the fifth or sixth year, counting by the whorls of branches.

[1] *Vide* Hosmer's gray squirrel.

J. Hosmer cut off his little pitch pine grove west of Clamshell, and left the single large old pine which seeded it to do him the same service again; and here now, where for the second time (since) he has sown winter-rye, I see the ineffectual oak sprouts uplifting a few colored leaves still and blushing for him.

The squirrels have no notion of starving in a hard winter, and therefore they are unceasingly employed in the fall in foraging. Every thick wood, especially evergreens, is their storehouse against necessity, and they pack it as thickly as they can with nuts and seeds of all kinds. The squirrel which you see at this season running so glibly along the fence with his tail waving over his head, with frequent pauses on a post or stone, which you watch, perhaps, for twenty or thirty rods, has probably a nut or two in his mouth which he is conveying to yonder thicket.

Evidently a great deal depends on the locality and other conditions of a stump to affect its durability. The oak stump at Clamshell cut some twenty years since barely shows a trace of the axe, while the chestnut stump on Hubbard's hill, cut more than fifty years ago, is much better preserved.

Oct. 31. P. M. — To Wheeler's artificial pine wood.

Exclusive and dense white pine woods are not nearly so common in this town as the same kind of pitch pine woods. They are more likely to have oaks in them. There is a dense birch wood in Witherell Vale.

Among old stumps I have not named those white pine ones used as fences with their roots. I think that some of these must be older than any left in the ground. I remember some on the Corner road, which apparently have not changed for more than thirty years, and are said to be ninety years old. Lying thus high and dry, they are almost indestructible, and I can still easily count the rings of many of these. I count one hundred and twenty-six rings on one this afternoon, and who knows but it is a hundred years since it was cut? They decay much faster left upright in the ground than lying on their sides on the surface, supposing it open land in both cases.

Perhaps these great pine roots which grew in a swamp were provided with some peculiar quality by which to resist the influence of moisture and so endure the changes of the weather.

Yes, these dense and stretching oak forests, whose withered leaves now redden and rustle on the hills for many a New England mile, were all planted by the labor of animals. For after some weeks of close scrutiny I cannot avoid the conclusion that our modern oak woods sooner or later spring up from an acorn, not where it has fallen from its tree, for that is the exception, but where it has been dropped or placed by an animal. Consider what a vast work these forest-planters are doing!

I do not state the facts exactly in the order in which they were observed, but select out of very numerous observations extended over a series of years the most important ones, and describe them in their natural order.[1]

---

[1] [Evidently written for his lecture on the Succession of Forest Trees.]

So far as our noblest hardwood forests are concerned, the animals, especially squirrels and jays, are our greatest and almost only benefactors. It is to them that we owe this gift. It is not in vain that the squirrels live in or about every forest tree, or hollow log, and every wall and heap of stones.

Looked at the white pine grove set out by the father of Francis Wheeler some twenty-two or three years ago southwest of his house. They are in three or four irregular rows some eighteen rods long by four wide, — some one hundred trees, covering half an acre of sandy hillside. Probably not so many trees as Emerson's, but making more show. They are trimmed up. There are neither small white nor pitch pines beneath them, but I see that the seeds of the pitch pines which grow below them have been blown *through* this grove and come up thickly along its outer edge.

Look at a pure strip of old white pine wood on the hillside west of this. There are no little white pines coming up under them, but plenty of them in the open hollows around and under its edge. This I commonly notice. White pines, it is true, may come up in the more open parts of any wood, whether a pine or oak or mixed wood, in more open places caused by cutting, for instance; but the pitch pine requires much more of an opening.

I see by the road east of White Pond a large white pine wood with some oaks in it. There are no little white pines where it is dense, but one rod off across the road eastward there is a dense row concealing the lower rail (many quite under it) for many rods, — the only place where they are allowed to grow there.

Many a man's field has a dense border of pitch pines which strayed into it when the adjacent woods were of that species, though they are now hardwood.

Consider what a demand for arrowheads there must be, that the surface of the earth should be thus sprinkled with them, — the arrowhead and all the disposition it implies toward both man and brute. There they lie, pointed still, making part of the sands of almost every field.

I cut two shrub oaks (in different places) which have respectively ten and twenty rings. The last was a large and old one in a hedge.[1]

I first noticed the pitch pine twigs cut off by squirrels the 16th. Think how busy they were about that time in every pitch pine grove all over the State, cutting off the twigs and collecting the cones! While the farmer is digging his potatoes and gathering his corn he little thinks of this harvest of pine cones which the squirrel is gathering in the neighboring woods still more sedulously than himself.

I saw on the 28th, close by the stump of the easternmost big chestnut at Flint's Pond, the *Phallus impudicus*.

I hear the sound of the flail in M. Miles's barn, and gradually draw near to it from the woods, thinking many things. I find that the thresher is a Haynes of Sudbury, and he complains of the hard work and a lame back. Indeed, he cannot stand up straight. So all is not gold that glitters. This sound is not so musical after I have withdrawn. It was as well to have heard this music afar off. He complains also that the weather is not fit for his

[1] *Vide* [p. 208].

work, — that it is so muggy that he cannot dry the sheaves, and the grain will not fly out when struck. The floor, too, is uneven, and he pointed out one board more prominent on which he had broken two or three swingles.

He thought that there were larger trees in Sudbury, on what was John Hunt's land, now occupied by Thompson, near the old store, than in Inches Woods. Said there was a tree by the roadside on the farm of the late William Read in West Acton which nobody there-abouts knew the name of, but he had been South, and knew it to be a China-berry tree planted by a robin, for they are very fond of its fruit.

IV

NOVEMBER, 1860

(ÆT. 43)

Nov. 1. 2 P. M. — To Tommy Wheeler wood-lot.

A perfect Indian-summer day, and wonderfully warm. 72 + at 1 P. M. and probably warmer at two.

The butterflies are out again, — probably some new broods. I see the common yellow and two *Vanessa Antiopa*, and yellow-winged grasshoppers with blackish edges.

A striped snake basks in the sun amid dry leaves. Very much gossamer on the withered grass is shimmering in the fields, and flocks of it are sailing in the air.

Measure some pine stumps on Tommy Wheeler's land, about that now frosty hollow, cut as I judge from sprouts four years ago.

First the pitch pine: —

1 is	18½	inches [in] diameter and has	145 (?)	rings
2	18	"	"	"	137	"
3	20	"	"	"	128	"
4	21	"	"	"	148	"
5	21	"	"	"	140	"
6	22¾	"	"	"	160 + 4 (Counted the last 64 at home)
7	20	"	"	"	167 or 168 (?)

7)141¼   7)1026 + 4

Average 20   Average 147 + 1, or 148

That is, they all together averaged in growth from

first to last about a fifteenth of an inch in a year. But they grew very slowly indeed for the last fifty or more years. They did nearly half (?) their growing in the first third of their existence. For example, (I measure now on that side where I counted, *i. e.* the broadest, so that my figures are not absolutely but relatively true), —·

No. 2 grew 5 inches in first 32 years
  5   "   4½   "   "   50 and 3⅝ in second 50
  6   "   7¼   "   "   50 " 2½   "   "
  7   "   4½   "   "   50 " 2¾   "   "

          21¼   182   3)8½   150
  A little more than ⅕ inch a year.   Average ¹⁄₁₈ inch.

The 7th grew only something less than three inches (which was all of the sap) in the last sixty-seven or eight years, or one twenty-second of an inch a year only. Indeed, in one case, the 6th, the outside had grown only one and one fourth inches in sixty-four years, or about one fiftieth of an inch in a year, just one inch in the last fifty-three years, or one fifty-third of an inch a year, — equal to the finest scales. I should say that they averaged but one thirty-sixth part of an inch the third or last fifty years.

  1st 50   2d 50   3d 50
  ⅕ inch   ¹⁄₁₈   ¹⁄₃₆

That is, their rate of growth the three successive periods of fifty years diminishes in geometrical progression, the quotient being two.

The seven pitch pine stumps measured on the 30th averaged thirty-four years and had grown a tenth of an inch in a year. This is a perfect and remarkable agreement, and quite unlooked for. They were a mile apart,

and I was not reminded of those previous measurements until I chanced to compare them afterward.

I may therefore take this to be [the] average growth
of a pitch pine for the first fifty years. But I have not
yet taken into the account the fact that, though the
thickness of the layer is less, its superficies, or extent,
is greater, as the diameter of the tree increases. Let us
compare the three portions of wood.
If the diameter at the end of the first
fifty years is four, the second fifty,
six, and the third fifty, seven, then
the amount of wood added each
term will be (to omit very minute
fractions) twelve and a half, fifteen
and a half, and ten respectively.[1] So
that, though in the second fifty the
rings are twice as near together, yet considerably more
wood is produced than in the first, but in the third fifty
the tree is evidently enfeebled, and it probably is not
profitable (so far as bulk is concerned) to let it grow
any more.

The very oldest trees whose rings I have counted
(i. e. these pitch pines and the oaks on Eb. Hubbard's
hill) grew thus slowly at last, which I think indicates
that a tree has a definite age after which it grows more
languidly or feebly, and thus gradually ceases to grow
at all, — dies and decays. I should say that these
pitch pines flourished till they were about a hundred
years old, and that they then began to grow with less

[1] Or, actually averaging eight trees under Nov. 10th, it is 7, 10+,
10—.

vigor, though their old age (in this sense) might be a third or more of their whole life. Two or three more were dead or nearly dead when sawed four years ago, and I saw the rotted stumps of some others.

There were twenty or thirty of the pitch pines, — though I measured the largest of them, — and they were all but one or two perfectly sound to the core, and the inmost rings were the plainest. The sap was only from one and three quarters to three inches thick, and was the most decayed. (It was one and three quarters inches thick in No. 6.) The bark was generally from two to two and three quarters inches thick. This would have added four and three quarters to the average diameter of the trees, or made it twenty-four and three quarters. That is, where sawed off, which was rather low, or say eight to ten inches above ground.

There were also as many or more large white pines mixed with them. One of 24 inches diameter had 78 rings; second, 31 inches, 96 rings. Also one hemlock 21 inches, 81 rings. This had grown with remarkable equality throughout [1] and was very easy to count. An oak (probably black), 14 inches, 94 rings.

About a hundred and fifty years ago, then, there came up in and around this hollow in the woods a grove of pitch pines. Perhaps some came up twenty or thirty years earlier, which have now died and decayed. When the first had grown for about sixty years, many white pines sprang up amid and under them, as we see happen to-day.

---

[1] And so it is generally.

I occasionally (or frequently) see white pines springing up in a sprout-land when other trees have failed
to fill it up for some years.

No. 6, having 164 rings and having been cut four
years, sprang up at least one hundred and sixty-eight
years ago, or about the year 1692, or fifty-seven years
after the settlement, 1635.

In another case I counted fifteen rings (with a microscope) within the last quarter of an inch, which was
at the rate of one sixtieth of an inch in a year, — equal,
I think, to the finest scales ordinarily used.

WHITE PINE WOODS

> The small dense grove of Clark's (?), north of Boze's [sic]
> Meadow.
> Near road, southwest of Tarbell's.
> Abel Hosmer's, north and northwest of house.
> Mason's pasture (south of this, younger white pine with cedars
> intermixed).
> The Holden Swamp woods as seen from north (except south-
> west part).
> Northeast part of Baker Farm, quite young.
> Behind Martial Miles's, southwest of cold pond-hole.
> East side Second Division Brook, very extensive.

I have seen that a great many pitch pine cones
have been cut off this fall, but it chances that I have
not seen where they were eaten or stripped. I conclude,
therefore, that they must be collected into some hole
in a tree or in the earth, — there can hardly be a doubt
of this, — and possibly some are buried as nuts are.
What stores of them there must be collected in some
places now!

PITCH PINE WOODS

Young, north of Loring's Pond.

Just beyond Concord bound on right hand, this side Wetherbee's, extensive and large. (Tarbell says that when he came to town in '26 these were just about as large as his now. Sixty to seventy years old, then.)

Heywood's small grove southeast of Peter's.

Large, southeast Copan.

Beyond Nathan Barrett's, both sides road, large.

Hill behind Abner Buttrick's.

Lane south of second Garfield house.

Southwest of Brooks's Pigeon-Place.

North G. M. Barrett's, by College Road.

Northeast of Sam Barrett's mill.

Northwest of Sam Barrett's mill, west of pond.

Nov. 2. P. M. — To D. Wetherbee's old oak lot. As several days past, it has been cloudy and misty in the morning and fairer and warmer, if not Indian summer, in the afternoon; yet the mist lingers in drops on the cobwebs and grass until night.

HARDWOOD LOTS

Wetherbee's.

Blood's.

G. M. Barrett's hillside, behind house.

Walnuts (young) of Smith's Hill, Lincoln.

   "   "   " Annursnack, above orchard.

   "   " Fair Haven Hill slope.

   Also north side of path from Springs to bars.

   "   " site of Britton's shanty.

   South side of Bear Hill, Lincoln.

Saw off a very large and old-looking shrub oak on a pitch pine plain, twelve or more feet in height and three and one half inches in diameter (the wood) at one foot from the ground, where it has just twenty-seven rings. The first fourteen rings occupied one and a quarter inches from the centre, where the whole radius was but one and three quarters. It evidently began to grow more slowly when fifteen years old.

Wetherbee's oak lot may contain four or five acres.[1] The trees are white, red, scarlet, and swamp white oaks, maple, white pine, and ash. They are unusually large and old. Indeed, I doubt if there is another hereabouts of oaks as large. It is said that Wetherbee left them for the sake of mast for pigeons.

I measure a white oak at three feet from the ground, — eight feet four and one half inches in circumference. Another white oak at same height is six and three quarters in circumference; a red oak is six feet two inches in circumference; another, eight and a half; another, seven and four twelfths; and the scarlet oaks are of the same character, though the above were the largest, or among the largest. These oaks, though they form a wood, are some of them about as spreading as a pasture oak (*i. e.* one or two white ones near the outside), but generally they rise much higher before they branch. The white oaks have peculiarly smooth *tawny-white* boles for eight or ten feet up, the coarser flakes of the bark having scaled off so far. The red oaks, as well as scarlet, have a coarser and rougher, more deeply furrowed bark, and the trees rise higher before branching (commonly). One not very large had no limb for thirty feet or more, standing aslant. In the lowest part, on the brook, they were swamp white oaks and maples. The maples, being old, had a

[1] He says eight.

rough, dark, scaly bark. There were a few white pines straggling into this wood (only one large one).

Many of the oaks have been cut, and I counted about one hundred and ten rings on one small white oak, from which I should infer that the trees would average much more than that, perhaps between a hundred and fifty and two hundred years. Such a wood has got to be very rare in this neighborhood. Even the gray brushy tops of this attract your attention at a distance.

As you approach the wood, and even walk through it, the trees do not affect you as large, but as surely as you go quite up to one you are surprised. The very lichens and mosses which cover the rocks under these trees seem, and probably are in some respects, peculiar. Such a wood, at the same time that it suggests antiquity, imparts an unusual dignity to the earth.

It is pleasing to see under the trees great rocks covered with polypody, which has caught a great crop of shining brown oak leaves to contrast with its green. This oak wood is now bare and the leaves just fairly fallen.

This is probably one of those woods, like Ebby Hubbard's, which was never cut off but only cut out of.

I think it would be worth the while to introduce a school of children to such a grove, that they may get an idea of the primitive oaks before they are all gone, instead of hiring botanists to lecture to them when it is too late. Why, you do not now often meet with a respectable oak stump even, for they too have decayed.

I see a this year's sound red oak acorn tucked into a crevice in the bark of a white oak a foot or more from the ground.

Even in this old oak wood there is to be observed a resemblance to the primitive woods. The ground, never having been cleared nor cultivated, has a more primitive look; there are more ferns on it, and the rocks are far greener, with these and with lichens, never having been burned and bleached white by sun and fire.

Lee of the Corner speaks of an oak lot of his in Sudbury, which he bought in '31 and cut off (last and all of it last winter), but from the older stumps no sprouts have come up, but good ones from the younger.

You see the tufts of indigo now broken off and dropped exactly bottom up in the pastures, as if an industrious farmer had been collecting it by handfuls, which he had dropped thus.

It would be just as sensible for them to treat their young orchards or nurseries of apple trees in the same way, *i. e.*, to burn them over and raise rye there a year or two, thinking to do them good.

As for the *Vaccinia*, I am disposed to agree with those who derive the name from *bacca*, a berry, for one species or another of this large family is the berry of berries in most northern parts of the world. They form an under-shrub, or sort of lower forest, even throughout our woodlands generally, to say nothing of open fields and hills. They form a humble and more or less dormant, but yet vivacious forest under a forest, which bides its time.

This wonderful activity of the squirrels in collecting and dispersing and planting nuts and acorns, etc., etc., every autumn is the more necessary since the trees on whose fruit they mainly live are not annual plants like the wheat which supplies *our* staff of life. If the wheat crop fails this year, we have only to sow more the next year, and reap a speedy harvest, but if the forests were to be planted only at intervals equal to the age of the trees, there would be danger, what with fires and blight and insects, of a sudden failure and famine. It is important that there be countless trees in every stage of growth, — that there be an annual planting, as of wheat. Consider the amount of work they have to do, the area to be planted!

More or less rainy to-day.

I hear that geese went over to-day, alighted in Walden.

Nov. 4. P. M. — To Tommy Wheeler's lot.

As I go over John Hosmer's High Level, there being considerable wind, I notice for the first time that peculiar blueness of the river agitated by the wind and contrasting with the tawny fields, a fall phenomenon. Tarbell's white pine grove northwest of the Irishman's, in the swamp, and some thirty to forty years old, is so dense that there is no growth under it, only a tawny carpet of pine-needles.

In the Tommy Wheeler lot south of the old pitch pine hollow, I see the stumps of many white pines and oaks which were cut some four years ago, and no fire has been set there. These oak stumps have generally fifty-three or fifty-four rings, though some pitch pines and oaks are much older; but I scarcely see a stump of this age even which has sent up any shoots. I notice one. The sprouts are from a much younger growth. It is evident that all the larger stumps were too old and

effete, young as they were. In two or three cases I notice
these stumps of oaks cut some four years ago and having
fifty-three or four rings (from which no shoot has put
forth), two together, half inclosing in a semicircle a
very old and almost completely decayed stump, which,
of course, was cut some fifty-eight years ago. These
sprouts are rarely sound quite to the core. Perhaps the
rest are sprouts whose stumps have quite disappeared,
and this, *i. e.* the great age of the roots, may account for
its sending up no more sprouts. I see, then, that the
stumps of trees which were cut sixty years ago are still
very common to be seen in our woods.

I have but little doubt that if Wetherbee's old oak
lot should now be cut no sprouts would come up from
the stumps. It is by seeds that oaks would have to be
renewed there, if at all; but rather it is time for a different growth, *i. e.* for pines, and if he contemplates the
removal of these oaks he should be considering how to
favor the growth of pines there. They are already
appearing thinly on various sides within that wood.

I frequently notice the seeds of small fruits and weeds
left on stumps by birds and mice and even foxes (in
their excrement).

There is *primitive wood* which has never been
touched by the civilized man. We have none of this.

Then there is *primitive woodland, i. e.*, which has
never been cut clean off, and which in age now is mostly
second growth.

Then there is *primitive copsewood, i. e.*, which has
been cut clean off but suffered to grow up again without
further clearing or burning.

Then copsewood of other kinds.

Sophia brings me the drawer which held her acorns (almost all red oak). It is seventeen and a half inches by twelve and a half and two inches deep, and I count, crawling about on the bottom, one hundred and seventy-three great full-grown grubs with brown heads, which have come out of the acorns by a hole, oftenest at the edge of the cup on one side. And many of the grubs had been thrown away, and probably some had crawled away within a month, and no doubt more are still to come out. Also the bottom of this box is covered with four or five times as many minute pink grubs which may be the progeny of the former: here are at least eight hundred and sixty-five (or say one thousand) grubs to about four quarts of acorns *with their cups* (the box was hardly more than half full). I find that sixty red oak acorns with their cups make one pint. There were, therefore, about five hundred acorns to one hundred and seventy-three large grubs already out in the box, to say nothing of those that have been thrown and have crawled away, nor of the seven or eight hundred *young* grubs and probably more yet to be produced. Not quite half of the acorns, then, have grubs in them.[1] Now add the squirrels, jays, crows, and other birds and quadrupeds that feed on them, and the effect of the winter's cold and rain, and how many of the acorns of this year will be fit to plant next spring?

[1] Nov. 22, about a third as many more grubs have come out of these acorns, — both large and small grubs, — which will make nearly half as many large grubs as acorns ; and each of these large grubs has been the destruction of an acorn, so that already one half of these acorns have been destroyed by worms.

It appears that nearly half of these red oaks have already manifestly been destroyed by worms. It is evident that there will be at least two grubs to one of these acorns, though of course the grubs will not always be with the acorn. This is one of the nut weevils, and since they come from eggs laid by a beetle, it would seem that many eggs must have been *recently* laid.

White birch seed has but recently begun to fall. I see a quarter of an inch of many catkins bare. May have begun for a week. To-day also I see distinctly the tree sparrows, and probably saw them, as supposed, some days ago. Perhaps they feed on the birch seed as the linarias do. Thus the birch begins to shed its seed about the time our winter birds arrive from the north.

Nov. 5. P. M. — To Blood's oak lot.

Measure the great white oak near the bars of the bridle-road just beyond the northeast corner of the Holden (?) farm. At the ground it is about nineteen feet in circumference. At three feet from the ground it is eleven feet and seven inches in circumference, and the same at five feet and apparently more above this. It is about sixteen feet to the lowest limb. The whole trunk standing aslant. It has a black and quite rough bark, not at all like that of the white oaks of Wetherbee's and Blood's lots. There is a large open space amid the huckleberry bushes beneath it, covered with a short and peculiarly green sward, and this I see is the case with other oaks a quarter of a mile off.

There is a large chestnut in the lot east of this, and I observe that its top is composed of many small branches and twigs disposed very regularly and densely, brush-wise, with a firm, distinct, more than semicircular edge against the horizon, very unlike the irregular, open, and more scraggy-twigged oak.

Blood's oak lot may contain about a dozen acres. It consists of red, black, white, and swamp white oaks, and a very little maple. The following are some of the largest that I saw. I measured one black oak which was, at three feet high, four feet eight inches in circumference; another, five feet six inches; and another the same. A red oak was six feet three inches; another, seven feet four inches; another, seven feet four inches; another, seven feet. One swamp white oak was six feet four inches. A white oak was seven feet seven inches, and another the same. The diameter of a third at one foot from ground (sawed off) was thirty-one and a half inches average.

This is quite a dense wood-lot, even without consider-ing the size of the trees, and I was rather surprised to see how much spread there was to the tops of the trees in it, especially to the white oaks. The trees here rise far higher before branching, however, than in open land; some black oaks (if not others) were very straight and thirty to forty feet high without a limb. I think that there was not so much difference in color between the trunks of black and red oaks as commonly. The red oaks were oftener smooth, or smoothish, the largest of them. I saw very little decay. Considering their num-ber and closeness, the trees were on the whole larger than I should have expected, though of course not nearly so large as the largest pasture oaks, — one to two and a half feet in diameter, or say generally (the sizable trees) a foot and a half in diameter. This will probably do for a specimen of a primitive oak forest hereabouts. Such probably was the size and aspect of the trees.

As for its age, I saw the stump of a white oak (not quite so large as those I measured) which had been sawed off at about one foot from the ground within four or five years, perfectly level and sound to the core, and thirty-one and a half inches in diameter. The first thirty-three (?) rings were so close and indistinct as to be impossible to count exactly (occupying three quarters of an inch of the centre); the rest was perfectly distinct. In all one hundred and forty-seven rings; or, by inches from middle, thirty-nine, nine, six, seven, five, eleven, six, four, four, five, six, nine, ten, twelve, and then three quarters of an inch left. From which it appears that it grew much the fastest at about the age of eighty-nine years and very much the slowest for the first thirty-three years.

I am struck by the fact that the more slowly trees grow at first, the sounder they are at the core, and I think that the same is true of human beings. We do not wish to see children precocious, making great strides in their early years like sprouts, producing a soft and perishable timber, but better if they expand slowly at first, as if contending with difficulties, and so are solidified and perfected. Such trees continue to expand with nearly equal rapidity to an extreme old age.

Another white oak stump, not so large but somewhat decayed, had one hundred and sixty and more rings. So that you may say this wood is a hundred to a hundred and sixty years old.

I was struck by the orderly arrangement of the trees, as if each knew its own place; and it was just so at Wetherbee's lot. This being an oak wood, and like that, somewhat meadow [*sic*] in the midst, the swamp white oaks with a very few maples occupied that part, and I think it likely that a similar selection of the ground might have been detected often in the case of the other oaks, as the white compared with the red. As if in the natural state of things, when sufficient time is given, trees will be found occupying the places most suitable to each, but when they are interfered with, some are prompted to grow where they do not belong and a certain degree of confusion is produced. That is, our forest generally is in a transition state to a settled and normal condition.

Many young white pines — the largest twenty years old — are distributed through this wood, and I have no doubt that if let alone this would in a hundred years look more like a pine wood than an oak one.

Hence we see that the white pine may introduce itself into a primitive oak wood of average density.

The only sounds which I heard were the notes of the jays, evidently attracted by the acorns, and the only animal seen was a red squirrel, while there were the nests of several gray squirrels in the trees.

Last evening, the weather being cooler, there was an arch of northern lights in the north, with some redness. Thus our winter is heralded.

It is evident that the pasture oaks are commonly the survivors or relics of old oak woods, — not having been set out of course, nor springing up often in the bare pasture, except sometimes along fences. I see that on the outskirts of Wetherbee's and Blood's lots are some larger, more spreading and straggling trees, which are not to be distinguished from those. Such trees are often found as stragglers beyond a fence in an adjacent lot. Or, as an old oak wood is very gradually thinned out, it becomes open, grassy, and park-like, and very many owners are inclined to respect a few larger trees on account of old associations, until at length they begin to value them for shade for their cattle. These are oftenest white oaks. I think that they grow the largest and are the hardiest. This final arrangement is in obedience to the demand of the cow. She says, looking at the oak woods: " Your tender twigs are good, but grass is better. Give me a few at intervals for shade and shelter in storms, and let the grass grow far and wide between them."

No doubt most of those white pines in pastures which branch close to the ground, their branches curving out and upward harpwise without one erect leading shoot, were broken down when young by cows. The cow does not value the pine, but rubs it out by scratching her head on it.

Nov. 6. Sawed off half of an old pitch pine stump at Tommy Wheeler's hollow. I found that, though the surface was entire and apparently sound except one or two small worm-holes, and the sap was evidently decaying, yet within, or just under the surface, it was extensively honeycombed by worms, which did not eat out to the surface. Those rings included in the outmost four or five inches were the most decayed, — including the sap-wood.

Nov. 7. To Cambridge and Boston.

Nov. 8. 2 P. M. — To Mt. Misery *via* sugar maples and Lee's Bridge.

The white oak near the English cress at three feet is nine feet and one twelfth in circumference and has a rough and dark bark. By its branching so low, it suggests that it may have stood in comparatively open ground most of its life, or such as the outmost oaks in Blood's wood toward his house.

I notice along the Corner road, beyond Abiel Wheeler's, quite a number of little white pines springing up against the south wall, whose seed must have been blown from Hubbard's Grove some fifty rods east. They extend along a quarter of a mile at least. Also a wet and brushy meadow some forty rods in front of Garfield's is being rapidly filled with white pines whose seeds must have been blown an equal distance.

We need not be surprised at these results when we consider how persevering Nature is, and how much time she has to work in, though she works slowly. A great pine wood may drop many millions of seeds in one year, and if only half a dozen are conveyed a quarter of a mile and lodge against some fence, and only one comes up and lives there, yet in the course of fifteen or twenty years there are fifteen or twenty young trees there, and they begin to make a show and betray their origin. It does not imply any remarkable rapidity or success in Nature's operations.

In the wood north of the sugar maples a hickory but two feet in circumference has eighty-six rings. A white oak twenty-six inches [in] diameter has one hundred and twenty-eight rings.

The sugar maples occupy, together with oaks of the same size, about thirty rods, or say ten rods by three. The largest about five inches [in] diameter, but generally quite small. They have sprung from quite small stumps, commonly not bigger than themselves at most. They are peculiar among maples in retaining yet a part of their leaves, — a delicate fawn(?)-color, pale brown.

There is quite a pitch pine wood on the lane beyond the second Garfields, but though there are *very* few little white pines under it (no large ones), these are under the densest part, and there are no little pitch pines, though they are common in the more open parts. Seed-bearing pines are distant here. I observe on the trunk of one of the largest of these pitch pines (which may be forty years old), standing on the outside the wood, minute or short branches, commonly mere tufts of needles in rings around the trunk, — reminding you even of the branches of the horse-tail, they are in this case so regular, — perfectly horizontal and six to twelve inches apart. Some are two or three years old, but only three to six inches long. These seem to represent the old whorls of branches. Perhaps, the tree growing slowly at the top, the dormant buds here are stimulated. I afterward see in another wood an outside pitch pine, a tall one, on which some of these tufts had apparently developed into branches four or five feet long, in imperfect whorls, the top being partly dead.

A white oak stump, roadside west of Abel Minott house site, nineteen and one half inches [in] diameter (wood), sixty-five rings. A pitch pine standing on opposite side more westerly is five and nine twelfths feet in circumference at three feet.

I observe on the west side of Mt. Misery, cut off apparently last winter, mulleins, very tall, sprung up, — as well as fire-weed and goldenrods. I saw an abundance of mulleins in a young wood-lot with much bare ground, burnt over a year or so ago, behind Mason's on the bridle-road, on the 5th, so that the mullein too might be called a fire-weed. But I notice that those plants so called, as the epilobium and senecio, and which are supposed to owe their origin to the fire, generally spring up on a surface made bare by whatever cause. They are the first weeds after a clearing or cutting.

On this same Mt. Misery (cut last winter), an oak stump (apparently black) eleven and one half inches [in] diameter, sixty-one rings; a white oak, thirteen inches, fifty-eight rings. I count four or more of these stumps, — which are as plain as usual, — and make from fifty-four to sixty-one rings, say average fifty-eight years. Yet in several of these instances they were manifestly sprouts, and there was the old stump cut 58 + 1 years ago.[1] These stumps did not show any trace of the axe, but there was one which lay on its side, apparently of the same date, but from which no sprout had come, which

[1] *Vide* Nov. 13.

was much better preserved and did show the traces of the axe plainly. These recent stumps, though only some sixty years old, had in no case sprouted again, and I think that this is because they are sprouts, and that the vitality of the stock was so nearly exhausted. These old stumps are frequently half inclosed in the recent stump. I think that I readily detected the sprout also by the greater breadth of the rings the first few years.

The stumps of trees which were cut in the last century — oaks at least — must be not uncommon in our woods.

Looking from this hill, I think that I see considerably more oak than pine wood.

Edward Hoar's pitch pine and white pine lot on the south side of this hill is evidently a new wood. You see the green moss, the cladonia, and birches (which I think do not spring up within an old wood), and even feel with your feet an old cow-path and see an old apple tree inclosed in the wood. Are not birches interspersed with pines a sign of a new wood?

When a pitch pine wood is cut, that fringe or edging of little pitch pines which commonly surrounds it may remain to grow up and in a measure represent it. Also, apparently, when for any reason, as from frost, land where the wood has been cut remains comparatively bare for several years and becomes only grassy, pitch pines (as well as white pines) may catch there thickly.

I constantly meet now with those tufts of indigo-weed (turned black) now broken off and dropped exactly bottom up, as it were dropped by a careful hand in woodland paths or in pastures, as if an industrious farmer or a simpler had been collecting it by handfuls and had dropped his parcels thus. The fact is that they grow up many stems close together, and their branches are so interlaced as not to be easily separated; so that the wind operates the more powerfully and breaks them all off together at the ground, and then, on account of their form, these parcels are deposited exactly bottom up commonly, and you see three or four to fifteen or more stems within a diameter of four or five inches, looking just as if somebody had plucked them and laid them together.[1] I also see the fly-away grass going over a wall or rock from time to time.

The *Salix sericea* has just blackened the ground with its leaves.

These are annual phenomena.

Dr. (?) Manasseh Cutler, in the first volume of the Boston Academy's Reports for 1785, speaks of whortle‑berries only in the half-converted or disparaging way in which the English do, — and have reason to, — saying that children love to eat them in milk. His eyes had not been opened to their significance; they were without honor in their native country. But I have no doubt that he ate them himself in secret.

Nov. 9.[2] 12 m. — To Inches' Woods in Boxboro.

This wood is some one and three quarters miles from West Acton, whither we went by railroad. It is in the east part of Boxboro, on both sides of the Harvard

---

[1] So these seeds and fly-away grass seed dispersed.
[2] *Vide* also Nov. 16.

turnpike. We walked mostly across lots from West
Acton to a part of the wood about half a mile north
of the turnpike, — and the woods appeared to reach
as much further north. We then walked in the midst
of the wood in a southwesterly by west direction,
about three quarters of a mile, crossing the turnpike
west of the maple swamp and the brook, and thence
south by east nearly as much[1] more, — all the way in
the woods, and chiefly old oak wood. The old oak wood,
as we saw from the bare hill at the south end, extends
a great deal further west and northwest, as well as north,
than we went, and must be at least a mile and a half[1]
from north to south by a mile to a mile and a quarter[1]
possibly from east to west. Or there *may* be a thousand[2]
acres[3] of old oak wood. The large wood is chiefly oak,
and that white oak, though black, red, and scarlet oak
are also common. White pine is in considerable quantity, and large pitch pine is scattered here and there,
and saw some chestnut at the south end. Saw no hemlock or birch to speak of.

Beginning at the north end of our walk, the trees
which I measured were (all at three feet from ground
except when otherwise stated): a black oak, ten feet [in]
circumference, trunk tall and of regular form; scarlet
oak, seven feet three inches, by Guggins Brook; white
oak, eight feet; white oak, ten feet, forks at ten feet;
white oak, fifteen feet (at two and a half feet, bulging
very much near ground; trunk of a pyramidal form;

---

[1] [Queried in pencil.]
[2] Four or five hundred.
[3] *Vide* [p. 227].

first branch at sixteen feet; this just north of turnpike
and near Guggins Brook); white oak, nine feet four
inches (divides to two at five feet); white oak, nine
feet six inches (divides to two at five feet); red oak,
eight feet (south of road); white pine, nine feet; a
scarlet or red oak stump cut, twenty and a half inches
[in] diameter, one hundred and sixty rings.

I was pleased to find that the largest of the white oaks,
growing thus in a dense wood, often with a pine or other
tree within two or three feet, were of pasture oak size and
even form, the largest commonly branching low. Very
many divide to two trunks at four or five feet only from
the ground. You see some white oaks and even some
others in the midst of the wood nearly as spreading as
in open land.

Looking from the high bare hill at the south end, the
limits of the *old* oak wood (so far as we could overlook
it) were very distinct, its tops being a mass of gray
brush, — contorted and intertwisted twigs and boughs,
— while the younger oak wood around it, or bounding
it, though still of respectable size, was still densely
clothed with the reddish-brown leaves.

This famous oak lot — like Blood's and Wetherbee's
— is a place of resort for those who hunt the gray squirrel. They have their leafy nests in the oak-tops.

It is an endless maze of gray oak trunks and boughs
stretching far around. The great mass of individual
trunks which you stand near is very impressive.

Many sturdy trunks (they commonly stand a little
aslant) are remarkably straight and round, and have so
much regularity in their roughness as to suggest smooth-

ness. The older or largest white oaks were of a rougher and darker bark than Wetherbee's and Blood's, though often betraying the same tendency to smoothness, as if a rough layer had been stripped off near the ground.

I noticed that a great many trunks (the bark) had been gnawed near the ground, — different kinds of oak and chestnut, — perhaps by squirrels.

Nov. 10. Cheney gives me a little history of the Inches Woods. He says it was a grant to Jekil (John (?) Jekil) by the crown, and that it amounted to half of Boxboro as well as much of Stow and Acton. That Jekil had a summer house where Squire Hosmer's house stands in Stow, before the Revolution, but at that time withdrew into Boston. It was a great event when he used to come out to Stow in the summer. Boxboro was a part of Stow then. Mr. Hosmer had charge of the lands for Inches, and the kitchen of his house was partly the old summer house of Jekil, and he also remembered an old negro named York, who had been a slave of Jekil, and he, the negro, said that twenty of the thirty acres bought of Inches by Hosmer, behind his house, was once fenced in with a paling or picket fence ten or fifteen feet high, and formed a park in which Jekil kept deer. The neighbors used to come and peep through the paling at the deer. Henderson Inches, hearing of these lands about the time of the Revolution, went to the heirs of Jekil and purchased the whole tract quite cheap, and they had been a fortune to the family since. Many farms have been made of parts of the wood, and thousands of dollars' worth of wood have been sold at a time.

Had realized maybe $150,000 from it. Cheney had heard that there were about four hundred acres of the Inches lands left. Henderson Inches died two or three years ago, and now his heirs wished to sell, but would not divide it, but sell in one body. Ruggles, Nourse, and Mason wished to buy, but not the whole. Except what has been sold, or generally, Inches would not have it. cut. He was sharp and stood out for his price, and also liked to keep it. Hence it is a primitive oak wood and said to be the most of one in Massachusetts.

Collier tells me that his sunflower-head (now dried) measures just twenty-one and a half inches [in] diameter, — the solid part.

Most think that Inches Wood was worth more twenty or thirty years ago, — that the oaks are now decayed within. Some have suggested that it would be much for the benefit of Boxboro to have it cut off and made into farms, but Boxboro people answer no, that they get a good deal more in taxes from it now than they would then.

How little there is on an ordinary map! How little, I mean, that concerns the walker and the lover of nature. Between those lines indicating roads is a plain blank space in the form of a square or triangle or polygon or segment of a circle, and there is naught to distinguish this from another area of similar size and form. Yet the one may be covered, in fact, with a primitive oak wood, like that of Boxboro, waving and creaking in the wind, such as may make the reputation of a county, while the other is a stretching plain with scarcely a tree on it. The waving woods, the dells and glades and green banks and smiling fields, the huge boulders, etc., etc., are not on the map, nor to be inferred from the map.

That grand old oak wood is just the most remarkable and memorable thing in Boxboro, and yet if there is a history of this town written anywhere, the history or even mention of this is probably altogether omitted, while that of the first (and may be last) parish is enlarged on.

What sort of cultivation, or civilization and improvement, is ours to boast of, if it turns out that, as in this instance, unhandselled nature is worth more even by our modes of valuation than our improvements are, — if we leave the land poorer than we found it ? Is it good economy, to try it by the lowest standards, to cut down all our forests, if a forest will pay into the town treasury a greater tax than the farms which may supplant it, — if the oaks by steadily growing according to their nature leave our improvements in the rear ?

How little we insist on truly grand and beautiful natural features! How many have ever heard of the Boxboro oak woods ? How many have ever explored them ? I have lived so long in this neighborhood and but just heard of this noble forest, — probably as fine an oak wood as there is in New England, only eight miles west of me.

I noticed young white pines springing up in the more open places and dells. There were considerable tracts of large white pine wood and also pine and oak mixed, especially on the hills. So I see that the character of a primitive wood may gradually change, as from oak to pine, the oaks at last decaying and not being replaced by oaks.

Though a great many of those white oaks of the Inches Wood branch quite as low and are nearly as spreading as pasture oaks, yet generally they rise up in stately columns thirty or forty or fifty feet, diminishing very little. The black and red and scarlet oaks are especially columnar and tall, without branches for a long distance, and these trees are shaped more in their trunks like an elm than a pasture oak. They commonly stand aslant at various angles. When, in the midst of this great oak wood, you look around, you are struck by the great mass of gray-barked wood that fills the air. The leaves of these old oaks are now fairly fallen, and the ground is densely covered with their rustling reddish-brown scales.

A peculiarity of this, as compared with much younger woods, is that there is little or no underwood and you walk freely in every direction, though in the midst of a dense wood. You walk, in fact, *under* the wood.

The wood not having been cut to any extent, and the adjacent country being very little occupied, I did not notice a single cart-path where a wheel-track was visible, — at most a slight vista, and one footpath. I knew that I was near the southwest edge by the crowing of a cock.

This wood is said to have been a great resort for pigeons. We saw one large pigeon-place on the top of the hill where we first entered it. Now used.

Seeing this, I can realize how this country appeared when it was discovered. Such were the oak woods which the Indian threaded hereabouts.

Such a wood must have a peculiar fauna to some extent. Warblers must at least pass through it in the spring, which we do not see here.

We have but a faint conception of a full-grown oak forest stretching uninterrupted for miles, consisting of sturdy trees from one to three and even four feet in diameter, whose interlacing branches form a complete and uninterrupted canopy. Many trunks old and hollow, in which wild beasts den. Hawks nesting in the dense tops, and deer glancing between the trunks, and occasionally the Indian with a face the color of the faded oak leaf.

Grimes said that he could almost clasp the loins of my lynx as it hung up by the heels before it was skinned; it was so slender there that a man with a large hand could have done it.

Richardson in his "Fauna Boreali-Americana," which I consulted at Cambridge on the 7th, says that the French-Canadians call the Canada lynx indifferently *Le Chat* or *Le Peeshoo*, and Charlevoix falsely calls it *Carcajou*, which is the wolverene, and hence much confusion and error among naturalists. "Seven to nine thousand are annually procured by the Hudson's Bay Company. It is found on the Mackenzie River as far north as latitude 66°." Easily killed by a stroke with a small stick on the back! (?) Breeds once a year and has two young. Never attacks man. A poor runner, but a good swimmer. Audubon and Bachman repeat Richardson. According to Pennant, Lawson and Catesby repeat the falsehoods about its dropping from trees on deer, etc.

Observed in the dropping of a fox the other day, with fur, some quarter-shaped (or triangular segments) seeds, and roughish, which may have been seeds of rose hips. They were white. So are the sweet-briar hips, but the common wild rose hips are brownish. Were they prinos seeds? If rose hips, then the fox enjoys what Manasseh Cutler in 1785 called "the conserve of hepps of the London dispensatory" without the sugar.

Elijah Wood, senior, tells me that about 1814 (or before 1815, in which year he was married, and while he still lived at his father's on Carlisle road), as he was riding to town on horseback in the evening alone to singing to prepare for Thanksgiving, he stopped to let his horse drink at the brook beyond Winn's, when he heard a cry from some wild beast just across the river. It affected him so that he did not stop to let his horse drink much. When he returned later, — now with others, — they all heard it, as if answering to their shouts, somewhat further up the river. It was also heard by some teamsters, and also an animal supposed to be the same was said to have been seen by a woman crossing the road just west of where Wood now lives. It was thought to be a wolverene.

I have now measured in all eight pitch pine stumps at the Tommy Wheeler hollow, sawed off within a foot of the ground.

I measured the longest diameter, and then at right angles with that, and took the average, and then selected that side of the stump on which the radius was of average length and counted the number of rings in each inch, beginning at the centre, thus: —

	1st inch	2	3	4	5	6	7	8	9	10	11	12	Radius	Rings, in all
1st tree	9—	12+	9—	7+	$11\frac{1}{2}$	$16\frac{1}{2}$ (?)	26 (?)	25	26	in $\frac{3}{8}$ inch 17			$9\frac{3}{8}$	158
2	10+	7+	6	$5\frac{1}{2}$	5	$6\frac{1}{2}$	$9\frac{1}{2}$	11	$13\frac{1}{2}$	19	33	in $\frac{5}{8}$ inch 38	$11\frac{5}{8}$	164
3	13—	11	9	11	15	21	16	20	28	32			10	176 (?); more correctly, 168
4	15	12	10	16	24	19	18	16	15	in $\frac{1}{8}$+ inch 3			$9\frac{1}{8}$+	148
5 diam. $19\frac{1}{2}$	12	12	9	9	11	23	17	21	32	in $\frac{3}{4}$ inch 25			$9\frac{3}{4}$	171 *I have* this; more correctly, 165
6	15	13	11	14	18	19	23	21	21	in $\frac{1}{2}$+ inch 16			$9\frac{1}{2}$+	171
7	13	11	11	11	22	29	42	in $\frac{5}{8}$ inch 24					$7\frac{5}{8}$	163
8	16	13	12	13	11	14	14	19	28	in $\frac{1}{4}$ inch 10			$9\frac{1}{4}$	About 150
	103	91	77	$86\frac{1}{2}$	$117\frac{1}{2}$	148	$165\frac{1}{2}$	133	$163\frac{1}{2}$	51	33		Av. R. about $9\frac{1}{2}$	Av. age 162 or 163 years
x	13—	11+	10—	11—	15—	18+	21—	19	23+	25+	33	Av. Diam. 19.		

Of these eight, average growth about one seventeenth of an inch per year.

Calling the smallest number of rings in an inch in each tree 1, the comparative slowness of growth of the inches is thus expressed, *viz.*: —

1	1.3	1.7	1.3	1.	1.6	2.3	3.7	3.6	3.7		
2	2.	1.4	1.2	1.1	1.	1.3	1.9	2.1	2.7	3.8	6.6
3	1.4	1.2	1.	1.2	1.7	2.3	1.6	2.2	3.1	3.4	
4	1.5	1.2	1.	1.6	2.4	1.9	1.8	1.6	1.5		
5	1.3	1.3	1.	1.	1.2	2.4	1.9	2.3	3.4		
6	1.4	1.2	1.	1.3	1.6	1.7	2.1	1.9	1.9	2.5	
7	1.2	1.	1.	1.	2.	2.6	3.8	3.6			
8	1.4	1.2	1.1	1.2	1.	1.3	1.3	1.7	2.5	3.6	

From the line x I calculate the average rate of growth in diameter (or radius) each successive ten years thus (in decimals of an inch): [1] —

1 to 10	10 to 20	20–30	30–40	40–50	50–60	60–70
(.77)	(.87)	(.96)	(.95)	(.78+)	(.66)	(.55+)

70–80	80–90	90–100	100–110	110–120	120–130
(.54−)	(.48−)	(.48+)	(.53−)	(.51)	(.43+)

130–140	140–150	150–160	160–170	170–180	180–190
(.43+)	(.403)	(.40)	(.36+)	(.30)	(.30)

Of course the error is great in proportion as the number of rings in an inch exceeds ten.

They grew in the first decade more than in any decade after their fiftieth year, and continued to grow with pretty regularly accelerated growth up to about the end of the third decade, or say about the twenty-ninth year, when they were increasing fastest in diameter, — 1.92 inches in ten years. They continued to

[1] It would have been much easier, as well as more correct if I had counted at first the number of rings to each inch.

grow at nearly the same rate through the fourth decade, and then their rate of growth very suddenly decreased, — *i. e.*, in fifth decade, or from the fortieth to the fiftieth years, when they grew only about the same as in the first decade. In the sixth and seventh decades the rate of growth steadily decreased as fast as it had increased in the first three decades, and it continued to decrease through the eighth, ninth, and tenth decades, though much more slowly. In the eleventh and twelfth decades, or from one hundred to one hundred and twenty years, the rate was accelerated, or they grew faster than from eighty to one hundred, but after the twelfth decade the rate of growth steadily decreased to the last, when it was less than one third what it was in the third decade.[1] When growing fastest, or between the twentieth and thirtieth year, the radius often was not increased one inch in ten years. But after they were one hundred and sixty years old they did not grow four tenths[2] of an inch in ten years — or one twenty-fifth [3] of an inch in one year.[4] On an average, by accurate observation these eight trees were gaining the most in diameter at about the thirtieth year, and least (with one exception) in the last ten years of their existence.

Many have inferred that it is most profitable to cut pitch pine when about thirty (or forty) years old, but they seem to forget that the most rapid increase in diameter when the tree is only ten or fifteen years old

---

[1] According to calculation, but *actually* still less.

[2] On an average, $\frac{28}{100}$.   [3] $\frac{1}{35}$

[4] And sometimes much less, as has been stated.

does not indicate so great bulk of wood added to the tree, as a much less increase in diameter when it is fifty or one hundred years old. Indeed these trees, slowly as they appeared to grow at last, increased in bulk far more rapidly in the last twenty years than in the first twenty, — or as thirty-six to ten.

The absolute area of the annual rings (which is in the same proportion as the bulk of wood formed) each ten years is (calculated from the measurement on the third page back): —

	1st 10 yrs.	2	3	4	5	6	7	8	9	10	11	12	13	14	15	16	17
1st tree	inch 3.9	7.9	16.5	28.1	23.2	21.6	18.1	15.7	15.7	18.8	18.8	19.7	20.5	20.5	14.		
2	3.1	17.3	39.3	53.4	43.2	44.8	41.4	33.	31.4	22.3	20.	20.	16.	12.	12.	12.	
3	2.4	6.7	15.6	19.5	19.2	18.4	16.5	17.4	25.5	24.5	23.6	21.3	19.	19.	18.8	18.7	18.7
4	2.1	5.	10.2	15.1	13.8	12.4	11.8	13.7	18.2	20.	22.7	26.7	29.5	35.6	29.7		
5*	2.6	6.8	13.6	22.3	25.4	18.2	15.	18.6	24.	23.	22.4	19.	16.7	16.7	17.2	18.1	18.1
6	2.1	4.7	8.7	14.4	15.7	15.7	15.7	18.	18.2	17.8	17.8	21.	22.4	24.2	25.4	23.4	21.3
7	2.4	6.7	12.	17.1	17.1	12.8	12.7	11.9	11.9	11.2	9.7	9.7	9.7	9.9	11.8	11.8	
8	2.	4.	7.8	13.1	16.5	22.2	25.2	25.2	29.2	2.8	24.7	20.2	19.1	19.1	14.9		
	20.6	59.1	123.7	183.0	174.1	166.1	156.4	153.5	174.1	165.6	159.7	157.6	152.9	157.0	143.8	84.0	58.1
Av.	2.6—	7.4—	15.5—	22.9—	21.7—	20.8—	19.5—	19.2—	21.8—	20.7—	20.—	19.9—	19.1	19.6	18.	16.8	19.4—

* By actually measuring the space covered by each successive ten rings for the fifth tree I got .9, .6, 1, 1.1, 1, .7, .5, .5, .56, .5, .5, .37, .25, .44, .25, .31, .25.

According to the above, most wood is made in the fourth decade, though there is but little decrease in amount afterward.

There is a loss of time if you cut at thirty or even forty years, for, supposing that a new pitch pine were at once to take the place of the old one, at the end of forty years more you would only have got $(2.6 + 7.4 + 15.5 + 22.9 =)$ 48.5 of wood more, instead of $(21.7 + 20.8 + 19.5 + 19.2 =)$ 81.2 more, which you would have had by this time if you had let the tree stand. Or if you had cut it at eighty years, you would only have 129.7 of wood after eighty years more, instead of the 155.9 that might have grown. Or even if you should cut every forty years, you would after one hundred and sixty years have got only 194 of wood to 285.6 that you might have had. From which I infer that the greater bulk of wood made in the third and fourth decade is so little more than that made in any succeeding ten years of the tree's age, and so much more than that made in the previous ten years, that if you want this kind of wood it is best to let the tree stand as long as it is sound and growing.

To be sure, the above calculation supposes the tree to increase in height in proportion to its age — which is hardly the case — and also that the same number of large trees can stand on the same area as of small ones. But even after these deductions, when we consider the proportionally greater value of large timber of this kind, it must be best to let it grow as long as it will.

The same is true until the last forty years makes less wood than the first forty. The first forty makes 48.5;

the last, 76.8. However, the time of cutting may depend
partly on the number of trees that stand on a given
area and also on whether they are wanted for fuel or
for lumber, many small being about as good for the
former use as a few large; *i. e.*, these trees made more
wood any other forty years than the first. Why, then,
employ them then only?

Nov. 10 *and* 11 were rainy, raising the river considerably on to the meadows.

Nov. 13. P. M. — To Mt. Misery.

A white birch (*Betula alba*) west edge of Trillium
Wood, two feet seven inches [in] circumference at three
feet.

On the Moore and Hosmer lot, cut in '52 (I think),
west of railroad, south of Heywood's meadow, an oak
stump fifteen and a half inches [in] diameter, ninety-
three rings; another, white oak, fourteen and a half
inches [in] diameter, ninety-four rings. In the first
case there were two stumps of same age, evidently
sprouts from an older stock, they curving around it, but
I observed only a slight hollow where apparently the old
stump had been. In the second case there was but one
stump, but that rather concave on one side where
there was a deep hollow in the earth. In both of these
cases the tenacious mould, covered slightly with a fine
greenish lichen, appeared heaved up about where the
old stump had been. It was a good hundred years since
that old stump was cut. The inmost rings of the recent
stumps were coarse, as with sprouts.

Near these apparently a black (?) oak, or maybe a chestnut (?), twenty inches [in] diameter and seventy-four rings, but the centre was within four inches of the westerly side.

A white oak standing by the fence west of Spanish Brook dam on Morse's lot, circumference six feet and two twelfths at three feet. Near by a hornbeam a foot and a half [in] circumference at three feet.

J. Baker's pitch pines south of upper wood-path north of his house abundantly confirm the rule of *young* white pines under pitch pines. That fine young white pine wood west of this is partly of these which were left when the pitch pines were cut.

Baker's hill between farm and Pleasant Meadow, oak (apparently a black), diameter twenty-six, seventy-one rings. The stumps here were cut some five or six years ago and have fifty to sixty rings. Commonly no sprouts from those of this age here.

On top of Mt. Misery, looked again at those old stumps (of the 8th). There are three or four quite plain, just showing themselves above the surface, with rounded, flaky, decaying and crumbling edge, close to the recent stump of the shoot or shoots which sprang from them and which were cut last winter. One of these recent stumps, counted to-night, gives sixty years, but the first two or three are uncertain. Hence this old stump is as old as the century.

There are several perfectly dry and exposed stumps on bare rocky shelves, or else lying on rocks on their sides, quite well preserved and showing the marks of the axe, which I have but little doubt are of the same age, preserved by being tipped out of the earth many years ago.[1]

Am surprised at the very slow growth of some hickory (stumps) along the wall on the top of this hill, — so fine I did not count quite accurately.

One was 10 inches in diameter with		104 rings
" " $6\frac{1}{2}$[2] "	"	*about* 115 "
" " $14\frac{1}{2}$ "	"	" 84 "
" " $11\frac{3}{4}$ "	"	121 "

I think that the oak stumps have lasted unusually long on this hill, on account of their having originally grown slowly here and since been so much exposed to the light and air over and amid the rocks.

Nov. 14. River two feet four inches above summer level (and at height) on account of rain of 10th and 11th and 12th.

The red maple on south edge of Trillium Wood is six feet three inches in circumference at three feet.

Yellow butterflies still.

Almost all holes in and about stumps have nutshells or nuts in them.

Nov. 16. This and yesterday Indian-summer days.
P. M. — To Inches Woods.

Walked over these woods again, — first from Harvard turnpike at where Guggins Brook leaves it, which is the east edge of the old wood, due north along near the edge of the wood, and at last more northwest along edge to the cross-road, a strong mile.

[1] *Vide* account of pine stump, April 5, 1859.
[2] Have this. *Vide* Nov. 19th.

I observe that the black, red, and scarlet oaks are generally much more straight and perpendicular than the white, and not branched below. The white oak is much oftener branched below and is more irregular, — curved or knobby.

The first large erect black oak measured on the 9th was by the path at foot of hill southeast of pigeon-place. Another, more north, is (all at three feet when not otherwise stated) ten and a half [feet] in circumference.

There is not only a difference between most of the white oaks within Blood's wood and the pasture oaks without, — the former having a very finely divided and comparatively soft tawnyish bark, and the latter a very coarse rugged and dark-colored bark, — but there is here a similar difference within this wood; *i. e.,* some of the white oaks have a hard, rugged bark, in very regular oblong squares or checkers (an agreeably regular *roughness* like a coat of mail), while others have a comparatively finely divided and soft bark.

I see one white oak shaped like this: —

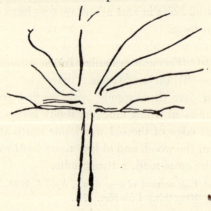

It happens oftenest here, I think, that the very largest
white oaks have the most horizontal branches and branch
nearest the ground, which would at first suggest that *these*
trees were a different variety from the more upright and
rather smaller ones, but it may be that these are older,
and for that reason had more light and room and so
temptation to spread when young.

Northwesterly from pigeon-place (near base of
hill), —

A white oak $6\frac{3}{4}$ in circumference

    "   "   " $8\frac{4}{12}$

    "   "   " $6\frac{11}{12}$

The last one grows close against a rock (some three
feet high), and it has grown over the top and sides of
this rock to the breadth of twelve and eighteen inches
in a thin, close-fitting, saddle-like manner, very remarkable and showing great vigor in the tree.

Here, too, coming to water, I see the swamp white
oak rising out of it, elm-like in its bark and trunk. Red
maples also appear here with them. It is interesting
to see thus how surely the character of the ground determines the growth. It is evident that in a wood that
has been let alone for the longest period the greatest
regularity and harmony in the disposition of the trees
will be observed, while in our ordinary woods man has
often interfered and favored the growth of other kinds
than are best fitted to grow there naturally. To some,
which he does not want, he allows no place at all.

Hickories occasionally occur, — sometimes scaly-
barked, if not shagbarks, — also black birch and a few
little sugar maples.

Still going north, a white pine nine feet [in] circumference.

The wood at the extreme north end (along the road) is considerably smaller. After proceeding west along the road, we next went west by south through a maple and yellow birch swamp, in which a black oak eight feet and four twelfths [in] circumference, a red maple six feet and a half, a black birch seven feet, a black birch eight feet. And in the extreme northwesterly part of the wood, close to the road, are many large chestnuts, — one eleven and three quarters feet [in] circumference with many great knobs or excrescences, another twelve and seven twelfths.

We next walked across the open land by the road to the high hill northeast of Boxboro Centre. In this neighborhood are many very large chestnuts, of course related to the chestnut wood just named. 1st, along this road just over the north wall, beyond a new house, one $13\frac{11}{12}$ feet in circumference; 2d, 16, a few rods more west by the wall; then, perhaps fifty or sixty rods more west and maybe eight or ten rods north from the road, along a wall, the 3d, $15\frac{2}{12}$; and then, near the road, southwest from this, the 4th, $15\frac{4}{12}$; and some rods further north, toward hill and house of O. and J. Wetherbee, the 5th, $13\frac{7}{12}$; then northeast, in lower ground (?), the 6th, 16 feet, at ground $21\frac{2}{3}$; then, near base of hill, beyond house, the 7th, $16\frac{2}{12}$ at two feet from ground; next, some rods west of the hill, the 8th, $17\frac{8}{12}$ at three feet, at ground $23\frac{1}{2}$; and then, a considerable distance north and further down the hill, the 9th, $13\frac{4}{12}$. (There [were] also four other good-sized chestnuts

Old Chestnut Trees on a Hilltop in Boxboro

on this hillside, with the last three.) Or these nine trees
averaged about 15¼ feet in circumference. The 3d tree
had a limb four or five feet from the ground, which
extended horizontally for a rod toward the south, declining a little toward the earth, and this was nine feet
in circumference about eighteen inches from the tree.
The 7th had a large limb broken off at one foot above
the ground on the side, whose stump prevented measuring at the ordinary height. As I remember, the 8th was
the finest tree.

These nine (or thirteen) trees are evidently the relics
of one chestnut wood of which a part remains and makes
the northwest part of Inches Wood, and the trees are all
within about a quarter of a mile southeast and northwest, the first two being by themselves at the southeast.

The chestnut is remarkable for branching low, occasionally so low that you cannot pass under the lower
limb. In several instances a large limb had fallen out
on one side. Commonly, you
see great rugged strips of bark,
like straps or iron clamps made
to bind the tree together, three
or four inches wide and as many
feet long, running more or less
diagonally across the trunk and
suggesting a very twisted grain,
while the grain of the recent bark
beneath them may be perpendicular. Perhaps this may
be owing to old portions of the bark which still adhere,
being wrenched aside by the unequal growth of the
wood. I think that all these old trunks show this.

Frank Brown tells me of a chestnut in his neighborhood nineteen feet and eight(?) inches in circumference
at three feet.

White oaks within a wood commonly, at Wetherbee's
and Blood's woods, have lost the outside rough and
rugged bark near the base, like a jacket or vest cast off,
revealing that peculiar smooth tawny-white inner garment or shirt. Probably the moisture and shade of a
wood softens the bark and causes it to scale off. Apparently outside trees do not lose this outer bark, but
it becomes far more rugged and dark exposed to the
light and air, forming a strong coat of mail such as
they need.

Most of the white oaks in Inches Wood are of a slight
ashy tinge and have a rather loose, scaly bark, but the
larger, losing this below, become tawny-white.

Having returned into Inches Wood, not far west of
the meadow (which is west of the brook), at the angle
made by the open land, a black oak stump recently
cut, about one foot high and twenty-one inches in diameter, had only one hundred and six rings. A white
oak only nine inches in diameter near by had eighty
rings. I suspect that the smaller white oaks are much
older comparatively (with the large) than their size
would indicate, as well as sounder and harder wood. A
white oak at three feet, six and one half in circumference. A black oak had been recently cut into at the
west base of Pigeon Hill, and I counted about eighty-
five rings in the outside three inches. The tree (wood
only) was some twenty-three inches in diameter.

Looking at this wood from the Boxboro hill, the

white pines appeared to be confined chiefly to the higher land, forming a ridge from north to south. Young white pines have very generally come in (a good many being twenty feet high or more), though in some places much more abundantly than in others, all over this oak wood, though not high enough to be seen at a distance or from hills (except the first-named larger trees); but though there are very many large pitch pines in this wood, especially on the hills or moraines, young pitch pines are scarcely to be seen. I saw some only in a dell on the south side the turnpike. If these oaks were cut off with care, there would very soon be a dense white pine wood there. The white pines are not now densely planted, except in some more open places, but come up straggingly every two or three rods. The natural succession is rapidly going on here, and as fast as an oak falls, its place is supplied by a pine or two. I have no doubt that, *if entirely let alone*, this which is now an oak wood would have become a white pine wood.

Measured on the map, this old woodland is fully a mile and a half long from north to south — one mile being north [of] the turnpike — and will average half a mile from east to west. Its extreme width, measuring due east and west, is from Guggins Brook on the turnpike to the first church. (It runs considerably further southeast, however, on to the high hill.) There is a considerable tract on the small road south [of] the turnpike covered with second growth. There is, therefore, some four hundred acres of this old wood.

There is a very little beech and hemlock and yellow birch in this wood. Many large black birches at the northwest end. Chestnuts at the northwest and south-east ends.

The bark of the oaks is very frequently gnawed near the base by a squirrel or other animal.

Guggins Brook unites with Heather Meadow Brook, and then with Fort Pond Brook just this side of West Acton, and thus the water of this old oak wood comes into the Assabet and flows by our North Bridge. The seeds of whatever trees water will transport, provided they grow there, may thus be planted along our river.

I crossed the brook in the midst of the wood where there was no path, but four or five large stones had evidently been placed by man at convenient intervals for stepping-stones, and possibly this was an old Indian trail.

You occasionally see a massive old oak prostrate and decaying, rapidly sinking into the earth, and its place is evidently supplied by a pine rather than an oak.

There is now remarkably little life to be seen there. In my two walks I saw only one squirrel and a chickadee. Not a hawk or a jay. Yet at the base of very many oaks were acorn-shells left by the squirrels. In a perfectly round hole made by a woodpecker in a small dead oak five feet from the ground, were three good white oak acorns placed.

In the midst of the wood, west of the brook, is a natural meadow, — i. e. in a natural state, — a narrow strip without trees, yet not very wet. Evidently swamp white oaks and maples might grow there. The greater part of this wood is strewn with large rocks, more or less flat or table-like, very handsomely clothed with moss and polypody. The surface of the ground is finely diversified, there being hills, dells, moraines, meadows, swamps, and a fine brook in the midst of all. Some parts are very thickly strewn with rocks (as at the northwest), others quite free from them. Nowhere any monotony.

It is very pleasant, as you walk in the shade below, to see the cheerful sunlight reflected from the maze of oak boughs above. They would be a fine sight after one of those sticking snows in the winter.

On the north end, also, the first evidence we had that we were coming out of the wood — approaching its border — was the crowing of a cock.

Nov. 17. P. M. — To Blood's woods.

Sawed off a branch of creeping juniper two inches [in] diameter with fifteen rings.

On one square of nine rods in Blood's wood, which seemed more dense than the average, are thirteen sizable trees. This would give about two hundred and thirty to an acre, but probably there are not more than one hundred and eighty to an acre, take the wood through. This is but little more than one to a square rod. Yet this is a quite dense wood. That very solid white oak stump recently sawed in this wood was evidently a seedling, the growth was so extremely slow at first. If I found the case to be the same with the other oaks here, I should feel sure that these were all seedlings and therefore had been preceded by pines or at least some dense evergreens, or possibly birches. When I find a dense oak wood, whether sprouts or seedlings, I affirm that evergreens once stood [there] and, if man does not prevent, will grow again. This I must believe until I find a dense oak wood planted under itself or in open land.

Minot Pratt's elm is sixteen and a quarter feet [in] circumference at three feet.

These tawny-white oaks are thus by their color and character the lions among trees, or rather, not to compare them with a foreign animal, they are the cougars or panthers — the American lions — among the trees, for nearly such is that of the cougar which walks beneath and amid or springs upon them. There is plainly this harmony between the color of our chief wild beast of the cat kind and our chief tree.

How they do things in West Acton. As we were walking through West Acton the other afternoon, a few rods only west of the centre, on the main road, the Harvard turnpike, we saw a rock larger than a man could lift, lying in the road, exactly in the wheel-track, and were puzzled to tell how it came there, but supposed it had slipped off a drag, — yet we noticed that it was peculiarly black. Returning the same way in the twilight, when we had got within four or five rods of this very spot, looking up, we saw a man in the field, three or four rods on one side of that spot, running off as fast as he could. By the time he had got out of sight over the hill it occurred to us that he was blasting rocks and had just touched one off; so, at the eleventh hour, we turned about and ran the other way, and when we had gone a few rods, off went two blasts, but fortunately none of the rocks struck us. Some time after we had passed we saw the men returning. They looked out for themselves, but for nobody else. This is the way they do things in West Acton. We now understood that the big stone was blackened by powder.

Silas Hosmer tells me how —— and —— sold the Heywood lot between the railroad and Fair Haven. They lotted it off in this wise: *i. e.* in triangles, and, carry-ing plenty of liquor, they first treated all round, and then proceeded to sell at auction, but the purchasers, excited with liquor, were not aware when the stakes were pointed out that the lots were not as broad in the rear as in front, and the wood standing cost them as much as it should have done delivered at the door.

I frequently see the heads of teasel, called fuller's thistle, floating on our river, having come from factories above, and thus the factories which use it may distribute its seeds by means of the streams which turn their machinery, from one to another. The one who first cultivated the teasel extensively in this town is said to have obtained the seed when it was not to be pur-chased — the culture being monopolized — by sweep-ing a wagon which he had loaned to a teasel-raiser.

The growth of very old trees, as appears by calculating the bulk of wood formed, is feebler at last than when in middle age, or say in pitch pine at one hundred and sixty than at forty or fifty, especially when you consider the increased number of leaves, and this, together with the fact that old stumps send up no shoots, shows that trees are not indefinitely long-lived.

I have a section of a chestnut sprout — and not at

all a rank one — which has 6 rings in the first inch, or
4 rings in five eighths of an inch, but a section of a
chestnut seedling has 10 rings in five eighths of an inch.

A section of a white oak sprout, far from rank, has
4 rings in first five eighths of an inch; of a seedling
ditto, 16 or 17 in first five eighths of an inch; of a seedling ditto, 8 — in first five eighths of an inch; of a very
slow-grown sprout, 6 — in first five eighths of an inch.
Or in the white oaks the proportion is as five to twelve.

The first seedling oak has the rough and tawny light-
brown bark of an old tree, while the first sprout is quite
smooth-barked.

A seedling white birch has 10 rings in first seven
eighths of an inch.

A sprout white birch has 5 rings in first seven eighths
of an inch. The first has the white bark of an old tree;
the second, a smooth and reddish bark.

When a stump is sound to the pith I can commonly
tell whether it was a seedling or a sprout by the rapidity
of the growth at first. A seedling, it is true, may have
died down many times till it is fifteen or twenty years
old, and so at last send up a more vigorous shoot than at
first, but generally the difference is very marked.

Nov. 19. P. M. — To Mt. Misery.

Saw off a hickory stump which is scarcely six and a
half inches in diameter and has nearly a hundred rings.
(It is the one of November 13th, and then called about
115 (??). Counting it now in the evening, I make 92.)
It is surprising how quickly this wood decays. This
tree was cut last winter, and then evidently was per-

fectly sound, as appears from the surface, but on sawing it off three inches lower I find that it is rotted entirely through and is soft and no part sound, so that I cannot count it on the new face. In less than one year this stump is worthless, even for fuel!

I look again at the old oak stumps on this hill. One evidently, *i. e. surely*, a sprout (the older stump beside it), a white oak, grew nearly $1\frac{3}{8}$ inches in the first twelve years; another oak, a sprout (with older stump), $1\frac{5}{8}$ inches in the first eleven or twelve years; a white oak (without an older stump), $1\frac{5}{8}$ inches in the first twelve years; probably the last a sprout also, for, as seen on last page, a white oak seedling grows only $\frac{5}{8}$ of an inch in twelve years. There was also a hickory sprout stump of the same age with the others, though of course the old stump was long since gone. It was plainly seen to be a sprout by the very rapid growth at first and the concave form of one side.

My rule of small white pines under pitch pines is so true of E. Hoar's land that he very easily got a hundred white pines there to set by his house.

Mr. Bradshaw says that he got a little auk in Wayland last week, and heard of two more, one in Weston and the other in Natick. Thinks they came with the storm of the 10th and 11th.

He tells me of a small oak wood of old trees called More's, half a mile east of Wayland, behind the grave-yard.

Nov. 20. P. M. — To R. W. E.'s hill.

I see a pitch pine several years old on the west slope

of the railroad embankment, sixty rods by pacing from
the nearest pitch pine, which was in Trillium Wood.
I have seen several such. This tree would soon sow itself in our yards if they were neglected.

In the Moore and Hosmer lot which I surveyed in
'49–'50, beyond Heywood meadow, a white oak stump
ten inches [in] diameter with seventy rings (cut in winter
of '49–'50), evidently a sprout, though the old stump
appears to have been entirely overgrown and so concealed.

I see, on the southwest or railroad side, near top,
of Emerson's hill, a great many oak stumps (which were
sprouts) with the older stump still very plain.

One (probably black oak) with 35 rings cut some 2 years = 37.
2d,   "   "   "   "   "   "   "   "   "   " = 37.
3d,   "   "   "   "   "   "   "   "   "   " = 37.

(This last *old* stump being small and almost overgrown between the stumps of the sprouts and seen — a
sliver of it — in a hole between them.) Also lower
down-hill, toward railroad, old chestnut stumps with the
stumps of sprouts of R. W. E.'s cutting twenty-five to
thirty and odd years old, cut some dozen years ago;
stumps, then, some forty years old.

Also, on the pond end of the hilltop, amid the piles
of stones, where I suppose was a pasture once, I see oak
stumps cut just thirty-eight years ago beside the stumps
of their sprouts cut last winter, and here are many
sprouts coming up the second time; but on the other
end [of] the hill I notice no sprouts the second time.
There were many oaks where these piles of stone are,
some seventy or eighty years ago, then, at least, and I

think that if this ever was a pasture they must have been preceded by pines. These oak stumps, cut about thirty-eight years ago, are quite fresh, especially the white oak on the top of this rocky hill. So at Mt. Misery. Such is evidently a favorable locality for their preservation. Indeed, it is very common to see oak stumps forty years old in such places. They are the rule here.

Decidedly finger-cold to-night.

Nov. 21. If you cut a dense mixed wood of pine and oak in which no little pines have sown themselves, it is evident that a wood exclusively of oak sprouts may succeed, as I see is the case with part of R. W. E.'s hill-side toward the pond.

I see a little pitch pine which bore a cone at twenty-two inches from the ground when it was only seven or eight years old. It is now a dozen years old and has borne two more since, and scattered the seed.

P. M. — To Fair Haven Hill.

On what was Stow's lot, southwest the Boiling Spring, adjacent to Wheeler's field, I count the rings of four oak stumps which are from eighteen to twenty-two inches in diameter. They are all about 120, and the oaks are evidently all from the seed. This was both a pine and oak wood, and I suspect that about one hundred and twenty years [ago] pines were cut or burned or blown down or decayed there and these oaks succeeded. These stumps are now in the very best condition for counting, having been cut nine or ten years ago. But not so with the pitch pine stumps

(one is twenty-three inches in diameter) cut about
a year later on what was R. Brown's, higher up. Their
sap and more is covered with green and red cockspur
lichens so thickly you cannot see the rings. On this
lot (now open Wheeler lot) are not only these old pitch
pine stumps (a few), but the stumps of oak sprouts
forty-four years old, with the older stumps by their
side, or half overgrown, yet quite plain, which last there
were cut (44 + 9 =) 53 years ago. No sprouts from
them.

In early times probably less wood was cut at once;
commonly only the winter's wood for the owners' use.
This Brown lot was variously treated apparently.

See young beeches near the upper edge of Stow's,
about midway on Wheeler, near where some stones
have been hauled into Stow's from Wheeler's land.

Another finger-cold evening, which I improve in
pulling my turnips — the usual amusement of such
weather — before they shall be frozen in. It is worth
the while to see how green and lusty they are yet,
still adding to their stock of nutriment for another
year; and between the green and also withering leaves
it does me good to see their great crimson round or
scalloped tops, sometimes quite above ground, they are
so bold. They remind you of rosy cheeks in cool weather,
and indeed there is a relationship. All kinds of har-
vestry, even pulling turnips when the first cold weather
numbs your fingers, are interesting, if you have been
the sower, and have not sown too many.

Got a section to-day of a white cedar railroad sleeper
which I am told came from the eastward and was

brought up from Charlestown. First count gives 254 rings; second, on opposite side, where the centre is less plain, 246 rings; average, 250. Its diameter is 16¼ inches, or nearly 31 rings to an inch. This is the oldest, as well as slowest-growing, tree that I have counted the rings of. I see other sleepers nearly as old. Some smaller, or say 10½ inches in diameter, had 125 rings in the first three inches and then grew much faster; as if they were at first part of a very dense thicket and grew very slowly, but afterward, prevailing over the rest, grew faster. This sleeper had, of course, been cut a year at least. It may not have been the butt end of the log, or at any rate it must have been several years old before it reached the height at which it was cut, so that it must have begun to exist before the settlement of Jamestown. It was a flourishing young cedar of at least some fifteen summers when the Pilgrims came over. Thus the cars on our railroad, and all their passengers, roll over the trunks of trees *sleeping* beneath them which were planted years before the first white man settled in New England.

Nov. 22. P. M. — To northwest part of Sudbury.

The *Linaria Canadensis* is still freshly blooming. It is the freshest flower I notice now.

Considerable ice, lasting all day, on the river meadows and cold pools.

I measure the stump of that white pine which I used to see on the Marlborough road. It is thirty inches in diameter and has 85 rings.

There are two small clumps of laurel close to the

left side this road, by the woods, just this side the Sudbury line, going to Maynard's.

Here is a dense oak wood. I see many little white
pines sprung up along its edge in the road, but scarcely
one within the wood. They, too, want light and air,
though not so much as the pitch pine.

All the sound white oak acorns that I see now have
sprouted, and many have sent a root down into the
earth. This is often four inches long. But I see no
black nor scarlet nor red oak acorns sprouted, though
I find sound ones. The white are evidently very much
more sensitive and tender than they.

This is a very beautiful November day, — a cool but
clear, crystalline air, through which even the white
pines with their silvery sheen are an affecting sight. It
is a day to behold and to ramble over the hard (stiffen-
ing) and withered surface of the tawny earth. Every
plant's down glitters with a silvery light along the
Marlborough road, — the sweet-fern, the lespedeza,
and bare blueberry twigs, to say nothing of the weather-
worn tufts of *Andropogon scoparius*. A thousand bare
twigs gleam like cobwebs in the sun. I rejoice in the
bare, bleak, hard, and barren-looking surface of the
tawny pastures, the firm outline of the hills, so convenient to walk over, and the air so bracing and
wholesome. Though you are finger-cold toward night,
and you cast a stone on to your first ice, and see the
unmelted crystals under every bank, it is glorious
November weather, and only November fruits are out.
On some hickories you see a thousand black nuts
against the sky.

There is quite a white cedar swamp behind the old tavern south of Maynard's.

You walk fast and far, and every apple left out is grateful to your invigorated taste. You enjoy not only the bracing coolness, but all the heat and sunlight that there is, reflected back to you from the earth. The sandy road itself, lit by the November sun, is beautiful. Shrub oaks and young oaks generally, and hazel bushes and other hardy shrubs, now more or less bare, are your companions, as if it were an iron age, yet in simplicity, innocence, and strength a golden one.

(Day before yesterday the rustling of the withered oak leaves in the wind reminded me of the similar sound produced by snow falling on them.)

It is glorious to consider how independent man is of all enervating luxuries; and the poorer he is in respect to them, the richer he is. Summer is gone with all its infinite wealth, and still nature is genial to man. Though he no longer bathes in the stream, or reclines on the bank, or plucks berries on the hills, still he beholds the same inaccessible beauty around him. What though he has no juice of the grape stored up for him in cellars; the air itself is wine of an older vintage, and far more sanely exhilarating, than any cellar affords. It is ever some gouty senior and not a blithe child that drinks, or cares for, that so famous wine.

Though so many phenomena which we lately admired have now vanished, others are more remarkable and interesting than before. The smokes from distant chimneys, not only greater because more fire is required, but more distinct in the cooler atmosphere, are a very pleasing sight, and conduct our thoughts quickly to the roof and hearth and family beneath, revealing the homes of men.

Maynard's yard and frontage, and all his barns and fences, are singularly neat and substantial, and the highroad is in effect converted into a private way through his grounds. It suggests unspeakable peace and happiness. Yet, strange to tell, I noticed that he had a tiger instead of a cock for a vane on his barn, and he himself looked overworked. He had allowed the surviving forest trees to grow into ancestral trees about his premises, and so attach themselves to him as if he had planted them. The dusty highway was so subdued that it seemed as if it were lost there. He had all but stretched a bar across it. Each traveller must have felt some misgivings, as if he were trespassing.

However, the farmer's life expresses only such content as an ox in his yard chewing the cud.

What though your hands are numb with cold, your sense of enjoyment is not benumbed. You cannot now find an apple but it is sweet to taste.

Simply to see to a distant horizon through a clear air, — the fine outline of a distant hill or a blue mountain-top through some new vista, — this is wealth enough for one afternoon.

We journeyed into the foreign land of Sudbury to see how the Sudbury men — the Hayneses, and the Puffers, and the Brighams — live. We traversed their pastures and their wood-lots, and were home again at night.

Nov. 23. George Minott tells me that sixty years ago wood was only two or three dollars a cord here — and some of that hickory. Remembers when Peter Wheeler, sixty or more years ago, cut off all at once over a hundred acres of wood stretching from Flint's Pond to Goose Pond, — since cut again in part by Britton, and owned now partly by the Stows.

Most of us are still related to our native fields as the navigator to undiscovered islands in the sea. We can any autumn discover a new fruit there which will surprise us by its beauty or sweetness. So long as I saw one or two kinds of berries in my walks whose names I did not know, the proportion of the unknown seemed indefinitely if not infinitely great.

Famous fruits imported from the tropics and sold in our markets — as oranges, lemons, pineapples, and bananas — do not concern me so much as many an unnoticed wild berry whose beauty annually lends a new charm to some wild walk, or which I have found to be palatable to an outdoor taste.

The tropical fruits are for those who dwell within the tropics; their fairest and sweetest parts cannot be exported nor imported. Brought here, they chiefly concern those whose walks are through the market-place. It is not the orange of Cuba, but the checkerberry of the neighboring pasture, that most delights the eye and the palate of the New England child. What if the Concord Social Club, instead of eating oranges from Havana, should spend an hour in admiring the beauty of some wild berry from their own fields which they never attended to before? It is not the foreignness or size or nutritive qualities of a fruit that determine its absolute value.

It is not those far-fetched fruits which the speculator imports that concerns us chiefly, but rather those which you have fetched yourself in your basket from some far hill or swamp, journeying all the long afternoon in the hold of a basket, consigned to your friends at home, the first of the season.

We cultivate imported shrubs in our front yards for the beauty of their berries, when yet more beautiful berries grow unregarded by us in the surrounding fields.

As some beautiful or palatable fruit is perhaps the noblest gift of nature to man, so is a fruit with which a man has in some measure identified himself by cultivating or collecting it one of the most suitable presents to a friend. It was some compensation for Commodore Porter, who may have introduced some cannon-balls and bombshells into ports where they were not wanted, to have introduced the Valparaiso squash into the United States. I think that this eclipses his military glory.

As I sail the unexplored sea of Concord, many a dell and swamp and wooded hill is my Ceram and Amboyna.

At first, perchance, there would be an abundant crop of rank garden weeds and grasses in the cultivated land, — and rankest of all in the cellar-holes, — and of pin-weed, hardhack, sumach, blackberry, thimble-berry, raspberry, etc., in the fields and pastures. Elm, ash, maples, etc., would grow vigorously along old garden limits and main streets. Garden weeds and grasses would soon disappear. Huckleberry and blueberry bushes, lambkill, hazel, sweet-fern, barberry, elder, also shad-bush, choke-berry, andromeda, and thorns, etc., would rapidly prevail in the deserted pastures. At the same time the wild cherries, birch, poplar, willows, checkerberry would reëstablish themselves. Finally the pines, hemlock, spruce, larch, shrub oak, oaks, chestnut, beech, and walnuts would occupy the site of Concord once more. The apple and perhaps all exotic trees and shrubs and a great part of the indigenous ones named above would have disappeared, and the laurel and yew would to some extent be an underwood here, and perchance the red man once more thread his way through the mossy, swamp-like, primitive wood.

Nov. 24. P. M. — To Easterbrooks's.

Under the two white oaks by the second wall southeast of my house, on the east side the wall, I am surprised to find a great many sound acorns still, though every one is sprouted, — frequently more than a dozen on the short sward within a square foot, each with its radicle two inches long penetrated into the earth. But many have had their radicle broken or eaten off, and many have it now dead and withered. So far as my observation goes there, by far the greatest number of white oak acorns were destroyed by decaying (whether in consequence of frost or wet), both before and soon after falling. Not nearly so many have been carried off by squirrels and birds or consumed by grubs, though the number of acorns of all kinds lying under the trees is now comparatively small to what it was early in October.

It is true these two trees are exceptions and I do not find sound ones nearly as numerous under others.

Nevertheless, the sound white oak acorns are not so *generally* and *entirely* picked up as I supposed. However, there are a great many more shells or cups than acorns under the trees; even under these two trees, I think, there are not more than a third as many of any kind — sound or hollow — as there were, and generally those that remain are a very small fraction of what there were. It will be worth the while to see how many of these sprouted acorns are left and are sound in the spring. It is remarkable that all sound white oak acorns (and many which are not now sound) are sprouted, and that I have noticed no other kind sprouted, — though I have not seen the chestnut oak and little chinquapin at all. It remains to be seen how many of the above will be picked up by squirrels, etc., or destroyed by frost and grubs in the winter.

The first spitting of snow — a flurry or squall — from out a gray or slate-colored cloud that came up from the west. This consisted almost entirely of pellets an eighth of an inch or less in diameter. These drove along almost horizontally, or curving upward like the outline of a breaker, before the strong and chilling wind. The plowed fields were for a short time whitened with them. The green moss about the bases of trees was very prettily spotted white with them, and also the large beds of cladonia in the pastures. They come to contrast with the red cockspur lichens on the stumps, which you had not noticed before. Striking against the trunks of the trees on the west side they fell and accumulated in a white line at the base. Though a slight touch, this was the first wintry scene of the season. The air was so filled with these snow pellets that we could not see a hill half a mile off for an hour. The hands seek the warmth of the pockets, and fingers are so benumbed that you cannot open your jack-knife. The rabbits in the swamps enjoy it, as well as you. Methinks the winter gives them more liberty, like a night. I see where a boy has set a box trap and baited it with half an apple, and, a mile off, come across a snare set for a rabbit or partridge in a cow-path in a pitch pine wood near where the rabbits have nibbled the apples which strew the wet ground. How pitiable that the most that many see of a rabbit should be the snare that some boy has set for one!

The bitter-sweet of a white oak acorn which you nibble in a bleak November walk over the tawny earth is more to me than a slice of imported pineapple. We do not think much of table-fruits. They are especially for aldermen and epicures. They do not feed the imagination. That would starve on them. These wild fruits, whether eaten or not, are a dessert for the imagination. The south may keep her pineapples, and we will be content with our strawberries.

Nov. 25. I count the rings in a spruce plank from the railroad bridge, which extend five and a half inches from the centre of the tree, and make them 146, — $\frac{1}{26}$ + to a ring. This is slower growth than I find in a black spruce to-day at —

Ministerial Swamp, P. M. — It is $10\frac{1}{2}$ feet high, $2\frac{1}{2}$ inches [in] diameter just above ground, and has 21 rings, $\frac{1}{17}$ inch to a ring. A larch near by is 21 feet high, $2\frac{13}{16}$ inches [in] diameter, and has 20 rings, which makes $\frac{1}{14}$ + to a ring. The larch has made nearly twice as much wood as the spruce in the same time.

The cones of the spruce which I see are still closed. A few sugar maple seeds still hang on.

Last night and to-day are very cold and blustering. Winter weather has come suddenly this year. The house was shaken by wind last night, and there was a general deficiency of bedclothes. This morning some windows were as handsomely covered with frost as ever in winter. I wear mittens or gloves and my greatcoat. There is much ice on the meadows now, the broken edges shining in the sun. Now for the phenomena of winter, — the red buds of the high blueberry and the purple berries of the smilax.

As I go up the meadow-side toward Clamshell, I see a very great collection of crows far and wide on the meadows, evidently gathered by this cold and blustering weather. Probably the moist meadows where they feed are frozen up against them. They flit before me in countless numbers, flying very low on account of the strong northwest wind that comes over the hill, and a cold gleam is reflected from the back and wings of each, as from a weather-stained shingle. Some perch within three or four rods of me, and seem weary. I see where they have been pecking the apples by the meadow-side. An immense cohort of cawing crows which sudden winter has driven near to the habitations of man. When I return after sunset I see them collecting and hovering over and settling in the dense pine woods west of E. Wood's, as if about to roost there. Yesterday I saw one flying over the house, its wings so curved by the wind that I thought it a black hawk.

How is any scientific discovery made? Why, the discoverer takes it into his head first. He must all but see it.

I see several little white pines in Hosmer's meadow just beyond Lupine Hill, which must have sprung from seed which came some fifty rods, — probably blown so far in the fall. There are also a few in the road beyond Dennis's, which probably were blown from his swamp wood. So that there is nothing to prevent their springing up all over the village in a very few years — but our own plows and spades. They have also come up quite numerously in the young woodland north of J. P. B.'s Cold Pool (probably blown from the wood south of the pond), though they are evidently half a dozen years younger than the oaks there. I look at this large white pine wood by the pool to see if little ones come up under it. What was recently pasture comes up within a rod of this high wood on the north side, and, though the fence is gone, the different condition and history of the ground is very apparent by the different aspect of the little pines. There the old white pines are dense, and there are no little ones under them, but only a rod north they are very abundant, forming a dense thicket only two or three feet high bounded by a straight line on the south (or east and west), where the edge of the open land was within a rod of the great pines. Here they sprang up abundantly in the open land close by, but not at all under the pines. Yet within the great wood, wherever it is more open from any cause, I see a great many little pines springing up. Though they are thin and feeble comparatively, yet most of them will evidently come to be trees. White pines will spring up in the more open parts of a white pine wood, even under pines, though they are thin and feeble just in proportion to the density of the larger pines, and, where the large trees are quite dense, they will not spring up at all.

How commonly you see pitch pines, white pines, and birches filling up a pasture, and, when they are a dozen or fifteen years old, shrub and other oaks beginning to show themselves, inclosing apple trees and walls and fences gradually and so changing the whole aspect of the region. These trees do not cover the whole surface equally at present, but are grouped very agreeably after natural laws which they obey. You remember, perhaps, that fifteen years ago there was not a single tree in this pasture, — not a germinating seed of one, — and now it is a pretty dense forest ten feet high. I confess that I love to be convinced of this inextinguishable vitality in Nature. I would rather that my body should be buried in a soil thus wide-awake than in a mere inert and dead earth. The cow-paths, the hollows where I slid in the winter, the rocks, are fast being enveloped and becoming rabbit-walks and hollows and rocks in the woods.

How often you make a man richer in spirit in proportion as you rob him of earthly luxuries and comforts!

I see much oak wood cut at thirty years of age, — sprout wood.

Many stumps which have only twenty-five or thirty rings send up no shoots, because they are the sprouts from old stumps, which you may still see by their sides, and so are really old trees and exhausted. The chopper should foresee this when he cuts down a wood.

The bass by Dugan's cut a year ago. It is hard to count, so indistinct its rings, but I make 46 to 50 in a diameter of some twenty inches. The sprouts are quite peculiar, so light an ash-color with red tips and large blunt red buds.

The old pitch pines (*vide* back two or three weeks) one hundred and sixty years old, that stood on the south side of the Tommy Wheeler hollow, were twenty-three in number on a space about twelve rods by three (or thirty-six rods), with half a dozen white pines and as many oaks, the last two say twenty to fifty years younger than the pitch pines. Probably some of the pitch pines have died and left no trees, so that it may originally have been a pretty dense grove of pitch pines. There were as many more pitch pines (not to mention the oaks and white pines) on the other side of the hollow. These were on a slope toward the north. Now, four years after they were cut, this hillside is covered with hazel bushes, huckleberries, young oaks, red maples, *Viburnum nudum*, and a few little white pines, but the hollow below them has little beside grass (fine sedge) in it. It will be long before anything catches there. It is remarkable that no pitch pines grew there before, nor oaks, and very few white pines, which were the only trees there.

Some pitch pines have shed their seeds.

Nov. 26. P. M. — To E. Hubbard's Wood.
I see in the open field east of Trillium Wood a few

pitch pines springing up, from seeds blown from the
wood a dozen or fifteen rods off. Here is one just
noticeable on the sod — though by most it would be
mistaken for a single sprig of moss — which came
from the seed this year. It is, as it were, a little green
star with many rays, half an inch in diameter, lifted an
inch and a half above the ground on a slender stem.
What a feeble beginning for so long-lived a tree! By
the next fall it will be a star of greater magnitude, and
in a few years, if not disturbed, these seedlings will alter
the face of nature here. How significant, how ominous,
the presence of these green moss-like stars is to the
grass, heralding its doom! Thus from pasture this portion of the earth's surface becomes forest. These which
are now mistaken for mosses in the grass may become
lofty trees which will endure two hundred years, under
which no vestige of this grass will be left.

In Hubbard's Wood at north end I measure the
stump of either a red or black oak: 21 inches [in] diameter and 141 rings.

I examine quite a number of oak stumps thereabouts
and find them all seedlings. This, of course, must be
the case with old forests generally, for in the beginning
the trees were not cut.

A red oak about in middle of the wood 6½ feet circumference at 3 ft.
A canoe birch,   45 inches   "   " " "
Another "   "   45½ "   "   " " "
A white oak on the east
    side rather toward south,   7 feet   "   " " "

Some of the white oaks have a very loose scaly bark,
commencing half a dozen feet from the ground. I see

pitch pine bark four to five inches thick at the ground.
There are in this wood many little groves of white
pines two to four feet high, quite dense and green, but
these are in more open spaces, and are vigorous just in
proportion to the openness. There are also seedling
oaks and chestnuts ten to thirty years old, yet not
nearly so numerous as the pines. The large wood is
mixed oak and pine, — more oak at the north and more
pine, especially pitch pine, at the south. The prospect
is that in course of time the white pines will very greatly
prevail over all other trees here. This is also the case
with Inches', Blood's, and Wetherbee's woods.

If I am not mistaken, an evidence of more openness
where the little pines are is to be found in the greater
prevalence of pyrola and lycopodiums there. There are
even some healthy *Juniperus repens* in the midst of
these woods. Though the pitch pines are the prevailing
trees at the south end, I see no young pitch pines under
them.

Perhaps this is the way that a natural succession
takes place. Perhaps oak seedlings do not so readily
spring up and thrive within a mixed white pine and oak
wood as pines do, — in the more open parts, — and
thus, as the oaks decay, they are replaced by pines
rather than by oaks.

But where did the pitch pines stand originally ? Who
cleared the land for its seedlings to spring up in ? It is
commonly referred to very poor and sandy land, yet I
find it growing on the best land also. The expression
" a pitch pine plain " is but another name for a poor and
sandy level. It grows both on the sand and [in] the

swamp, and the fact that it grows on the sand chiefly is not so much evidence that it prefers it as that other trees have excluded it from better soil. If you cut down the pines on the pitch pine plain, oaks will come up there too. Who knows but the fires or clearings of the Indians may have to do with the presence of these trees there ? They regularly cleared extensive tracts for cultivation, and these were always level tracts where the soil was light — such as they could turn over with their rude hoes. Such was the land which they are known to have cultivated extensively in this town, as the Great Fields and the rear of Mr. Dennis's, — sandy plains. It is in such places chiefly that you find their relics in any part of the county. They did not cultivate such soil as our maple swamps occupy, or such a succession of hills and dales as this oak wood covers. Other trees will grow where the pitch pine does, but the former will maintain its ground there the best. I know of no tree so likely to spread rapidly over such areas when abandoned by the aborigines as the pitch pines — and next birches and white pines.

While I am walking in the oak wood or counting the rings of a stump, I hear the faint note of a nuthatch like the creak of a limb, and detect [it] on the trunk of an oak much nearer than I suspected, and its mate or companion not far off. This is a constant phenomenon of the late fall or early winter; for we do not hear them in summer that I remember.[1] I heard one not long since in the street.

I see one of those common birch fungi on the side of

[1] In '61 hear one occasionally a month earlier than this.

a birch stake which has been used to bound a lot sold
at auction, three feet or more from the ground, and its
face is toward the earth as usual, though the birch is
bottom up.

I saw that nuthatch to-day pick out from a crevice
in the bark of an oak trunk, where it was perpendicular,
something white once or twice and pretty large. May it
not have been the meat of an acorn ? Yet commonly
they are steadily hopping about the trunks in search of
insect food. Possibly some of those acorn-shells I see
about the base of trees may have been dropped from
the crevices in the bark above by birds — nuthatch or
jay — as well as left by squirrels.

Mother says that Lidy Bay, an Indian woman (so
considered), used to live in the house beyond Cæsar's
and made baskets, which she brought to town to sell,
with a ribbon about her hat. She had a husband.

The value of these wild fruits is not in the mere possession or eating of them, but in the sight or enjoyment
of them. The very derivation of the word " fruit "
would suggest this. It is from the Latin *fructus*, meaning that which is *used* or *enjoyed*. If it were not so, then
going a-berrying and going to market would be nearly
synonymous expressions. Of course it is the spirit in
which you do a thing which makes it interesting, whether
it is sweeping a room or pulling turnips. Peaches are un-
questionably a very beautiful and palatable fruit, but the
gathering of them for the market is not nearly so interesting as the gathering of huckleberries for your own use.

A man fits out a ship at a great expense and sends
it to the West Indies with a crew of men and boys,

and after six months or a year it comes back with a load of pineapples. Now, if no more gets accomplished than the speculator commonly aims at, — if it simply turns out what is called a successful venture, — I am less interested in this expedition than in some child's first excursion a-huckleberrying, in which it is introduced into a new world, experiences a new development, though it brings home only a gill of huckleberries in its basket. I know that the newspapers and the politicians declare otherwise, but they do not alter the fact. Then, I think that the fruit of the latter expedition was finer than that of the former. It was a more fruitful expedition. The value of any experience is measured, of course, not by the amount of money, but the amount of development we get out of it. If a New England boy's dealings with oranges and pineapples have had more to do with his development than picking huckleberries or pulling turnips have, then he rightly and naturally thinks more of the former; otherwise not.

Do not think that the fruits of New England are mean and insignificant, while those of some foreign land are noble and memorable. Our own, whatever they may be, are far more important to us than any others can be. They educate us, and fit us to live in New England. Better for us is the wild strawberry than the pineapple, the wild apple than the orange, the hazelnut or pignut than the cocoanut or almond, and not on account of their flavor merely, but the part they play in our education.

In the Massachusetts Historical Collections, First Series, volume x, Rev. John Gardner of Stow furnishes

a brief historical notice of that town in a letter dated
1767. He says, " The Indian names of this place were
Pompociticut and Shabbukin, from two notable hills."

I anticipated the other day that if anybody should
write the history of Boxboro, once a part of Stow, he
would be pretty sure to omit to notice the most interesting thing in it — its forest — and lay all the stress
on the history of its parish; and I find that I had con-
jectured rightly, for Mr. Gardner, after telling us who
was his predecessor in the ministry and where he
himself was settled, goes on to say: " As for any re-
markables, I am of the mind there have been the fewest
of any town of our standing in the Province. . . . I
can't call to mind above one thing worthy of publick
notice, and that is the grave of Mr. John Green," who,
it appears, " was made . . . clerk of the exchequer "
by Cromwell. " Whether he was excluded the Act of
Oblivion or not I cannot tell," says Mr. Gardner. At
any rate he tells us that he returned to New England,
" lived and died, and lies buried in this place." I can
assure Mr. Gardner that he was not excluded from the
act of oblivion.

However, Boxboro was less peculiar for its woods a
hundred years ago.

I have been surprised when a young man who had
undertaken to write the history of a country town, —
his native place, — the very name of which suggested
a hundred things to me, referred to it, as the crowning
fact of his story, that that town was the residence of
General So-and-so and the family mansion was still
standing.

Nov. 28. P. M. — To Annursnack.

Looking from the hilltop, I should say that there
was more oak woodland than pine to be seen, especially
in the north and northeast, but it is somewhat difficult
to distinguish all in the gleaming sunlight of mid-
afternoon. Most of the oak, however, is quite young.
As for pines, I cannot say surely which kind is most
prevalent, not being certain about the most distant
woods. The white pine is much the most dispersed,
and grows oftener in low ground than the pitch pine
does. It oftenest forms mixed woods with oak, etc.,
growing in straight or meandering lines, occasionally
swelling into a dense grove. The pitch pines commonly
occupy a dry soil — a plain or brow of a hill, often the
site of an old grain-field or pasture — and are much
the most seclusive, for, being a new wood, oaks, etc.,
have had no opportunity to grow up there, if they could.
I look down now on the top of a pitch pine wood
southwest of Brooks's Pigeon-place, and its top, so
nearly level, has a peculiarly rich and crispy look in
the sun. Its limbs are short and its plumes stout as compared with the white pine and are of a yellowish green.

There are many handsome young walnuts ten or
twelve feet high scattered over the southeast side of
Annursnack, or above the orchard. How came they
there? Were they planted before a wood was cut? It
is remarkable how this tree loves a hillside.

Behind G. M. Barrett's barn a scarlet oak stump
$18\frac{1}{2}$ inches [in] diameter and about 94 rings, which
has sent up a sprout two or three years since. On the
plain just north of the east end of G. M. B.'s oaks,

many oaks were sawed off about a year ago. Those I
look at are seedlings and very sound and rings very distinct and handsome. Generally no sprouts from them,
though one white oak sprout had been killed by frost.
One white oak, 17 inches [in] diameter, has 100 rings.
A second,   16½   "   "   "   also 100   "

The last has two centres which coalesced at the
thirtieth ring, which went round them both including
old bark between them. This was an instance of natural grafting.

Many seem to be so constituted that they can respect
only somebody who is dead or something which is
distant.

The less you get, the happier and the richer you are.
The rich man's son gets cocoanuts, and the poor man's,
pignuts; but the worst of it is that the former never
goes a-cocoanutting, and so he never gets the cream
of the cocoanut as the latter does the cream of the
pignut.

That on which commerce seizes is always the very
coarsest part of a fruit, — the mere husk and rind, in
fact, — for her hands are very clumsy. This is what
fills the holds of ships, is exported and imported, pays
duties, and is finally sold at the shops.

It is a grand fact that you cannot make the finer
fruits or parts of fruits matter of commerce. You may
buy a servant or slave, in short, but you cannot buy a
friend. You can't buy the finer part of any fruit — i. e.
the highest use and enjoyment of it. You cannot buy
the pleasure which it yields to him who truly plucks it;
you can't buy a good appetite even.

What are all the oranges imported into England to the hips and haws in her hedges ? She could easily spare the one, but not the others. Ask Wordsworth, or any of her poets, which is the most to him.

The mass of men are very easily imposed on. They have their runways in which they always travel, and are sure to fall into any pit or box trap set therein. Whatever a great many grown-up boys are seriously engaged in is considered great and good, and, as such, is sure of the recognition of the churchman and statesman. What, for instance, are the blue juniper berries in the pasture, which the cowboy remembers so far as they are beautiful merely, to church or state ? Mere trifles which deserve and get no protection. As an object of beauty, though significant to all who really live in the country, they do not receive the protection of any community. Anybody may grub up all that exist. But as an article of commerce they command the attention of the civilized world. I read that " several hundred tons of them are imported annually from the continent" into England to flavor gin with; "but even this quantity," says my author, " is quite insufficient to meet the enormous consumption of the fiery liquid, and the deficiency is made up by spirits of turpentine." Go to the English Government, which, of course, is representative of the people, and ask, What is the use of juniper berries ? The answer is, To flavor gin with. This is the gross abuse of juniper berries, with which an enlightened Government — if ever there shall be one — will have nothing to do.

Let us make distinctions, call things by the right names.

Nov. 29. Get up my boat, 7 A. M. Thin ice of the night is floating down the river. I hear that some boys went on to Goose Pond on the 26th and skated. It must have been thin.

P. M. — To Fair Haven Hill.

The pitch pine twigs have been so generally cut off by the squirrels for the sake of the cones that I easily detect the fertile trees, when going through a pitch pine wood, by seeing the green twigs strewn on the ground beneath. But few of the trees bear, and these are the ones.

The Bear Garden pitch pines are so generally open that young pitch pines of all sizes are intermixed with the others. There are many small white pines beside, but few if any seed-bearing ones.

I proceed through Potter's young wood south of this grove (toward Fair Haven Hill-side) and here I find by the stumps what I remember, — that a pitch pine wood was cut, some ten or twelve years ago, judging from the state of the stumps. It was for density, apparently, such a grove as now stands northward of this. It is a very poor soil. Shrub oaks chiefly appear to have succeeded to the pines, and now the growth consists of oaks, shrub and others (the latter four to six feet high), pitch pines two to ten feet high, and white birches. The soil is but poorly clad, owing to its barrenness and the prevalence of shrub oak at first. Probably the largest of these young pitch pines were such as stood in the open wood when it was cut — as they now do northward; but apparently the majority have been sown since, as others are still being sown by the large pitch pines there are left here and there quite numerously, the ground is still so open and bare on account of the feeble growth of the oaks. The white birches have as yet done the best, the pines next. It will ere long be a mixed oak and pitch pine wood, the pines not standing so dense as in new woods, though pretty thick in spots. This shows how a mixed wood of this character may arise, owing first to the existence of young pitch pines under the old when cut, — the latter being so open as to admit of their growth, — and secondly to the barren soil and shrub oaks, which fail to cover it for a long time, so that even after six or eight years pitch pines may catch there from seed-bearing trees which are left.

I am pleased to find an evidence that the pitch pine wood cut down here a dozen years ago was just such a *new* wood as that now standing on [the] north. It is this. Along the southwest edge of this portion of the lot, where the almost abrupt descent begins, I see many stones which were cast over the edge of the bank in great heaps when it was cultivated.

The small pitch pine grove above the western Fair Haven spring fully proves my theory of white pines in pitch pine, though there is hardly a seed-bearing white pine there. Young white pines are rapidly spreading up Fair Haven Hill-side, though the nearest seed-bearing white pines are across the river, thirty to sixty rods off.

I remember when this hillside above the spring was clear of wood. In fact, I was here when this field was cleared and the brush burned, some thirty-five years ago. Yet I now see a good many hickories both within and without the pines, five feet high, more or less. I feel about sure that these are not from stumps or old roots which have existed in the ground so long. How then did they come here ? The[y] even keep in advance of the pines on some sides a rod or two further into the open land. I am constrained to believe that they were planted there by quadrupeds or birds. If so, the wal- nut differs from the oak in the mode of its spreading; for I do not see oaks anywhere thus springing up in groves in grass ground, in advance of pines. It will be worth the while to ascertain the age of these exactly.

It is remarkable that the walnut loves a hillside so. I saw such a grove yesterday on Annursnack. Here is another of still larger trees a little lower down the hill; and there is a much more extensive one on the similar slope of Smith's Hill. Are animals more likely to plant walnuts in open land than acorns ? or is it that walnuts are more likely to live there when planted ? What a lover of the hills is this tree! I may be mistaken about those on Smith's Hill, after all.

Fair Haven Pond is skimmed over, all but the channel.

Can that be the skeleton of a raccoon which I find (killed not long since) on the Cliff Hill? Measured by my book it — the body from shoulder to tail — is 15½ inches long; tail, 13½; hind leg, 14½. *Vide* skull and foot.

If a man has spent all his days about some business, by which he has merely got to be rich, as it is called, *i. e.*, has got much money, many houses and barns and wood- lots, then his life has been a failure, I think; but if he has been trying to better his condition in a higher sense than this, has been trying to invent something, to be somebody, — *i. e.*, to invent and get a patent for himself, — so that all may see his originality, though he should never get above board, — and great inventors, you know, commonly die poor, — I shall think him comparatively successful.

From the Cliff I see more oak than pine.

Every interest, as the codfish and the mackerel, gets represented but the huckleberry interest. The first discoverers and explorers of the land make report of this fruit, but the last make comparatively little account of them.

You would say that some men had been tempted to live in this world at all only by the offer of a bounty by the general government — a bounty on living — to any one who will consent to be *out* at this era of the world, the object of the governors being to create a nursery for their navy. I told such a man the other day that I had got a Canada lynx here in Concord, and his instant question was, " Have you got the reward for him ? " What reward ? Why, the ten dollars which the State offers. As long as I saw him he neither said nor thought anything about the lynx, but only about this reward. " Yes," said he, " this State offers ten dollars reward." You might have inferred that ten dollars was something rarer in his neighborhood than a lynx even, and he was anxious to see it on that account. I have thought that a lynx was a bright-eyed, four-legged, furry beast of the cat kind, very *current*, indeed, though its natural gait is by leaps. But he knew it to be a draught drawn by the cashier of the wildcat bank on the State treasury, payable at sight. Then I reflected that the first money was of leather, or a whole creature (whence *pecunia*, from *pecus*, a herd), and, since leather was at first furry, I easily understood the connection between a lynx and ten dollars, and found that all money was traceable right back to the original wildcat bank. But the fact was that, instead of receiving ten dollars for the lynx which I had got, I had paid away some dollars in order to get him. So, you see, I was away back in a gray antiquity behind the institution of money, — further than history goes.

This reminded me that I once saw a cougar recently killed at the Adirondacks which had had its ears clipped. This was a ten-dollar cougar.

Yet, though money can buy no fine fruit whatever, and we are never made truly rich by the possession of it, the value of things generally is commonly estimated by the amount of money they will fetch. A thing is not valuable — *e. g.* a fine situation for a house — until it is convertible into so much money, that is, can cease to be what it is and become something else which you prefer. So you will see that all prosaic people who possess only the commonest sense, who believe strictly in this kind of wealth, are speculators in fancy stocks and continually cheat themselves, but poets and all discerning people, who have an object in life and know what they want, speculate in real values. The mean and low values of anything depend on it[s] convertibility into something else — *i. e.* have nothing to do with its intrinsic value.

This world and our life have practically a similar value only to most. The value of life is what anybody will give you for living. A man has his price at the South, is worth so many dollars, and so he has at the North. Many a man here sets out by saying, I will make so many dollars by such a time, or before I die, and that is his price, as much as if he were knocked off for it by a Southern auctioneer.

We hear a good deal said about moonshine by so-called practical people, and the next day, perchance, we hear of their failure, they having been dealing in fancy stocks; but there really never is any moonshine of this kind in the practice of poets and philosophers; there never are any hard times or failures with them, for they deal with permanent values.

V

DECEMBER, 1860

(ÆT. 43)

Dec. 1. P. M. — To Fair Haven Hill.

Yesterday, rain, raising river somewhat. Examined the young hickories on Fair Haven Hill slope to see how old they are. I sawed off three at two or three inches below the surface, and also higher up. These were about three feet high. The rings are very hard to discern, but I judge the smallest of them (which is about one inch in diameter and three feet high) to be seven years old. The other two are probably older, yet not nearly so old as the pines whose beginning I remember. It therefore must be that these hickories have sprung up from nuts within seven to twenty-five years past. They are most numerous in openings four or five rods over amid the pines, and are also found many rods from the pines in the open pasture, and also especially along walls, though yet very far from other trees of any kind. I infer, therefore, that animals plant them, and perhaps their growing along walls may be accounted for in part by the fact that the squirrels with nuts oftenest take that road. What is most remarkable is that they should be planted so often in open land, on a bare hillside, where oaks rarely are. I do not know of a grove of oaks springing up in this manner, — with broad intervals of bare sward between them, and away from pines.

How is this to be accounted for? Yet I did notice oak seedlings coming up in this manner in Potter's open field beyond Bear Garden.

It is wonderful how much these hickories have endured and prevailed over. Though I searched the whole hillside, not only for the smallest, but the most perpendicular and soundest, each of the three that I sawed off had died down once at least, years ago. Though it might not betray any scar above ground, on digging I found it an inch below the surface.

Most of these small ones consist of several stems from one root, and they are often of such fantastic forms and so diseased that they seem to be wholly dead at a little distance, and yet evidently many of them make erect, smooth, and sound trees at last, all defects smoothed over or obliterated. Some which have thus died down and sprung up again are in the form of rude harps and the like. These had great tap-roots considerably larger just beneath the surface than the stock above, and they were so firmly set in the ground that, though the tree was scarcely an inch in diameter and you had dug around it to the depth of three or four inches, it was impossible to pull one up; yet I did not notice any side roots, so high. They are iron trees, so rigid and so firm set are they. It may be that they are more persistent at the root than oaks, and so at last succeed in becoming trees in these localities where oaks fail. They may be more persevering. Perhaps, also, cattle do not browse them, but do oaks. It will be very suggestive to a novice just to go and dig up a dozen seedling oaks and hickories and see what they have had to contend with. Theirs is like the early career of genius.

Measured a great red maple near the south end of E. Hubbard's swamp, dividing in two at the ground, the largest trunk 7 feet and 10 inches at three feet and draped for three or four feet up with the pulmonaria (?) lichen. This the largest I know. Another is $5\frac{1}{2}$ feet, a third $5\frac{1}{4}$, a fourth in open land just south of turnpike $6\frac{1}{6}$.

Dec. 2. P. M. — To Smith's Hickory Hill-side.

I come *via* Britton's to see if I can find a seedling hickory under half a dozen years old. After searching long amid the very numerous young hickories at Britton's shanty and Smith's Hill I fail to find one so recently planted. I find many at the last place only one or two feet, but they invariably have great roots, and old stubs which have died down are visible at or beneath the surface of the ground. It is very common — almost the rule — to find from one to three from one root each one inch in diameter and two or three feet high, while the common stock beneath the ground is two inches in diameter. Pulling at one at Britton's, which was two feet and a quarter in height, it came up easily, to my surprise, and I found that it had broken off at just one foot below the surface, being quite decayed there. It was three quarters of an inch in diameter at the surface, and increased regularly for five or six inches downward till it was one inch in diameter. There was the stub of an old shoot, and the root was suddenly enlarged to about one and a half inches in diameter and held about

the same to where it broke off, at a foot below the surface. There was another stub about three inches above
the ground, and the more recent growth above this was
the work of about four years. This last had died, and
this year two shoots had put out at six and eight inches
above the ground and had grown two and four inches
respectively. Here were evident, then, at the very least,
four efforts to rise to a tree.

The first stub was about the diameter of the whole tree at present (above ground). Call it, then,	4 years
The second was probably two years old when it died (at least)	2
The third (forming the present tree)	4
The fourth (growth of this year)	1
	11

This little hickory, two feet and a quarter high and
three quarters of an inch in diameter, standing in open
land, was then at least eleven years old. What more
the root would have revealed if I had dug deeper, I
do not know. The fact that the lowest observed stub
was nearly six inches below the surface, showing
plainly to the eye that the earth had been heaped up
about, was significant and suggested that this root
might have survived in the ground through clearing
and burning and subsequent cultivation. I remember
well when the field was cultivated, I should think
within ten or twelve years. It must be seventeen or
eighteen years since the woods were cut here; since
which time a peach orchard (which I selected) has been

raised, a premium obtained for it, and the trees died and gone some years ago, also an apple orchard. The hickories are on the site and in the midst of these; and what makes it the more likely that these hickories may be from roots of young seedlings left in the ground is the fact that there are sprouts from several large chestnut stumps in the midst of the orchard, which, by their size, have probably been cut down once or twice since the tree was cut, and yet survived. What is true of these chestnut sprouts may be true of the hickories.

On Smith's Hill I selected a large and healthy-looking one (hickory), sawed it off, and found it nearly dead. It was four years old. It had been cut down before to a stub, which showed five years more. I did not look beneath the surface. The leading shoot was perfectly withered and dead. The same was very commonly the case, except when the tree had got above a certain height. I do not think that a single hickory has been planted in either of these places for some years at least. Indeed, why should squirrels bring the nuts to these particular localities where other hickories already stood? which they must do, supposing them to be planted still, and not to be all of one age.

They seem to be able to resist fire, cultivation, and frost. The last is apparently their great enemy at present. It is astonishing how many efforts they make, how persistent they are. Thus much is certain, at least.

In surrounding young wood they are common, and have got up three or four times as high. It may be that when pine and oaks and hickories, young and old, are cut off and the land cleared, the two former are exterminated but the hickories are tough and stubborn and do not give up the ground. I cannot as yet account for their existence in these two localities otherwise. Yet I still think that some must have been planted on Fair Haven Hill *without the pines* in a manner in which oaks are not, within a dozen years. Or perchance, if the oaks are *so* planted, they fail to come up?

In Stow's wood at Saw Mill Brook an old chestnut stump. Two sprouts from this were cut three years ago and have forty-two rings. From the stumps of the sprouts, other sprouts three years old have grown. The old stump was cut there forty-five years ago. The centre of the stumps of each of these sprouts is hollow for one and a half inches in diameter. See a chestnut stump, a seedling sawed off, with seventy-five rings and no sprout from it. Commonly the sprouts stand in a circle around the stump, — often a dozen or more of them.

Dec. 3.[1] P. M. — To Hill.

The hickory which was blown down by the wall has been cut up into lengths. The end of one some twelve feet from ground *apparently* is sixteen inches in diameter and has 112 rings distinct, the first 50 within five and three quarters inches. The bark is one inch thick.

Measured the three white oaks on the southeast side of hill.

---

[1] [Under date of March 22, 1861, Thoreau wrote to Daniel Ricketson: "I took a severe cold about the 3d of December, which at length resulted in a kind of bronchitis, so that I have been confined to the house ever since." — *Familiar Letters*, p. 376; Riv. 435.]

The northernmost   at three feet is 10 feet in circumference.
   " southeasternmost "   "   "   " 10⅓ "   "
   " southwesternmost "   "   "   " 11½ "   "

I find no young hickories springing up on the *open* hillside. Yet, if they do so elsewhere, why should they not here, where nuts are abundant? But, under and about the hickory which stands near the white oak (under the north side of the hill), there are many small hickories two to four feet high amid the birches and pines, — the largest of which birches and pines have been lately cut off.

I am inclined to think now that both oaks and hickories are occasionally planted in open land a rod or two or more beyond the edge of a pine or other wood, but that the hickory roots are more persistent under these circumstances and hence oftener succeed there.

As for the planting of acorns, it is to be observed that they do not require to be buried but merely transported and dropped on the surface in a suitable place. All the sound white oak acorns that I can find have now sent down their radicle under these circumstances, though, no doubt, far the greatest part of them will be killed this winter.

Talking with Walcott and Staples to-day, they declared that John Brown did wrong. When I said that I thought he was right, they agreed in asserting that he did wrong because he threw his life away, and that no man had a right to undertake anything which he knew would cost him his life. I inquired if Christ did not foresee that he would be crucified if he preached such doctrines as he did, but they both, though as if it was their only escape, asserted that they did not believe that he did. Upon which a third party threw in, "You do not think that he had so much foresight as Brown." Of course, they as good as said that, if Christ *had* foreseen that he would be crucified, he would have "backed out." Such are the principles and the logic of the mass of men.

It is to be remembered that by good deeds or words you encourage yourself, who always have need to witness or hear them.

Dec. 4. The first snow, four or five inches, this evening.

Talk about slavery! It is not the peculiar institution of the South. It exists wherever men are bought and sold, wherever a man allows himself to be made a mere thing or a tool, and surrenders his inalienable rights of reason and conscience. Indeed, this slavery is more complete than that which enslaves the body alone. It exists in the Northern States, and I am reminded by what I find in the newspapers that it exists in Canada. I never yet met with, or heard of, a judge who was not a slave of this kind, and so the finest and most unfailing weapon of injustice. He fetches a slightly higher price than the black man only because he is a more valuable slave.

It appears that a colored man killed his would-be kidnapper in Missouri and fled to Canada. The bloodhounds have tracked him to Toronto and now demand him of her judges. From all that I can learn, they are playing their parts like judges. They are servile, while the poor fugitive in their jail is free in spirit at least.

This is what a Canadian writes to the *New York Tribune* : "Our judges may be compelled to render a judgment adverse to the prisoner. Depend upon it, they will not do it unless *compelled* [his italics].[1] And then the poor fellow will be taken back, and probably burned to death by the brutes of the South." Compelled! By whom? Does God compel them? or is it some other master whom they serve? Can't they hold out a little longer against the *tremendous pressure*? If they are fairly represented, I would n't trust their courage to defend a setting hen of mine against a weasel. Will this excuse avail them when the real day of judgment comes? They have not to fear the slightest bodily harm: no one stands over them with a stick or a knife even [?]. They have at the worst only to resign their places and not a mouse will squeak about it. And yet they are likely to assist in tying this victim to the stake! Would that his example might teach them to break their own fetters! They appear not to know what kind of justice that is which is to be done though the heavens fall. Better that the British Empire be destroyed than that it should help to reënslave this man!

This correspondent suggests that the "good people" of New York may rescue him as he is being carried back. There, then, is the only resort of justice, — not where the judges are, but where the mob is, where human hearts are beating, and hands move in obedience to their impulses. Perhaps his fellow-fugitives in Toronto

---

[1] [The brackets are Thoreau's.]

may not feel compelled to surrender him. Justice, departing from the Canadian soil, leaves her last traces among these.

What is called the religious world very generally deny virtue to all who have not received the Gospel. They accept no god as genuine but the one that bears a Hebrew name. The Greenlander's *Pirksoma* [?] (he that is above), or any the like, is always the name of a false god to them.

C. says that Walden was first frozen over on the 16th December.

Dec. 22. This evening and night, the second important snow, there having been sleighing since the 4th, and now, —

Dec. 23, — there is seven or eight inches of snow at least. Larks were about our house the middle of this month.

Dec. 26. Melvin sent to me yesterday a perfect *Strix asio*, or red owl of Wilson, — not at all gray. This is now generally made the same with the *nævia*, but, while some consider the red the old, others consider the red the young. This is, as Wilson says, a bright "nut brown" like a hazelnut or dried hazel bur (not *hazel*). It is twenty-three inches [in] alar extent by about eleven long. Feet extend one inch beyond tail. Cabot makes the old bird red; Audubon, the young. How well fitted these and other owls to withstand the winter! a mere core in the midst of such a muff of feathers! Then the feet of this are feathered finely to the claws, looking like the feet of a furry quadruped. Accordingly owls are common here in winter; hawks, scarce.

It is no worse, I allow, than almost every other practice which custom has sanctioned, but that is the worst of it, for it shows how bad the rest are. To such a pass our civilization and division of labor has come that A, a professional huckleberry-picker, has hired B's field and, we will suppose, is now gathering the crop, perhaps with the aid of a patented machine; C, a professed cook, is superintending the cooking of a pudding made of some of the berries; while Professor D, for whom the pudding is intended, sits in his library writing a book, — a work on the Vacciniæ, of course. And now the result of this downward course will be seen in that book, which should be the ultimate fruit of the huckleberry-field and account for the existence of the two professors who come between D and A. It will be worthless. There will be none of the spirit of the huckleberry in it. The reading of it will be a weariness to the flesh. To use a homely illustration, this is to save at the spile but waste at the bung. I believe in a different kind of division of labor, and that Professor D should divide himself between the library and the huckleberry-field.

Dec. 30. *Sunday.* I saw the crows a week ago perched on the swamp white oaks over the road just beyond Wood's Bridge, and many acorns and bits of bark and moss, evidently dropped or knocked off by them, lay on the snow beneath. One sat within twenty feet over my head with what looked like a piece of acorn in his bill.

To-day I see that they have carried these same white oak acorns, cups and all, to the ash tree by the riverside, some thirty rods southeast, and dropped them there. Perhaps they find some grubs in the acorns, when they do not find meat. The crows now and of late frequent thus the large trees by the river, especially swamp white oak, and the snow beneath is strewn with bits of bark and moss and with acorns (commonly worthless). They are foraging. Under the first swamp white oak in Hubbard's great meadow (Cyanean) I see a little snap-turtle (shell some one and a quarter inches in diameter — on his second year, then) on its back on the ice — shell, legs, and tail perfect, but head pulled off, and most of the inwards with it by the same hole (where the neck was). What is left smells quite fresh, and this head must have been torn off to-day — or within a day or two. I see two crows on the next swamp white oak westward, and I can scarcely doubt that they did it. Probably one found the young turtle at an open and springy place in the meadow, or by the river, where they are constantly preying, and flew with it to this tree. Yet it is possible (?) that it was frozen to death when they found it.

I also saw under the oak where the crows were one of those large brown cocoons of the *Attacus Cecropia*, which no doubt they had torn off.

Eben Conant's sons tell me that there has been a turtle dove associating with their tame doves and feeding in the yard from time to time for a fortnight past. They saw it to-day.

The traveller Burton says that the word *Doab*, " which

means the land embraced by the bifurcation of two streams, has no English equivalent." ("Lake Regions of Central Africa," page 72.)

It is remarkable how universally, as it respects soil and exposure, the whortleberry family is distributed with us, one kind or another (of those of which I am speaking) flourishing in every soil and locality, — the Pennsylvania and Canada blueberries especially in elevated cool and airy places — on hills and mountains, and in openings in the woods and in sprout-lands; the high blueberry in swamps, and the second low blueberry in intermediate places, or almost anywhere but in swamps hereabouts; while we have two kinds confined to the Alpine tops of our highest mountains. The family thus ranges from the highest mountain-tops to the lowest swamps and forms the prevailing small shrubs of a great part of New England. Not only is this true of the family, but *hereabouts* of the genus *Gaylussacia*, or the huckleberries proper, alone. I do not know of a spot where any shrub grows in this neighborhood but one or another species or variety of the *Gaylussacia* may also grow there. It is stated in Loudon (page 1076) that all the plants of this order "require a peat soil, or a soil of a close cohesive nature," but this is not the case with the huckleberry. The huckleberry grows on the tops of our highest hills; no pasture is too rocky or barren for it; it grows in such deserts as we have, standing in pure sand; and, at the same time, it flourishes in the strongest and most fertile soil. One variety is peculiar to quaking bogs where there can hardly be said to be any soil beneath, not to mention another but unpalatable species, the hairy huckleberry, which is found in bogs. It extends through all our woods more or less thinly, and a distinct species, the dangle-berry, belongs especially to moist woods and the edges of swamps.

Such care has nature taken to furnish to birds and quadrupeds, and to men, a palatable berry of this kind, slightly modified by soil and climate, wherever the consumer may chance to be. Corn and potatoes, apples and pears, have comparatively a narrow range, but we can fill our basket with whortleberries on the summit of Mt. Washington, above almost all the shrubs with which we are familiar, — the same kind which they have in Greenland, — and again, when we get home, with another species in Beck Stow's Swamp.

I find that in Bomare's "Dictionnaire Raisonné" the *Vitis Idæa* (of many kinds) is called "raisin des bois." Our word "berry," according to lexicographers, is from the Saxon *beria*, a grape or cluster of grapes; but it must acquire a new significance here, if a new word is not substituted for it.

According to Father Rasles' Dictionary, the Abenaki word for bluets [1] was, fresh, *satar* (in another place *saté*, *tar*); dry, *sakisatar*.

First there is the early dwarf blueberry, the smallest of the whortleberry shrubs with us, and the first to ripen its fruit, not commonly an erect shrub, but more or less reclined and drooping, often covering the earth with a sort of dense matting. The twigs are green, the flowers commonly white. Both the shrub and its

1 [See p. 300.]

fruit are the most tender and delicate of any that we have.

The *Vaccinium Canadense* may be considered a more northern form of the same.

Some ten days later comes the high blueberry, or swamp blueberry, the commonest stout shrub of our swamps, of which I have been obliged to cut down not a few when running lines as a surveyor through the low woods. They are a pretty sure indication of water, and, when I see their dense curving tops ahead, I prepare to wade, or for a wet foot. The flowers have an agreeable sweet and berry-promising fragrance, and a handful of them plucked and eaten have a subacid taste agreeable to some palates.

At the same time with the last the common low blueberry is ripe. This is an upright slender shrub with a few long wand-like branches, with green bark and pink-colored recent shoots and glaucous-green leaves. The flowers have a considerable rosy tinge, of a delicate tint.

The last two more densely flowered than the others.

The huckleberry, as you know, is an upright shrub, more or less stout depending on the exposure to the sun and air, with a spreading, bushy top, a dark-brown bark, and red recent shoots, with thick leaves. The flowers are much more red than those of the others.

As in old times they who dwelt on the heath remote from towns were backward to adopt the doctrines which prevailed there, and were therefore called heathen in a bad sense, so we dwellers in the huckleberry pastures, which are our heath lands, are slow to adopt the notions

of large towns and cities and may perchance be nick-
named huckleberry people. But the worst of it is that the
emissaries of the towns care more for our berries than
for our salvation.

In those days the very race had got a bad name, and
ethnicus was only another name for heathen.

All our hills are or have been huckleberry hills, the
three hills of Boston and, no doubt, Bunker Hill among
the rest.

In May and June all our hills and fields are adorned
with a profusion of the pretty little more or less bell-
shaped flowers of this family, commonly turned toward
the earth and more or less tinged with red or pink and
resounding with the hum of insects, each one the fore-
runner of a berry the most natural, wholesome, palatable that the soil can produce.

The early low blueberry, which I will call "bluet,"
adopting the name from the Canadians, is probably the
prevailing kind of whortleberry in New England, for the
high blueberry and huckleberry are unknown in many
sections. In many New Hampshire towns a neighboring mountain-top is the common berry-field of many
villages, and in the berry season such a summit will be
swarming with pickers. A hundred at once will rush
thither from all the surrounding villages, with pails and
buckets of all descriptions, especially on a Sunday,
which is their leisure day. When camping on such
ground, thinking myself quite out of the world, I have
had my solitude very unexpectedly interrupted by such
an advent, and found that the week-days were the only
Sabbath-days there.

Blueberry Blossoms

For a mile or more on such a rocky mountain-top this will be the prevailing shrub, occupying every little shelf from several rods down to a few inches only in width, and then the berries droop in short wreaths over the rocks, sometimes the thickest and largest along a seam in a shelving rock, — either that light mealy-blue, or a shining black, or an intermediate blue, without bloom. When, at that season, I look from Concord toward the blue mountain-tops in the horizon, I am reminded that near at hand they are equally blue with berries.

The mountain-tops of New England, often lifted above the clouds, are thus covered with this beautiful blue fruit, in greater profusion than in any garden.

What though the woods be cut down, this emergency was long ago foreseen and provided for by Nature, and the interregnum is not allowed to be a barren one. She is full of resources: she not only begins instantly to heal that scar, but she consoles (compensates?) and refreshes us with fruits such as the forest did not produce. To console us she heaps our baskets with berries.

The timid or ill-shod confine themselves to the land side, where they get comparatively few berries and many scratches, but the more adventurous, making their way through the open swamp, which the bushes overhang, wading amid the water andromeda and sphagnum, where the surface quakes for a rod around, obtain access to those great drooping clusters of berries which no hand has disturbed. There is no wilder and richer sight than is afforded from such a point of view, of the edge of a blueberry swamp where various wild berries are intermixed.

As the sandalwood is said to diffuse its perfume around the woodman who cuts it, so in this case Nature rewards with unexpected fruits the hand that lays her waste.

VI

1861

(ÆT. 43–44)

Jan. 3. The third considerable snow-storm.

The berries which I celebrate appear to have a range — most of them — very nearly coterminous with what has been called the Algonquin Family of Indians, whose territories are now occupied by the Eastern, Middle, and Northwestern States and the Canadas, and completely surrounded those of the Iroquois, who occupied what is now the State of New York. These were the small fruits of the Algonquin and Iroquois families. The Algonquins appear to have described this kind of fruits generally by words ending in the syllables *meenar.*

It is true we have in the Northern States a few wild plums and inedible crab-apples, a few palatable grapes and nuts, but I think that our various species of berries are our *wild fruits* to be compared with the more celebrated ones of the tropics, and that, taking all things into consideration, New England will bear comparison with the West India Islands. I have not heard of any similar amusement there superior to huckleberrying here, the object not being merely to get a shipload of something which you can eat or sell.

Why should the Ornamental Tree Society confine its labors to the highway only? An Englishman laying out his ground does not regard simply the avenues and walks. Does not the landscape deserve attention?

What are the natural features which make a township handsome? A river, with its waterfalls and meadows, a lake, a hill, a cliff or individual rocks, a forest, and ancient trees standing singly. Such things are beautiful; they have a high use which dollars and cents never represent. If the inhabitants of a town were wise, they would seek to preserve these things, though at a considerable expense; for such things educate far more than any hired teachers or preachers, or any at present recognized system of school education. I do not think him fit to be the founder of a state or even of a town who does not foresee the use of these things, but legislates chiefly for oxen, as it were.

Far the handsomest thing I saw in Boxboro was its noble oak wood. I doubt if there is a finer one in Massachusetts. Let her keep it a century longer, and men will make pilgrimages to it from all parts of the country; and yet it would be very like the rest of New England if Boxboro were ashamed of that woodland.

I have since heard, however, that she is contented to have that forest stand instead of the houses and farms that might supplant [it], because the land pays a much larger tax to the town now than it would then.

I said to myself, if the history of this town is written, the chief stress is probably laid on its parish and there is not a word about this forest in it.

It would be worth the while if in each town there were a committee appointed to see that the beauty of the town received no detriment. If we have the largest boulder in the county, then it should not belong to an individual, nor be made into door-steps.

As in many countries precious metals belong to the crown, so here more precious natural objects of rare beauty should belong to the public.

Not only the channel but one or both banks of every river should be a public highway. The only use of a river is not to float on it.

Think of a mountain-top in the township — even to the minds of the Indians a sacred place — only accessible through private grounds! a temple, as it were, which you cannot enter except by trespassing and at the risk of letting out or letting in somebody's cattle! in fact the temple itself in this case private property and standing in a man's cow-yard, — for such is commonly the case!

New Hampshire courts have lately been deciding — as if it was for them to decide — whether the top of Mt. Washington belonged to A or to B; and, it being decided in favor of B, as I hear, he went up one winter with the proper officer and took formal possession of it. But I think that the top of Mt. Washington should not be private property; it should be left unappropriated for modesty and reverence's sake, or if only to suggest that earth has higher uses than we put her to. I know it is a mere figure of speech to talk about temples nowadays, when men recognize none, and, indeed, associate the word with heathenism.

It is true we as yet take liberties and go across lots, and steal, or "hook," a good many things, but we naturally take fewer and fewer liberties every year, as we

meet with more resistance. In old countries, as England, going across lots is out of the question. You must
walk in some beaten path or other, though it may [be]
a narrow one. We are tending to the same state of things
here, when practically a few will have grounds of their
own, but most will have none to walk over but what the
few allow them.

Thus we behave like oxen in a flower-garden. The
true fruit of Nature can only be plucked with a delicate
hand not bribed by any earthly reward, and a fluttering
heart. No hired man can help us to gather this crop.

How few ever get beyond feeding, clothing, sheltering,
and warming themselves in this world, and begin to
treat themselves as human beings, — as intellectual and
moral beings! Most seem not to see any further, — not
to see over the ridge-pole of their barns, — or to be
exhausted and accomplish nothing more than a full
barn, though it may be accompanied by an empty head.
They venture a little, run some risks, when it is a question of a larger crop of corn or potatoes; but they are
commonly timid and count their coppers, when the
question is whether their children shall be educated.
He who has the reputation of being the thriftiest farmer
and making the best bargains is really the most thrift-
less and makes the worst. It is safest to invest in
knowledge, for the probability is that you can carry
that with you wherever you go.

But most men, it seems to me, do not care for Nature
and would sell their share in all her beauty, as long as
they may live, for a stated sum — many for a glass of
rum. Thank God, men cannot as yet fly, and lay waste

the sky as well as the earth! We are safe on that side
for the present. It is for the very reason that some do
not care for those things that we need to continue to
protect all from the vandalism of a few.

We cut down the few old oaks which witnessed the
transfer of the township from the Indian to the white
man, and commence our museum with a cartridge-box
taken from a British soldier in 1775!

He pauses at the end of his four or five thousand
dollars, and then only fears that he has not got enough
to carry him through, — that is, merely to pay for what
he will eat and wear and burn and for his lodging for
the rest of his life. But, pray, what does he stay here
for? Suicide would be cheaper. Indeed, it would be
nobler to found some good institution with the money
and then cut your throat. If such is the whole upshot
of their living, I think that it would be most profitable
for all such to be carried or put through by being discharged from the mouth of a cannon as fast as they
attained to years of such discretion.

As boys are sometimes required to show an excuse
for being absent from school, so it seems to me that
men should show some excuse for being here. Move
along; you may come upon the town, sir.

I noticed a week or two ago that one of my white
pines, some six feet high with a thick top, was bent under
a great burden of very moist snow, almost to the point
of breaking, so that an ounce more of weight would
surely have broken it. As I was confined to the house
by sickness, and the tree had already been four or five
days in that position, I despaired of its ever recovering

itself; but, greatly to my surprise, when, a few days after, the snow had melted off, I saw the tree almost perfectly upright again.

It is evident that trees will bear to be bent by this cause and at this season much more than by the hand of man. Probably the less harm is done in the first place by the weight being so gradually applied, and perhaps the tree is better able to bear it at this season of the year.

Jan. 8. Trees, etc., covered with a dense hoar frost. It is not leaf-like, but composed of large spiculæ — spear-like — on the northeast sides of the twigs, the side from which the mist was blown. All trees are bristling with these spiculæ on that side, especially firs and arbor-vitæ.

They taught us not only the use of corn and how to plant it, but also of whortleberries and how to dry them for winter, and made us baskets to put them in. We should have hesitated long to eat some kinds, if they had not set us the example, knowing by old experience that they were not only harmless but salutary. I have added a few to my number of edible berries by walking behind an Indian in Maine, who ate such as I never thought of tasting before. Of course they made a much greater account of wild fruits than we do.

It appears from the above evidence[1] that the Indians used their dried berries commonly in the form of huckleberry cake, and also of huckleberry porridge or pudding. What we call huckleberry cake, made of Indian meal

[1] [The "evidence" was omitted from the Journal.]

and huckleberries, was evidently the principal cake of the aborigines, and was generally known and used by them all over this part of North America, as much or more than plum-cake by us. They enjoyed it all alone ages before our ancestors heard of Indian meal or huckleberries.

We have no national cake so universal and well known as this was in all parts of the country where corn and huckleberries grew.

If you had travelled here a thousand years ago, it would probably have been offered you alike on the Connecticut, the Potomac, the Niagara, the Ottawa, and the Mississippi.

Botanists have long been inclined to associate this family in some way with Mt. Ida, and, according to Tournefort arrange [*sic*] whortleberries were what the ancients meant by the vine of Mt. Ida, and the common English raspberry is called *Rubus Idæus* from the old Greek name. The truth of it seems to be that blueberries and raspberries flourish best in cool and airy situations on hills and mountains, and I can easily believe that something like them, at least, grows on Mt. Ida. But Mt. Monadnock is as good as Mt. Ida, and probably better for blueberries, though it does not [*sic*] mean "bad rock," — but the worst rocks are the best for blueberries and for poets.

Jan. 11. Horace Mann brings me the contents of a crow's stomach in alcohol. It was killed in the village within a day or two. It is quite a mass of frozen-thawed apple, — pulp and skin, — with a good many pieces of skunk-cabbage berries one fourth inch or less in diameter, and commonly showing the pale-brown or blackish outside, interspersed, looking like bits of acorns, — never a whole or even half a berry, — and two little bones as of frogs (?) or mice (?) or *tadpoles;* also a street pebble a quarter of an inch in diameter, hard to be distinguished in appearance from the cabbage seeds.

I presume that every one of my audience knows what a huckleberry is, — has seen a huckleberry, gathered a huckleberry, and, finally, has tasted a huckleberry, — and, that being the case, I think that I need offer no apology if I make huckleberries my theme this evening.

What more encouraging sight at the end of a long ramble than the endless successive patches of green bushes, — perhaps in some rocky pasture, — fairly blackened with the profusion of fresh and glossy berries ?

There are so many of these berries in their season that most do not perceive that birds and quadrupeds make any use of them, since they are not felt to rob us; yet they are more important to them than to us. We do not notice the robin when it plucks a berry, as when it visits our favorite cherry tree, and the fox pays his visits to the field when we are not there.

Jan. 14. Coldest morning yet; 20° (?).

Pliny says, " In minimis Natura praestat " (Nature excels in the least things). The *Wellingtonia gigantea,* the famous California tree, is a great thing; the seed from which it sprang, a little thing; and so are all seeds or origins of things.

Richard Porson said: "We all speak in metaphors. Those who appear not to do it, only use those which are worn out, and are overlooked as metaphors. The original fellow is therefore regarded as only witty; and the dull are consulted as the wise." He might have said that the former spoke a dead language.

John Horne Tooke is reported in "Recollections" by Samuel Rogers as having said: "Read few books well. We forget names and dates; and reproach our memory. They are of little consequence. We feel our limbs enlarge and strengthen; yet cannot tell the dinner or dish that caused the alteration. Our minds improve though we cannot name the author, and have forgotten the particulars." I think that the opposite would be the truer statement, books differ so immensely in their nutritive qualities, and good ones are so rare.

Gosse, in his "Letters from Alabama," says that he thinks he saw a large dragon-fly (*Æslona*), which was hawking over a brook, catch and devour some minnows about one inch long, and says it is known that "the larvae of the greater water-beetles (*Dyticidæ*) devour fish."

It is the discovery of science that stupendous changes in the earth's surface, such as are referred to the Deluge, for instance, are the result of causes still in operation, which have been at work for an incalculable period. There has not been a sudden re-formation, or, as it were, new creation of the world, but a steady progress according to existing laws. The same is true in detail also. It is a vulgar prejudice that some plants are "spontaneously generated," but science knows that they come from seeds, *i. e.* are the result of causes still in operation, however slow and unobserved. It is a common saying that "little strokes fall great oaks," and it does not imply much wisdom in him who originated it. The sound of the axe invites our attention to such a catastrophe; we can easily count each stroke as it is given, and all the neighborhood is informed by a loud crash when the deed is consummated. But such, too, is the rise of the oak; little strokes of a different kind and often repeated raise great oaks, but scarcely a traveller hears these or turns aside to converse with Nature, who is dealing them the while.

Nature is slow but sure; she works no faster than need be; she is the tortoise that wins the race by her perseverance; she knows that seeds have many other uses than to reproduce their kind. In raising oaks and pines, she works with a leisureliness and security answering to the age and strength of the trees. If every acorn of this year's crop is destroyed, never fear! she has more years to come. It is not necessary that a pine or an oak should bear fruit every year, as it is that a pea-vine should. So, botanically, the greatest changes in the landscape are produced more gradually than we expected. If Nature has a pine or an oak wood to produce, she manifests no haste about it.

Thus we should say that oak forests are produced by a kind of accident, *i. e.* by the failure of animals to reap the fruit of their labors. Yet who shall say that they have not a fair knowledge of the value of their labors — that the squirrel when it plants an acorn,

or the jay when it lets one slip from under its foot, has
not a transient thought for its posterity?

Possibly here, a thousand years hence, every oak will
know the human hand that planted it.

How many of the botanist's *arts* and inventions are
thus but the rediscovery of a lost art, *i. e.* lost to him
here or elsewhere!

Horace Mann told me some days ago that he found,
near the shore in that muddy bay by the willows in the
rear of Mrs. Ripley's, a great many of the *Sternothærus
odoratus*, assembled, he supposed, at their breeding-
time, or, rather, about to come out to lay their eggs.
He waded in [and] collected — I think he said — about
a hundred and fifty of them for Agassiz!

I see in the Boston *Journal* an account of robins in
numbers on the savin trees in that neighborhood,
feeding on their berries. This suggests that they may
plant its berries as well as the crows.

Jan. 15.   More snow last night, and still the first
that fell remains on the ground. Rice thinks that it is
two feet deep on a level now. We have had no thaw yet.

Rice tells me that he baits the "seedees" and the
jays and crows to his door nowadays with corn. He
thinks he has seen one of these jays stow away some-
where, without swallowing, as many as a dozen grains of
corn, for, after picking it up, it will fly up into a tree
near by and deposit so many successively in different
crevices before it descends.

Speaking of Roman wormwood springing up abundantly when a field which has been in grass for twenty years or more is plowed, Rice says that, if you carefully examine such a field before it is plowed, you will find very short and stinted specimens of wormwood and pigweed there, — and remarkably full of seed too!

Feb. 5. Horace Mann brings me a screech owl, which was caught in Hastings's barn on the meeting-house avenue. It had killed a dove there. This is a decidedly gray owl, with none of the reddish or nut brown of the specimen of December 26, though it is about the same size, and answers exactly to Wilson's mottled owl.

Rice brings me an oak stick with a woodpecker's hole in it by which it reached a pupa.

The first slight rain and thaw of this winter was February 2d.

Feb. 8. Coldest day yet; −22° at least (all we can read), at 8 A. M., and, [so far] as I can learn, not above −6° all day.

Feb. 15. A little thunder and lightning late in the afternoon. I see two flashes and hear two claps.

A kitten is so flexible that she is almost double; the hind parts are equivalent to another kitten with which the fore part plays. She does not discover that her tail belongs to her till you tread upon it.

How eloquent she can be with her tail! Its sudden swellings and vibrations! She jumps into a chair and then stands on her hind legs to look out the window; looks steadily at objects far and near, first turning her gaze to this side then to that, for she loves to look out a window as much as any gossip. Ever and anon she bends back her ears to hear what is going on within the room, and all the while her eloquent tail is reporting the progress and success of her survey by speaking gestures which betray her interest in what she sees.

Then what a delicate hint she can give with her tail! passing perhaps underneath, as you sit at table, and letting the tip of her tail just touch your legs, as much as to say, I am here and ready for that milk or meat, though she may not be so forward as to look round at you when she emerges.

Only skin-deep lies the feral nature of the cat, unchanged still. I just had the misfortune to rock on to our cat's leg, as she was lying playfully spread out under my chair. Imagine the sound that arose, and which was excusable; but what will you say to the fierce growls and flashing eyes with which she met me for a quarter of an hour thereafter? No tiger in its jungle could have been savager.

Feb. 21. I have just read a book called "Carolina Sports by Land and Water; including Incidents of Devil-Fishing, Wild-cat, Deer and Bear Hunting, Etc. By the Hon. Wm. Elliott."

The writer is evidently a regular sportsman, and describes his sporting with great zest. He was withal the inventor and institutor of devil-fishing, which consists in harpooning a monstrous salt-water fish, and represents himself in a plate harpooning him. His motive, however, was not profit or a subsistence, but sport.

However, I should have found nothing peculiar in the book, if it did not contain, near the end, so good an example of human inconsistency. I quote some sentences in the order in which they occur, only omitting the intermediate pages. After having described at length his own sporting exploits, using such words as these, for instance. Being in pursuit of a wildcat, he says (page 163): —

" It was at this moment that Dash, espying something in motion in the leafy top of a bay-tree, cracked off his Joe Manton with such good effect, that presently we heard a heavy body come tumbling through the limbs until it splashed into the water. Then came a stunning burst from the hounds — a clash from the whole orchestra in full chorus! — a growl from the assailed, with an occasional squeak on the part of the assailants, which showed that the game was not all on one side. We were compelled, all the while, to be delighted ear-witnesses only of the strife, which resulted in the victory of the hounds." This proved to be a raccoon, though they thought it the wildcat.

Again (page 168), being in pursuit of another cat, which had baffled them a long time with great cunning, he says: " The cat, with huge leaps, clambered up a tree; and now he had reached the very pinnacle, and as he gathered himself up to take a flying leap for a neighboring tree, I caught up my gun, and let slip at him in mid-flight. The arrowy posture in which he made his pitch, was suddenly changed, as the shot struck him to the heart; and doubling himself up, after one or two wild gyrations, into a heap, he fell dead, from a height of full fifty feet, into the very jaws of the dogs!"

Again (page 178), being [in] pursuit of a deer, which he had wounded, and his gun being discharged, he tried to run him down with his horse, but, as he tells us, "the noble animal refused to trample on his fellow quadruped," so he made up for it by kicking the deer in the side of the head with his spurred boot. The deer enters a thicket and he is compelled to pursue the panting animal on foot. "A large fallen oak lies across his path; he gathers himself up for the leap, and falls exhausted directly across it. Before he could recover his legs, and while he lay thus poised on the tree, I fling myself at full length upon the body of the struggling deer — my left hand clasps his neck, while my right detaches the knife; whose fatal blade, in another moment, is buried in his throat. There he lay in his blood, and I remained sole occupant of the field." Opposite is a plate which represents him in the act of stabbing the deer.

Page 267. — He tells us that his uncle once had a young wildcat, — a mere kitten, — but that, to prevent its worrying the poultry, "a cord was fastened round his neck, and a clog attached to the end." Still he would endeavor to catch the fowls.

"My uncle one day invited several of his friends, to witness this development of natural propensity in his savage pet. The kitten, with his clog attached, was let out of the box; and it was curious to observe with what stealthy pace he approached the spot where the poultry were feeding. They scarcely seemed to notice the diminutive thing that was creeping toward them; when, crouching low, and measuring exactly the distance which separated them, he sprang upon the back of the old rooster, and hung on by claw and teeth to the feathers, while the frightened bird dragged him, clog and all, over the yard. After several revolutions had been made, the cat let go his hold on the back of the fowl, and, with the quickness of lightning, *caught the head* in his mouth, clinched his teeth, shut his eyes, stiffened his legs, and hung on with the most desperate resolution, while the fowl, rolling over in agony, buffeted him with his wings. All in vain! In a few seconds more he was dead, and we looked with abhorrence on the savage animal, that had just taken his first degree in blood. In this case, there could have been no teaching — no imitation. It was the undoubted instinct of a cruel nature! We wondered that this young beast of prey should have known, from this instinct, *the vital part of its victim !* — and we wondered still more, that in the providence of God, he had seen fit to create an animal with an instinct so murderous. Philosophy is ready with her explanation, and our abhorrence may be misplaced, since from his very organization, he is compelled to destroy life *in order to live !* Yet, knowing this, our abhorrence still continues; whence we may draw the consolatory con- clusion — that the instincts of a man naturally differ from those of a wild-cat."

A few pages further (page 282) in a chapter called "Random Thoughts on Hunting," which is altogether a eulogy on that pursuit, he praises it because it devel- ops or cultivates among other qualities "the *observation*, that familiarizes itself with the nature and habits of the quarry — the *sagacity* that anticipates its projects of escape — and the *promptitude* that defeats them! — the rapid glance, the steady aim, the quick perception, the ready execution; these are among the faculties and qualities continually called into pleasing exercise."

Physician, heal thyself!

This plucking and stripping a pine cone is a business which he and his family understand perfectly. That is their *forte*. I doubt if you could suggest any improvement. After ages of experiment their instinct has settled on the same method that our reason would finally, if we had to open a pine cone with our teeth; and they were thus accomplished before our race knew that a pine cone contained any seed.

He does not prick his fingers, nor pitch his whiskers, nor gnaw the solid core any more than is necessary. Having sheared off the twigs and needles that may be in his way, — for like a skillful woodchopper he first secures room and verge enough, — he neatly cuts off the stout stem of the cone with a few strokes of his chisels, and it is his. To be sure, he may let it fall to the ground and look down at it for a moment curiously, as if it were not his; but he is taking note where it lies and adding it to a heap of a hundred more like it in his mind, and it now is only so much the more his for his seeming carelessness. And, when the hour comes to open it, observe how he proceeds. He holds it in his hands, — a solid embossed cone, so hard it almost rings at the touch of his teeth. He pauses for a moment perhaps, — but not because he does not know how to begin, — he only listens to hear what is in the wind, not being in a hurry.

He knows better than try to cut off the tip and work his way downward against a *chevaux-de-frise* of advanced scales and prickles, or to gnaw into the side for three quarters of an inch in the face of many armed shields. But he does not have to think of what he knows, having heard the latest æolian rumor. If there ever was an age of the world when the squirrels opened their cones wrong end foremost, it was not the golden age at any rate. He whirls the cone bottom upward in a twinkling, where the scales are smallest and the prickles slight or none and the short stem is cut so close as not to be in his way, and then he proceeds to cut through the thin and tender bases of the scales, and each stroke tells, laying bare at once a couple of seeds. And then he strips it as easily as if its scales were chaff, and so rapidly, twirling it as he advances, that you cannot tell how he does it till you drive him off and inspect his unfinished work.

Feb. 27. 2 p. m. — It is very pleasant and warm, and the ground half bare. As I am walking down the Boston road under the hill this side Clark's, it occurs to me that I have just heard the twitter of a bluebird. (C. heard one the 26th.) I stop and listen to hear it again, but cannot tell whether it comes from the buttonwoods high over my head or from the lower trees on the hilltop. It is not the complete bluebird warble, but the twitter only. And now it seems to come from Pratt's house, where the window is open, and I am not sure but it is a caged bird. I walk that way, and now think that I distinguish the minstrel in a black speck in the top of a great elm on the Common. Messer is shingling

Clark's barn; so, to make sure, I cross over and ask him if he has heard a bluebird to-day, and he says he has several times. When I get to the elm near Minott's I hear one warble distinctly. Miss Minott and Miss Potter have both died within a fortnight past, and the cottage on the hillside seems strangely deserted; but the first bluebird comes to warble there as usual.

Mother hears a robin to-day.

Buttonwood sap flows fast from wounds made last fall.

Feb. 28. P. M. — Down Boston road under the hill.

Air full of bluebirds as yesterday. The sidewalk is bare and almost dry the whole distance under the hill.

Turn in at the gate this side of Moore's and sit on the yellow stones rolled down in the bay of a digging, and examine the radical leaves, etc., etc.

Where the edges of grassy banks have caved I see the fine fibrous roots of the grass which have been washed bare during the winter extending straight downward two feet (and how much further within the earth I know not), — a pretty dense grayish mass.

The buttonwood seed has apparently scarcely begun to fall yet,[1] — only two balls under one tree, but they loose and broken.[2]

March 3. *Sunday.* Hear that there was a flock of

---

[1] Yes, many had been blown bare, for the balls do not fall often.

[2] Almost entirely fallen March 7th, leaving the dangling stems and bare receptacles.

geese in the river last night. See and hear song sparrows to-day; probably here for several days.

It is an exceedingly warm and pleasant day. The snow is suddenly all gone except heels, and — what is more remarkable — the frost is generally out of the ground, *e. g.* in our garden, for the reason that it has not been in it. The snow came December 4th, before the ground was frozen to any depth, has been unusually deep, and the ground has not been again exposed till now. Hence, though we have had a little very cold weather and a good deal of steady cold, the ground generally has not been frozen.

March 8. I just heard peculiar faint sounds made by the air escaping from a stick which I had just put into my stove. It sounded to my ear exactly like the peeping of the hylodes in a distant pool, a cool and breezy spring evening, — as if it were designed to remind me of that season.

Saw the *F. hyemalis* March 4th.

To continue subject of March 3d, —

It is remarkable that, though in ordinary winters, when the ground is alternately bare and covered with snow several times, or is not covered till after it is frozen, it may be frozen a foot or more in depth generally, yet, if it is kept covered with snow, though only a thin coating, from first to last, it will not be frozen at all.

For example, the ground was half bare on the 27th, the walk under the Boston road hills pretty fair on the

28th, and the 3d, after rain, the earth was bare, the ways were about settled, the melted snow and rain having been soaked up at once by the thirsty and open ground. There was probably no frost on level ground except where the earth had of late been partly exposed in the middle of the road. The recent rain and melting accordingly raised the river less than it otherwise would. There has been no breaking up of the frost on roads, — no bad travelling as usual, — but as soon as the snow is gone, the ways are settled.

In short, Nature uses all sorts of conveyances, from the rudest drag to a balloon, but she will get her seeds along in due season.

Is it not possible that Loudon is right as it respects the primitive distribution of the birch? Are not the dense patches always such as have sprung up in open land (commonly old fields cleared by man), as is the case with the pitch pine? It disappears at length from a dense oak or pine wood. Perhaps originally it formed dense woods only where a space had been cleared for it by a burning, as now at the eastward. Perhaps only the oaks and white pines could (originally) possess the soil here against all comers, maple succeeding because it does not mind a wet foot.

Suppose one were to take such a boxful of birch seed as I have described into the meeting-house belfry in the fall, and let some of it drop in every wind, but always more in proportion as the wind was stronger, and yet so husband it that there should be some left for every gale even till far into spring; so that this seed might be blown toward every point of the compass and to various distances in each direction. Would not this represent a single birch tree on a hill? Of which trees (though only a part on hills) we have perhaps a million. And yet some feel compelled to suppose that the birch trees which spring up after a burning are spontaneously generated — for want of seed! It is true [it] does not come up in great quantities at the distance I have spoken of, but, if only one comes up there this year, you may have a million seeds matured there a few years hence.

It is true that the greater part of these seeds fall near the trees which bore them, and comparatively few germinate; yet, when the surface is in a favorable condition, they may spring up in very unexpected places.

A lady tells me that she met Deacon S. of Lincoln with a load of hay, and she, noticing that as he drove under the apple trees by the side of the road a considerable part of the hay was raked off by their boughs, informed him of it. But he answered, "It is not mine yet. I am going to the scales with it and intend to come back this way."

March 11. C. says that Walden is almost entirely open to-day, so that the lines on my map would not strike any ice, but that there is ice in the deep cove. It will be open then the 12th or 13th. This is earlier than I ever knew it to open. Fair Haven was solid ice two or three days ago, and probably is still, and Goose Pond is to-day all ice. Why, then, should Walden have

broken up thus early? for it froze over early and the
winter was steadily cold up to February at least. I
think it must have been because the ice was uncommonly covered with snow, just as the earth was, and so,
as there was little or no frost in the earth, the ice also
was thin, and it did not increase upward with snow ice
as much as usual because there was no thaw or rain at
all till February 2d, and then very little. According to
all accounts there has been no skating on Walden the
past winter on account of the snow. It was unusually
covered with snow. This shows how many things are
to be taken into account in judging of such a pond. I
have not been able to go to the pond the past winter.
I infer that, if it has broken up thus early, it must be
because the ice was thin, and that it was thin not for
want of cold generally, but because of the abundance
of snow which lay on it.

The water is now high on the meadows and there is
no ice there, owing to the recent heavy rains. Yet C.
thinks it has been higher a few weeks since.

C. observes where mice (?) have gnawed the pitch
pines the past winter. Is not this a phenomenon of a
winter of deep snow only? as that when I lived at
Walden, — a hard winter for them. I do not commonly observe it on a large scale.

My Aunt Sophia, now in her eightieth year, says
that when she was a little girl my grandmother, who
lived in Keene, N. H., eighty miles from Boston, went
to Nova Scotia, and, in spite of all she could do, her dog
Bob, a little black dog with his tail cut off, followed
her to Boston, where she went aboard a vessel. Di-

rectly after, however, Bob returned to Keene. One day, Bob, lying as usual under his mistress's bed in Keene, the window being open, heard a dog bark in the street, and instantly, forgetting that he was in the second story, he sprang up and jumped out the chamber window. He came down squarely on all fours, but it surprised or shocked him so that he did not run an inch, —which greatly amused the children,—my mother and aunts.

The seed of the willow is exceedingly minute, — as I measure, from one twentieth to one twelfth of an inch in length by one fourth as much in width, — and is surrounded at base by a tuft of cotton-like hairs about one fourth of an inch long rising around and above it, forming a kind of parachute. These render it the most buoyant of the seeds of any of our trees, and it is borne the furthest horizontally with the least wind. It falls very slowly even in the still air of a chamber, and rapidly ascends over a stove. It floats the most like a mote of any, — in a meandering manner, — and, being enveloped in this tuft of cotton, the seed is hard to detect.

Each of the numerous little pods, more or less ovate and beaked, which form the fertile catkin is closely packed with down and seeds. At maturity these pods open their beaks, which curve back, and gradually discharge their burden like the milkweed. It would take a delicate gin indeed to separate these seeds from their cotton.

If you lay bare any spot in our woods, however

sandy, — as by a railroad cut, — no shrub or tree is surer to plant itself there sooner or later than a willow (commonly *S. humilis* or *tristis*) or poplar.

We have many kinds, but each is confined to its own habitat. I am not aware that the *S. nigra* has ever strayed from the river's brink. Though many of the *S. alba* have been set along our causeways, very few have sprung up and maintained their ground elsewhere.

The principal habitat of most of our species, such as love the water, is the river's bank and the adjacent river meadows, and when certain kinds spring up in an inland meadow where they were not known before, I feel pretty certain that they come from the river meadows. I have but little doubt that the seed of four of those that grow along the railroad causeway was blown from the river meadows, *viz. S. pedicellaris, lucida, Torreyana,* and *petiolaris.*

The barren and fertile flowers are usually on separate plants. I observe [?] that the greater part of the white willows set out on our causeways are sterile ones. You can easily distinguish the fertile ones at a distance when the pods are bursting. And it is said that no sterile weeping willows have been introduced into this country, so that it cannot be raised from the seed. Of two of the indigenous willows common along the brink of our river I have detected but one sex.

The seeds of the willow thus annually fill the air with their lint, being wafted to all parts of the country, and, though apparently not more than one in many millions gets to be a shrub, yet so lavish and persevering is Nature that her purpose is completely answered.

March 16. A severe, blocking-up snow-storm.

March 18. Tree sparrows have warbled faintly for a week.

When I pass by a twig of willow, though of the slenderest kind, rising above the sedge in some dry hollow early in December, or in midwinter above the snow, my spirits rise as if it were an oasis in the desert. The very name "sallow" (*salix*, from the Celtic *sal-lis*, near water) suggests that there is some natural sap or blood flowing there. It is a divining wand that has not failed, but stands with its root in the fountain.

The fertile willow catkins are those green caterpillar-like ones, commonly an inch or more in length, which develop themselves rapidly after the sterile yellow ones which we had so admired are fallen or effete. Arranged around the bare twigs, they often form green wands eight to eighteen inches long. A single catkin consists of from twenty-five to a hundred little pods, more or less ovate and beaked, each of which is closely packed with cotton, in which are numerous seeds so small that they are scarcely discernible by ordinary eyes.

I do not know what they mean who call this the emblem of despairing love! "The willow, worn by forlorn paramour!" It is rather the emblem of love and sympathy with all nature. It may droop, — it is so lithe, supple, and pliant, — but it never weeps. The willow of Babylon blooms not the less hopefully with us, though its other half is not in the New World at all, and never has been. It droops, not to represent David's tears, but rather to snatch the crown from Alexander's head. (Nor were poplars ever the weeping sisters of Phaëton, for nothing rejoices them more than the sight of the Sun's chariot, and little reck they who drives it.)

Ah, willow! willow! Would that I always possessed thy good spirits.

No wonder its wood was anciently in demand for bucklers, for, take the whole tree, it is not only soft and pliant but tough and resilient (as Pliny says?), not splitting at the first blow, but closing its wounds at once and refusing to transmit its hurts.

I know of one foreign species which introduced itself into Concord as [a] withe used to tie up a bundle of trees. A gardener stuck it in the ground, and it lived, and has its descendants.

Herodotus says that the Scythians divined by the help of willow rods. I do not know any better twigs for this purpose.

How various are the habits of men! Mother says that her father-in-law, Captain Minott, not only used to roast and eat a long row of little wild apples, reaching in a semicircle from jamb to jamb under the andirons on the reddened hearth (I used to buy many a pound of Spanish brown at the stores for mother to redden the jambs and hearth with), but he had a quart of new milk regularly placed at the head of his bed, which he drank at many draughts in the course of the night. It was so the night he died, and my grandmother discovered that he was dying, by his not turning over to reach his milk. I asked what he died of, and mother answered apoplexy! at which I did not wonder. Still this habit may not have caused it.

I have a cousin, also, who regularly eats his bowl of bread and milk just before going to bed, however late. He is a very stirring man.

You can't read any genuine history — as that of Herodotus or the Venerable Bede — without perceiving that our interest depends not on the subject but on the man, — on the manner in which he treats the subject and the importance he gives it. A feeble writer and without genius must have what he thinks a great theme, which we are already interested in through the accounts of others, but a genius — a Shakespeare, for instance — would make the history of his parish more interesting than another's history of the world.

Wherever men have lived there is a story to be told, and it depends chiefly on the story-teller or historian whether that is interesting or not. You are simply a witness on the stand to tell what you know about your neighbors and neighborhood. Your account of foreign parts which you have never seen should by good rights be less interesting.

March 22. A driving northeast snow-storm yesterday and last night, and to-day the drifts are high over the fences and the trains stopped. The Boston train due at 8.30 A. M. did not reach here till five this afternoon. One side of all the houses this morning was one color, — *i. e.* white with the moist snow plastered over them, — so that you could not tell whether they had blinds or not.

When we consider how soon some plants which

spread rapidly, by seeds or roots, would cover an area equal to the surface of the globe, how soon some species of trees, as the white willow, for instance, would equal in mass the earth itself, if all their seeds became full-grown trees, how soon some fishes would fill the ocean if all their ova became full-grown fishes, we are tempted to say that every organism, whether animal or vegetable, is contending for the possession of the planet, and, if any one were sufficiently favored, supposing it still possible to grow, as at first, it would at length convert the entire mass of the globe into its own substance.[1] Nature opposes to this many obstacles, as climate, myriads of brute and also human foes, and of competitors which may preoccupy the ground. Each suggests an immense and wonderful greediness and tenacity of life (I speak of the species, not individual), as if bent on taking entire possession of the globe wherever the climate and soil will permit. And each prevails as much as it does, because of the ample preparations it has made for the contest, — it has secured a myriad chances, — because it never depends on spontaneous generation to save it.

A writer in the *Tribune* speaks of cherries as one of the trees which come up numerously when the forest is cut or burned, though not known there before. This may be true because there was no one knowing in these matters in that neighborhood. But I assert that it *was* there before, nevertheless; just as the little oaks are in the pine woods, but never grow up to trees till the pines are cleared off. Scarcely any plant is more sure to come

[1] *Vide* Pliny on man's mission to keep down weeds.

up in a sprout-land here than the wild black cherry, and yet, though only a few inches high at the end of the first year after the cutting, it is commonly several years old, having maintained a feeble growth there so long. There is where the birds have dropped the stones, and it is doubtful if those dropped in pastures and open land are as likely to germinate. Yet the former rarely if ever get to be trees.

Rice told me a month ago that when the earth became bare the jays, though they still came round the house, no longer picked up the corn he had scattered for them. I suggested that it was because they were now able to vary their diet.

Of course natural successions are taking place where a swamp is gradually filling up with sphagnum and bushes and at length trees, i. e., where the soil is changing.

Botanists talk about the possibility and impossibility of plants being naturalized here or there. But what plants have not been naturalized? Of course only those which grow to-day exactly where the original plant of the species was created. It is true we do not know whether one or many plants of a given kind were originally created, but I think it is the most reasonable and simple to suppose that only one was, — to suppose as little departure as possible from the existing order of things. They commenced to spread themselves at once and by whatever means they possessed as far as they could, and they are still doing so. Many were common to Europe and America at the period of the discovery of the latter country, and I have no doubt that they had naturalized themselves in one or the other country. This is more philosophical than to suppose that they were independently created in each.

I suppose that most have seen — at any rate I can show them — English cherry trees, so called, coming up not uncommonly in our woods and under favorable circumstances becoming full-grown trees. Now I think that they will not pretend that they came up there in the same manner before this country was discovered by the whites. But, if cherry trees come up by spontaneous generation, why should they not have sprung up there in that way a thousand years ago as well as now?

If the pine seed is spontaneously generated, why is it not so produced in the Old World as well as in America? I have no doubt that it can be raised from the seed in corresponding situations there, and that it will seem to spring up just as mysteriously there as it does here. Yet, if it will grow so *after* the seed has been carried thither, why should it not before, if the seed is unnecessary to its production?

The above-mentioned cherry trees come up, though they are comparatively few, just like the red cherry, and, no doubt, the same persons would consider them as spontaneously generated. But why did Nature defer raising that species here by spontaneous generation, until we had raised it from the stones?

It is evident that Nature's designs would not be accomplished if seeds, having been matured, were simply dropped and so planted directly beneath their parent stems, as many will always be in any case. The next consideration with her, then, after determining to create a seed, must have been how to get it transported, though to never so little distance, — the width of the plant, or less, will often be sufficient, — even as the eagle drives her young at last from the neighborhood of her eyrie, — for their own good, since there is not food enough there for all, — without depending on botanists, patent offices, and seedsmen. It is not enough to have matured a seed which will reproduce its kind under favorable conditions, but she must also secure it those favorable conditions. Nature has left nothing to the mercy of man. She has taken care that a sufficient number of every kind of seeds, from a cocoanut to those which are invisible, shall be transported and planted in a suitable place.

A seed, which is a plant or tree in embryo, which has the principle of growth, of life, in it, is more important in my eyes, and in the economy of Nature, than the diamond of Kohinoor.

When we hear of an excellent fruit or a beautiful flower, the first question is if any man has got the seeds in his pocket; but men's pockets are only one of the means of conveyances which Nature has provided.

March 30. High water, — up to sixth slat (or gap) above Smith's second post. It is said to have been some nine inches higher about a month ago, when the snow first went off.

R. W. E. lately found a Norway pine cut down in Stow's wood by Saw Mill Brook.

According to Channing's account, Walden must have

skimmed nearly, if not entirely, over again once since the 11th or 12th, or after it had been some time completely clear. It seems, then, that in some years it may thaw and freeze again.

April 2. A drifting snow-storm, perhaps a foot deep on an average.

Pratt thought the cowslip was out the 4th.

April 6. Am surprised to find the river fallen some nine inches notwithstanding the melted snow. But I read in Blodget that the equivalent in water is about one tenth. Say one ninth in this case, and you have one and one third inches, and this falling on an unfrozen surface, the river at the same time falling from a height, shows why it was no more retarded (far from being absolutely raised).

There is now scarcely a button-ball to be seen on Moore's tree, where there were many a month ago or more. The balls have not fallen entire, but been decomposed and the seed dispersed gradually, leaving long, stringy stems and their cores dangling still. It is the storms of February and March that disperse them.

The (are they cinnamon?) sparrows are the finest singers I have heard yet, especially in Monroe's garden, where I see no tree sparrows. Similar but more prolonged and remarkable and loud.

April 7. Sunday. Round the two-mile square.

I see where the common great tufted sedge (*Carex stricta*) has started under the water on the meadows, now fast falling. The white maple at the bridge not quite out. See a water-bug and a frog. Hylas are heard to-day.

I see where the meadow flood has gone down in a bay on the southeast side of the meadow, whither the foam had been driven. A delicate scum now left an inch high on the grass. It is a dirty white, yet silvery, and as thin as the thinnest foil, often unbroken and apparently air-tight for two or three inches across and almost as light as gossamer. What is the material? It is a kind of paper, but far more delicate than man makes.

Saw in a roadside gutter at Simon Brown's barn a bird like the solitary tattler, with a long bill, which at length flew off to the river. But it may have been a small species of snipe.

April 8. Examine the pitch pines, which have been much gnawed or barked this snowy winter. The marks on them show the fine teeth of the mouse, and they are also nicked as with a sharp knife. At the base of each, also, is a quantity of the mice droppings. It is probably the white-footed mouse.

April 9. Small reddish butterflies common; also, on snow banks, many of the small fuzzy gnats and cicindelæ and some large black dor-bug-like beetles. The two latter are easily detected from a distance on the snow.

The phœbe note of chickadee.

White frosts these mornings.

Worm-piles in grass at Clamshell.

April 10. Purple finch.

April 11. Going to law. I hear that Judge Minott of Haverhill once told a client, by way of warning, that two millers who owned mills on the same stream went to law about a dam, and at the end of the lawsuit one lawyer owned one mill and the other the other.

April 16. Horace Mann says that he killed a bullfrog in Walden Pond which had swallowed and contained a common striped snake which measured one foot and eight inches in length.

Says he saw two blue herons (?) go over a fortnight ago.

He brought me some days ago the contents of a stake-driver's stomach or crop. It is apparently a perch (?), some seven inches long originally, with three or four pebble-shaped, compact masses of the fur of some very small quadruped, as a meadow mouse, some one fourth inch thick by three fourths in diameter, also several wing-cases of black beetles such as I see on the meadow flood.

He brought me also some time ago the contents of a black duck's crop (killed at Goose Pond), — green gobbets of fine grass (?) or weeds (?), apparently from the bottom of the pond (just then begun to spring up), but I have not yet examined these out of the bottle.

April 20. H. Mann brings me the hermit thrush.

April 21. Pratt collects very handsome tufts of *Hepatica triloba* in flower at Melrose, and the bloodroot out also there.

April 22. It was high water again about a week ago, — Mann thinks with[in] three or four inches as high as at end of winter.

He obtained to-day the buffle-headed duck, diving in the river near the Nine-Acre Corner bridge. I identify it at sight as my bird seen on Walden.

I hear a chip-bird.

April 23. Think I hear bay-wings. Toads ring.

April 25. Horace Mann brings me apparently a pigeon hawk. The two middle tail-feathers are not tipped with white and are pointed almost as a woodpecker's.

May 1. Water in our neighbors' cellars quite generally. May it not be partly owing to the fact that the ground was not frozen the last winter to any depth, and so the melted snow as well as rain has been chiefly absorbed by it? [1]

May 4. H. Mann brings me two small pewees, but not yellowish about eye and bill, and bill is all black. Also a white-throat sparrow, Wilson's thrush, and myrtle-bird.

May 5. Hear the seringo note.[2]

---

[1] Probably it was.

[2] [Pasted in at this point is a pencilled slip reading, "Strabo read as far as 306th p.," with memoranda apparently referring to the book.]

Hepatica and Bloodroot

May 11. A boy brings me a salamander from S. Mason's. Sent it to Mann. What kind?

SET OUT FOR MINNESOTA *via* Worcester.[1]

May 12. *Sunday.* In Worcester.

Rode to east side of Quinsigamond Pond with Blake and Brown and a dry humorist, a gentleman who has been a sportsman and was well acquainted with dogs. He said that he once went by water to St. John, N. B., on a sporting excursion, taking his dog with him; but the latter had such a remarkable sense of decency that, seeing no suitable place aboard the vessel, he did not yield to the pressing demands of nature and, as the voyage lasted several days, swelled up very much. At length his master, by taking him aside and setting him the example, persuaded him to make water only. When at length he reached St. John, and was leading his dog by a rope up a long hill there which led to the town, he was compelled to stop repeatedly for his dog to empty himself and was the observed of all observers. This suggested that a dog could be educated to be far more cleanly in some respects than men are.

He also states that a fox does not regard all dogs, — or, rather, avoid them, — but only hunting dogs. He one day heard the voices of hounds in pursuit of a fox and soon after saw the fox come trotting along a path in which he himself was walking. Secreting himself behind a wall he watched the motions of the fox, wishing to get a shot at him, but at that moment his dog, a spaniel, leapt out into the path and advanced to meet

[1] [See *Familiar Letters*, pp. 380, 383–393; Riv. 439, 443–455.]

the fox, which stood still without fear to receive him. They smelled of one another like dogs, and the sportsman was prevented from shooting the fox for fear of hitting his dog. So he suddenly showed himself in the path, hoping thus to separate them and get a shot. The fox immediately cantered backward in the path, but his dog ran after him so directly in a line with the fox that he was afraid to fire for fear of killing the dog.

May 13. Worcester to Albany.

The latter part of the day rainy. The hills come near the railroad between Westfield and Chester Village. Thereafter in Massachusetts they may be as high or higher, but are somewhat further off.

The leafing is decidedly more advanced in western Massachusetts than in eastern. Apple trees are greenish. Red elder-berry is apparently just beginning to bloom.

Put up at the Delavan House. Not so good as costly.

May 14. Albany to Suspension Bridge.

Albany to Schenectady a level pitch pine plain with also white pine, white birch, and shad-bush in bloom, with *hills* at last. No houses; only two or three huts on the edge of woods without any road. These were the last pitch pines that I saw on my westward journey.

It is amusing to observe how a kitten regards the attic, kitchen, or shed where it was bred as its castle to resort to in time of danger. It loves best to sleep on

some elevated place, as a shelf or chair, and for many
months does not venture far from the back door where
it first saw the light. Two rods is a great range for it,
but so far it is tempted, when the dew is off, by the
motions of grasshoppers and crickets and other such
small game, sufficiently novel and surprising to it. They
frequently have a wheezing cough, which some refer to
grasshoppers' wings across their windpipes. The kitten
has been eating grasshoppers.

If some member of the household with whom they
are familiar — their mistress or master — goes forth
into the garden, they are then encouraged to take a
wider range, and for a short season explore the more
distant bean and cabbage rows, or, if several of the
family go forth at once, — as it were a reconnaissance
in force, — the kitten does a transient scout duty outside,
but yet on the slightest alarm they are seen bounding
back with great leaps over the grass toward the castle,
where they stand panting on the door-step, with their
small lower jaws fallen, until they fill up with courage
again. A cat looks down with complacency on the
strange dog from the corn-barn window.

The kitten when it is two or three months old is full
of play. Ever and anon she takes up her plaything
in her mouth and carries it to another place, — a distant corner of the room or some other nook, as under
a rocker, — or perchance drops it at your feet, seeming
to delight in the mere carriage of it, as if it were her
prey — tiger-like. In proportion to her animal spirits
are her quick motions and sudden whirlings about on
the carpet or in the air. She may make a great show of

scratching and biting, but let her have your hand and she will presently lick it instead.

They are so naturally stealthy, skulking and creeping about, affecting holes and darkness, that they will enter a shed rather by some hole under the door-sill than go over the sill through the open door.

Though able to bear cold, few creatures love warmth more or sooner find out where the fire is. The cat, whether she comes home wet or dry, directly squeezes herself under the cooking-stove, and stews her brain there, if permitted. If the cat is in the kitchen, she is most likely to be found under the stove.

This (October 5) is a rainy or drizzling day at last, and the robins and sparrows are more numerous in the yard and about the house than ever. They swarm on the ground where stood the heap of weeds which was burned yesterday, picking up the seeds which rattled from it. Why should these birds be so much more numerous about the house such a day as this? I think of no other reason than because it is darker and fewer people are moving about to frighten them. Our little mountain-ash is all alive with them. A dozen robins on it at once, busily reaching after and plucking the berries, actually make the whole tree shake. There are also some little birds (I think purple finches) with them. A robin will swallow half a dozen berries, at least, in rapid succession before it goes off, and apparently it soon comes back for more.

The reason why naturalists make so little account

Thoreau's Grave

Thoreau's Grave

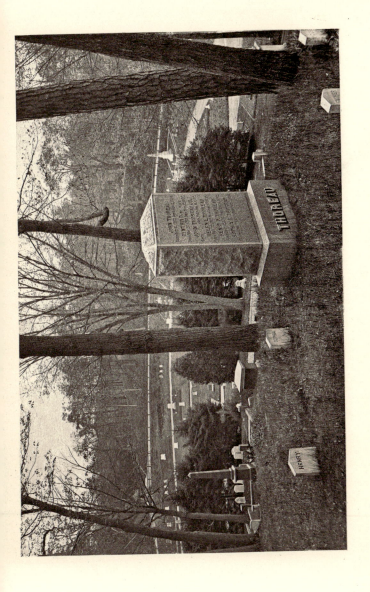

of color is because it is so insignificant to them; they
do not understand it. But the lover of flowers or animals
makes very much of color. To a fancier of cats it is not
indifferent whether one be black or gray, for the color
expresses *character*.

Prescott is not inclined to go to the wars again
(October, '61), and so Concord has no company to represent her at present. Cyrus Warren thinks that Derby,
the first lieutenant (and butcher that was), would do
for captain as well as Prescott, and adds, as his principal qualification, "There is n't one in the company
can cut up a crittur like him."

Henry Mitchell of the Coast Survey (page 317) [1] has
invented a new kind of pile, to be made of some heavy
and strong wood and "so cut that the lower portion
of it, for a space of six or eight feet, presents the appearance of a number of inverted frustums of cones,
placed one above another." When this is swayed to and
fro by the waves, instead of being loosened and washed
out, it sinks deeper and deeper. This, as Professor
Bache (in Coast Survey Report for 1859, page 30)
says, "is a device borrowed from nature, he [Mitchell]
having observed that certain seed vessels, by virtue of
their forms, bury themselves in the earth when agitated
by wind or water." No seeds are named, but they
must be similar to the seed of the porcupine grass of the
West.

[1] [*Report of the Superintendent of the Coast Survey, showing the
Progress of the Survey during the Year* 1859, Washington, 1860.]

Young Macey, who has been camping on Monadnock this summer, tells me that he found one of my spruce huts made last year in August, and that as many as eighteen, reshingling it, had camped in it while he was there.

See a large hornets' nest on a maple (September 29), the *half immersed* leaves turned scarlet.

Four little kittens just born; lay like stuffed skins of kittens in a heap, with pink feet; so flimsy and helpless they lie, yet blind, without any stiffness or ability to stand.

Edward Lord Herbert says in his autobiography, "It is well known to those that wait in my chamber, that the shirts, waistcoats, and other garments I wear next my body, are sweet, beyond what either easily can be believed, or hath been observed in any else, which sweetness also was found to be in my breath above others, before I used to take tobacco."

The kitten can already spit at a fortnight old, and it can mew from the first, though it often makes the motion of mewing without uttering any sound.

The cat about to bring forth seeks out some dark and secret place for the purpose, not frequented by other cats.

The kittens' ears are at first nearly concealed in the fur, and at a fortnight old they are mere broad-based triangles with a side foremost. But the old cat is ears for them at present, and comes running hastily to their

aid when she hears them mew and licks them into con-
tentment again. Even at three weeks the kitten cannot fairly walk, but only creeps feebly with outspread
legs. But thenceforth its ears visibly though gradually
lift and sharpen themselves.

At three weeks old the kitten begins to walk in a
staggering and creeping manner and even to play a
little with its mother, and, if you put your ear close,
you may hear it purr. It is remarkable that it will not
wander far from the dark corner where the cat has
left it, but will instinctively find its way back to it, probably by the sense of touch, and will rest nowhere else.
Also it is careful not to venture too near the edge of a
precipice, and its claws are ever extended to save itself
in such places. It washes itself somewhat, and assumes
many of the attitudes of an old cat at this age. By the
disproportionate size of its feet and head and legs
now it reminds you [of] a lion.

I saw it scratch its ear to-day, probably for the first
time; yet it lifted one of its hind legs and scratched
its ear as effectually as an old cat does. So this is in-
stinctive, and you may say that, when a kitten's ear
first itches, Providence comes to the rescue and lifts its
hind leg for it. You would say that this little creature
was as perfectly protected by its instinct in its infancy
as an old man can be by his wisdom. I observed when
she first noticed the figures on the carpet, and also put
up her paws to touch or play with surfaces a foot off.
By the same instinct that they find the mother's teat
before they can see they scratch their ears and guard
against falling.

After a violent easterly storm in the night, which clears up at noon (November 3, 1861), I notice that the surface of the railroad causeway, composed of gravel, is singularly marked, as if stratified like some slate rocks, on their edges, so that I can tell within a small fraction of a degree from what quarter the rain came. These lines, as it were of stratification, are perfectly parallel, and straight as a ruler, diagonally across the flat surface of the causeway for its whole length. Behind each little pebble, as a protecting boulder, an eighth or a tenth of an inch in diameter, extends northwest a ridge of sand an inch or more, which it has protected from being washed away, while the heavy drops driven almost horizontally have washed out a furrow on each side, and on all sides are these ridges, half an inch apart and perfectly parallel.

All this is perfectly distinct to an observant eye, and yet could easily pass unnoticed by most. Thus each wind is self-registering.

NOTE TO MAP OF CONCORD

The material used in this Map of Concord has been derived from a variety of sources. The town bounds, streets, and residences have been taken from a township map of Middlesex County made by H. F. Walling in 1856, reference also being had to a local map of Concord by the same engineer, dated 1852, on which credit for the surveys of White Pond and Walden Pond is given to " H. D. Thoreau, Civ. Eng^r." The course of the Concord River is drawn from an elaborate manuscript plan of Thoreau's, based on earlier surveys, showing the river from East Sudbury to Billerica Dam. This plan, on which Thoreau has entered the results of his investigation of the river in the summer of 1859, is now in the Concord Public Library. The outlines of Walden and White Ponds have also been taken from Thoreau's original surveys, now in the Concord Library. Loring's and Bateman's Ponds are according to surveys by Mr. Albert E. Wood of Concord, and Flint's Pond is from a survey for the Concord Water Works by Mr. William Wheeler, also of Concord.

All names of places are those used by Thoreau, no attention being given to other names perhaps more current either in his own time or at present. Only such names of residents are given as are mentioned in the Journal.

A few old wood roads, pasture lanes, etc. (Thoreau's preferred high-ways), are indicated, as to their general direction, by dotted lines.

The irregularity of the northeastern boundary of Concord arose from the fact that when Carlisle was set off from Concord in 1780, the farmers living on the border were given the option of remaining within the bounds of Concord or of being included in the new town. In 1903 the Massachusetts Legislature abolished this old division and continued the straight line forming the western half of the boundary directly to the river.

The identification of localities which were named by Thoreau apparently for his personal use alone has been accomplished, so far as it has proceeded, by a careful study of all the Journal references to each local-ity, an examination of a large number of Thoreau's manuscript surveys, and an extended personal investigation on the ground. Many of these localities are given more than one name in the Journal, and in a few cases the same name is given to different localities. Where doubt exists as to any particular location, the name is omitted from the map.

Hon. F. B. Sanborn, Judge John S. Keyes, Dr. Edward W. Emerson, the Misses Hosmer, and others among the older residents of Concord have been consulted in the preparation of the map, and have kindly supplied helpful information from their personal acquaintance with Thoreau.

H. W. Gleason.

December, 1906.

INDEX TO MAP OF CONCORD

Figures in parentheses correspond with figures on the map. A letter and figure combined indicate the space in which the locality may be found, this space being determined by the intersection of imaginary lines drawn from the corresponding letter and figure in the margin.

[1] This name is spelled "Heywood" by Thoreau.

2 This name was also given to a bay on the river in Sudbury.
3 This is the "Saw Mill Brook" most frequently mentioned by Thoreau.

INDEX

INDEX

"A stir is on the Worcester hills,"
verse, **1**, 122.
Abdallah, **2**, 190.
Abenaki language, **10**, 290, 291.
Abolition Society, **5**, 365.
Abolitionists, advised to assault the
church and press, **2**, 178.
About, Edmond, quoted, **10**, 234.
Abu Beker, **2**, 189.
Academy grants, **10**, 297.
Academy of Natural Sciences, Phil-
adelphia, **7**, 74.
Accident, nature's liability to, **5**, 176.
Account-books, old, **1**, 474, **6**, 77–80,
88, 94–96, 101.
Acerbi, **7**, 290.
Achilles, **1**, 366.
Acorns, **7**, 61, **14**, 103, 112, 113, 180;
edible, **3**, 56–59, **10**, 103, 104;
sprouting, **3**, 481, **14**, 264; Evelyn
on, **4**, 84, 85; shapes of, **6**, 477;
sketch of white oak, **7**, 35; after
falling, 47; sketch of scarlet oak
acorn, 47; the acorn of art, 62; as
food, 460; as food of squirrels, **10**,
129; weather prophets, 178; beauty
of, **11**, 208, 257, **12**, 320; a test of
soundness of, 150; destroyed by
worms, 157; falling after rain,
14, 96; decaying, 106, 107, 123,
124, 143, 263; with a double meat,
132; abundance of crop and large
number destroyed, 148; eating
white oak acorns, 154; mortality
of, 168; infested by grubs, 214; flavor of white oak, 265.
Acquaintance, **1**, 77.
Actions, lose distinction in hours of
vision, **1**, 447.
Acton, an historical monument in,
3, 101.
Actual, compared to ideal, **1**, 360.
Adam, the old and the new, **2**, 152,
153.
Adams, an expressman, **10**, 216.
Adams, of Waltham, **7**, 447.
Adams, Frank, **12**, 237.

Adams, John, **5**, 242; biography of,
3, 24.
Adams, John Quincy, of Carlisle, **14**,
78, 79, 83–86.
Adams, Paul, **6**, 31.
Adams, Rev. William, **7**, 182.
Adder, checkered, **6**, 308, 309, **14**, 168.
See also Snake, chicken.
Adder, water, **5**, 354, **8**, 412, 413, 424,
446, **10**, 416; carrying its young,
429. *See also* Snake, water.
Admetus, **1**, 391, **4**, 114, **6**, 185.
Adversity, thoughts induced by, **1**,
320.
Advice, futility of, **3**, 294, 295, **11**,
379, 380.
Æacus, **1**, 391, 392.
Ægina, **1**, 392.
Æschylus, a seer, **1**, 93; his genius,
93, 116; his "Prometheus Bound,"
94; intellectual solitude of, 117;
lack of discrimination in, 218.
Æsop, **1**, 470; fame of, **5**, 411.
Æsop's Fables, **7**, 469.
Africa, South, notes from Gordon
Cumming's book on, **2**, 130–133.
African, the, survival of, **1**, 446.
Afterglow, **4**, 240–243, 249, 262–264.
Afternoon, effect of, on man, **1**, 75.
Agassiz, Louis, on T. W. Harris, **4**,
439; on refractions on Lake Su-
perior, **6**, 140; on turtles, **8**, 342,
10, 399, 420; on intestinal worms
in the mouse, **8**, 362; on the haddock,
430; dinner with, **9**, 298, 299; on
development of the tortoise, 299;
showing a glow-worm to, **10**, 248;
in the Adirondacks, **11**, 119, 120.
Age, indispensable to youth, **1**, 413;
attitude toward nature in, **3**, 378;
Winckelmann on effects of, **9**, 242,
243.
Agrimonia Eupatoria, **4**, 194.
Aground, a boat, **2**, 78, 79.
Aikin, Dr. John, his "Arts of Life"
quoted, **7**, 460.
Air, a velvet cushion, **3**, 350; modi-

Apennines, the word, **3**, 229.

Aphides, **5**, 249; floating on the Assabet, 309; the father of all the, **9**, 8, 9.

Aphorisms, **1**, 342, 358, 438, **4**, 349.

Apocynum cannabinum, or Indian hemp, **8**, 447, 458, 466, **9**, 476, **11**, 3.

Apollo, **1**, 393, 394, **4**, 114.

Apollo Belvidere, **6**, 56.

Appearances, **4**, 45.

Appetite, **1**, 311, 312.

Apple-of-Peru, **7**, 483.

Apple blossoms, **2**, 30; fragrance of, **5**, 169.

Apple trees, wild, **2**, 92, 100, 106; bush compared to an hour-glass, 331; cows the foes of, **3**, 75; orchards, **4**, 181; scrubs, **5**, 179, 180; the "tea-tree," 338; best shape of a tree, **6**, 441; twigs eaten by partridges, **7**, 188; a tree carried on the shoulders, **8**, 312; roots of, **9**, 350, 351; a grafter of, 383, 384; decreasing in size, **10**, 12; reflections on an apple tree, 136; independence of, 137, 138; measured, 422, 428; low scrub, **11**, 76; hour-glass, 269.

Apples, fragrance of a sopsivine, **1**, 372, **4**, 271; an apple picked up in the road, **2**, 383; the noblest of fruits, **3**, 83, 84; early-harvest, **5**, 328; scent of, 373; frozen, 494; food of squirrels, **7**, 501; harvest of, **11**, 291–293; varieties at cattleshow, **12**, 356; compared with pears, **14**, 113, 114.

Apples, wild, **2**, 126, 127, **4**, 359; the native, **2**, 211; names proposed for, 212, 222, 223; fragrance of, 396; colors of, **7**, 508; eaten in the open air, 520, 526; spots on, **8**, 6; and the savage, 7.

Aquarium, Edward Emerson's, **12**, 151.

Arabian Nights, **1**, 344.

Arabic, names of plants from, **3**, 216.

Arabis, **7**, 319.

Arabis Canadensis, pods of, **6**, 410.

Arabs, prayers of, **9**, 252.

Aralia, spotted leaves of, **9**, 9. *See also* Sarsaparilla.

Aralia, bristly, berries of, **5**, 349.

Arbor-vitæ, **2**, 37, 200, **13**, 335; odor of, **6**, 209, 221.

Arbutus Uva-Ursi. See Bear-berry.

Arch, compared to stars, **4**, 152.

Archangelica, **9**, 60, **12**, 402, 403.

Archangelica atropurpurea, **4**, 138.

Architecture, in Canada, **2**, 75, 76; H. Greenough's letter on, **3**, 181–183; its inferiority to thought, **4**, 152; American taste for, 153; of youth and middle age, 227; terrene temples, **5**, 140; Gothic, 493; Numidian, 493; significance of the tent in, **7**, 461; of toadstools, **8**, 464.

Arctic regions, dreariness of, **7**, 59.

Arctostaphylos alpina, **11**, 42, 43.

Arctostaphylos Uva-Ursi. See Bear-berry.

Ardea minor. See Bittern, American.

Arenaria Grœnlandica, on Mt. Monadnock, **14**, 45.

Arethusa, adder's-tongue. *See Pogonia ophioglossoides.*

Arethusa bulbosa, **4**, 76, 200, **5**, 196; demands a poet, **4**, 81; a superb flower, **6**, 316, 317; fragrance of, 341.

Aristeus, **1**, 394.

Aristophanes, **13**, 195.

Aristotelean method, **12**, 372.

Aristotle, **1**, 150, 171, **9**, 299; his definition of art, **1**, 139; described by Degerando, 440; quoted, **2**, 150; his "History of Animals," **13**, 55; on spawning of fishes, 77, 78.

Arrowhead, *or* sagittaria, root of, **2**, 389; cropped by cows, **4**, 208; leaves of, 228, 264, **11**, 102, 103, **12**, 294; flowers of, **4**, 264, 5, 283, **12**, 300.

Arrowhead-maker, **1**, 453.

Arrowheads. *See* Indian arrowheads.

Arrow-wood, **4**, 203. *See also Viburnum dentatum.*

Art, highest condition of, **1**, 153; the true, 167; niggardliness of, compared with Nature, 270, 271; Grecian, 361, 362; limitation of, 367; kinship of, to Nature, 380; for art's sake, **3**, 30; beginnings of, **5**, 526; a gall, **7**, 10; defined, **10**, 80; a certain wildness in, compared with Nature's, **11**, 450; the product of leisure, **12**, 344.

Arthur, King, **1**, 23.

Artichokes, **12**, 410.

Artificial wants, encouragement of, **6**, 335, 336.

Artist, the, indifference of, **1**, 349.

Arts, lessons taught by the, **2**, 142.

Arum peltandrum, **11**, 127.

Arum triphyllum, **5**, 151, **8**, 415; berries of, **4**, 342, **9**, 51, 60, 92, **12**, 310; its beauty of form, 185.

Arundo, **5**, 382.

Arvicola Emmonsii. See Mouse, deer.

Ascension Island, **2**, 264, **12**, 33.

Asclepias, a substitute for hemp, **4**, 491. *See also* Milkweed.

Asclepias, four-leaved (*A. quadrifolia*), **4**, 138, **5**, 289.

Asclepias Cornuti. See Milkweed, common.

Asclepias incarnata. See Milkweed, water.

Asclepias obtusifolia, **4**, 205, 208, **8**, 404; pods of, **9**, 88.

Asclepias pulchra, **2**, 424.

Asclepias Syriaca. See Milkweed, common.

Ash, **5**, 176; harmony of form of, **10**, 43; fallen leaves of, 120; leaves of, in June, **13**, 336.

Ash, black, **2**, 197, **12**, 108; improperly named, **2**, 206.

Ash, mountain. *See* Mountain-ash.

Ash, white, **3**, 36, **12**, 108; keys of, **4**, 138; destroyed by lightning, 155, 156; anthers of, **9**, 377; an ancient scar on, **10**, 12.

Ashburnham, **2**, 74.

Ashly, Joe, **7**, 467.

Asmund, **3**, 203.

Asparagus, **10**, 510.

Aspen, **11**, 268, 269, 342, **13**, 305; showing spring's influence, **3**, 362; like green fires, **4**, 37; twigs kept in water, **5**, 5; leaves of, 122, 138; leafing of, **6**, 275, **7**, 351, 352; leaves of sprout, **9**, 113; fruit of, **10**, 420; leaves of, in June, **13**, 336. *See also* Poplar *and* Populus.

Aspen catkins, **3**, 419, **7**, 320, **8**, 277.

Aspidium cristatum, **12**, 386.

Aspidium Filix-fœmina, **9**, 483.

Aspiration, should exceed attainment, **1**, 352; fulfillment of, **10**, 202.

Asplenium, **9**, 483; likened to a breastpin, **11**, 333, 334.

"Assabet, The," verse, **1**, 84.

Assabet River, *or* North River, *or* North Branch, **4**, 154, **5**, 292; bathing-place in, **4**, 100; heaps of stones in, 152, 221, 222, **5**, 125; meadow on, **4**, 186, 187; character of, 188; bottom of, 211–214; walks in, 211–214, 220–223; expansiveness of, 310, 311; a beautiful scene on, **5**, 284; peculiarities of, **6**, 411; rise

and fall by fits and starts, **10**, 339, 340; physiography of, **12**, 238–248, 279–283; observing the Sabbath, 247; old dam in, **14**, 99.

Assabet stone bridge, **9**, 375, **12**, 245.

Assawampsett Pond, **7**, 473–479, **8**, 396, 397.

Associations, weight of in art-appreciations, **6**, 55–59.

Aster acuminatus, **4**, 347.

Aster cordifolius, **9**, 63.

Aster corymbosus, **5**, 424.

Aster lœvis, **10**, 35.

Aster, savory-leaved (*A. linariifolius* or *Diplopappus linariifolius*), **4**, 266, 267, **7**, 434, **11**, 205, 293.

Aster longifolius, **4**, 322, **5**, 476.

Aster macrophyllus, **9**, 25; fragrance of, **11**, 73.

Aster miser, **5**, 418, **9**, 6.

Aster multiflorus, **5**, 409.

Aster patens, **5**, 365, **8**, 464.

Aster puniceus, **5**, 423, 462, 476, **9**, 35.

Aster Tradescanti, **5**, 421, 422, **9**, 82.

Aster undulatus, **5**, 366, 423, **9**, 87; the latest aster, **5**, 449; compared with other species, 476; beauty of, **12**, 363.

Asters, **5**, 387, 412–415, **6**, 434, 463, **8**, 459; unidentified, **5**, 319, 406, 423, **6**, 447, 462, **7**, 7, 18; spots on an aster, **5**, 397; list of, in order of blooming, 397; fruit of the stars, 403, 404; unjustly despised, 408; an arrangement according to beauty, 413, 414; endurance of different species of, 473; ice-inclosed, **8**, 61, 62; commonest species Aug. 21, **9**, 12; lists of, in September, 51, 52, 89, 90; list of late September, 106; observed near Gloucester, **11**, 175, 176.

Astor Library, New York, **8**, 458 note.

Astrology, compared with astronomy, **4**, 470, 471.

Astronomer, mental blindness of the, **2**, 373.

Astronomy, course of the sun, **1**, 164; use of naked eye in, **2**, 294; compared with astrology, **4**, 470, 471; a fashionable study, **12**, 391.

Astyanax, **12**, 64.

"At midnight's hour I raised my head," verse, **1**, 407.

Atean, Joe, **5**, 424 and note, 425 note, 426.

Bear, white, **4**, 82.

Bear-berry (*Arctostaphylos Uva-Ursi* or *Arbutus Uva-Ursi*), **3**, 396, **4**, 54, **11**, 42, 43.

Beards, **6**, 97; **12**, 30.

Beatton, John, **9**, 133, 206; reminiscences of, **10**, 54; tomb of, 59; honesty of, 113.

Beauport (Quebec), **2**, 76.

Beauty, not far removed from ugliness, **1**, 119; composition of, 145; proportions of, 181; courage of votaries of, 308, 309; a utility, 449; perception of, a moral test, **4**, 126; pure forms of, compared to the picturesque, **6**, 55–59; appreciation of, disconnected from virtue, 58, 59; ornamental, 137; enjoyment of, **8**, 242; Winckelmann quoted on, **9**, 288; not to be far sought, **11**, 166; the garment of virtue, **12**, 367, 368.

Beaver, Montanus on, **6**, 136; William Wood on, **7**, 135; a victim to the fur trade, **12**, 121; described by Topsell, **13**, 152, 153.

Beaver-Hole Meadows, **12**, 269.

Beck, T. R., quoted, **8**, 466, **9**, 68.

Beck Stow's Swamp, **4**, 231.

Bed, Josh Piper's, **9**, 239; going to, **10**, 176.

Bedford, **1**, 91; the foreign land of, **2**, 6; inhabitants of, **3**, 3; bell of, **4**, 473.

Bedford (N. H.), **1**, 91.

Bee, mining, **13**, 287, 288.

Bee, tailor, **9**, 61.

Beech, beauties of, **3**, 94; verdure of, **5**, 173; fallen leaves of, 473, 474; leaf-buds of, **7**, 356; young, in autumn, **11**, 250; wood of, 250.

Beecher, Henry Ward, **11**, 438.

Bee-hunt, a, **4**, 368–373.

Bees, clover and, **2**, 272; importance of witch-hazel to, **3**, 60; working bees and maiden aunts, 71; a swarm of dead, 293, 294; bee-hunting, 296–299, **4**, 368–373; the squire's bee-chasing, **3**, 354, 355; on staminate flowers, 463; at work in spring, 465, 466; hum of, at sunrise, **4**, 257; flight of, after feeding, 371–373; voyages of, 374; incident of molasses, 404; finding the wax, **5**, 34; in the earliest flowers, 72; found with willow catkins, 81; in the skunk-cabbage, 96; carriers of pollen, 105; swarming, 209; a bee eating a flower, 361; attracted by the bass tree, **6**, 400, 404, 405; in the early flowers, **7**, 318; going in and out of a hole, 332; killing drones, **9**, 311; nest of, 469, 470; hum of, **10**, 346, 393; fond of ledum, **11**, 17; in high altitudes, 47, 48, 49 note; the first humming of, in the spring, **12**, 147, 148; droppings of, **13**, 202; sucking honey from the flowers, 278. *See also* Honey-bee.

Beetle, for woodchopping, **9**, 294.

Beetles, **5**, 33, **6**, 151, **7**, 292, **8**, 302, **9**, 348, **12**, 311, 312.

Beggar-ticks, **3**, 65, **5**, 448; as a symbol, **12**, 341.

"Behold, how, spring appearing," verse, **1**, 69.

Belcher-squelchers, **4**, 124.

Belief, **9**, 217.

Belknap, Jeremy, his History of New Hampshire quoted, **11**, 5, 58, 59.

Bell, Thomas, quoted, **10**, 437, 486, 487.

Bellew, F. A. T., **7**, 500.

Bellflower, clasping, **4**, 143.

Bellows, made from onion stems, **4**, 303.

Bellows Falls (Vt.), **9**, 74–76.

Bellows family, **9**, 77.

Bells, the Sabbath bell, **1**, 54, 55; a bright thought, 484; a bell heard on the horizon, **2**, 381; a factory bell, 485; vibratory hum of a bell, **3**, 68; the bell for evening meeting, 99; religion of, **4**, 443; melody of, **5**, 23; sound of, **7**, 307.

Bellwort, sessile-leaved, **7**, 18; a beautiful sight, **4**, 56.

Benignity, slimy, **5**, 264, 265.

Benjamin, William O., **6**, 71.

Bennet, Nehemiah, quoted, **7**, 474, 475, 484.

Bent, on cattle and salt, **14**, 9.

Benzo, his History of the West Indies, **5**, 27.

Bermudas, the, **5**, 21.

Berries, importance of, to children, **2**, 308; conditions of ripening of, **4**, 224; gem-like aspect of, 312; persistent in winter, 432; neglected fruit, **5**, 417; abundance of, **6**, 403; varieties of, 412; a profusion of, **8**, 444, 445; list of, the food of birds and mice, **13**, 158; of Mt.

time for seeing the larger, 444; granivorous, to some extent independent of the seasons, 459; migrations determined by food-supply, 459; notes vary with seasons, **4,** 31; impossible to imitate their notes with words, 31; list of, seen between April 28th and May 14th, 50, 51; color of young, 141; their hour for song, 182; which sing all summer, 190; songs of, in fog, 197, 198; their singing as affected by the weather, 245; summer silence of, 282; Frank Brown's collection of mounted, **5,** 78; the best authority on, 110; in the rain, 110; song of, the keynote of poetry, 144; exterminated by cutting down woods, 169; significance of meeting with a rare bird, 247; materials used for nests of, 276; young, suffering from heat, 290; August, 389; their nests similar to those of squirrels and mice, 480; wearing dress of Nature, 489; wintry notes of, **6,** 10; of the winter of 1853–54, 145, 146; inquisitiveness of, 204, **9,** 125; common April 21st, **6,** 211; early, seek early trees, 217; colors of small, lost by distance, 223; common about May 13th, 263; songs less loud in summer, 354; summaries of observations regarding, 389, 390, 413, 435, 436, 457; songs of, in August, 430, 440, 458; list of, seen in autumn, **7,** 30, 31; Masséna collection of, 74 and note; unidentified tracks of, on snow, 127; reason for entering yards in storms, 176; snow useful to, in finding weeds, 197; nests of, broken up, 252; effect of clouds on song of, 311; roosting-places of, 318, 319; on a cold and windy day, 336; stillness of, at noon, 353; digestion of birds of prey, 376; afraid of man, 510; as entomologists, **8,** 116; the return of the, 263; after storm, 333; agency of, in dispersing seeds, 335, 411; and the human ear, **9,** 274, 275; evening song of, 389; observed in Maine woods, 497; changing appearance of a flock in the air, **10,** 28; associations wakened by notes of, 304; distinguished with difficulty when flying, 338; keeping cool in hot weather, 423; in the White

Mountains, **11,** 34, 51; list of those heard in August, 1858, 104; the way to listen to, **12,** 21; protection of, 124, 125; singing to men, 144; berry-eating, 309, 310; influence of air-currents on flight of, 442, 443; their agency in preserving the equilibrium of nature, **13,** 295, 296; "matinade" of, 358; discriminators of fruits, **14,** 8; of Mt. Monadnock, 32–34, 67.

Birds, unidentified, **3,** 434, **4,** 328, 388, **5,** 51, 99, 146, 175, 246, 426, 458, 459, 468, 470, **6,** 28, 197, 198, 312, 313, 321, 343, 363, 369, 372, 459, 488, **7,** 62, 77, 94, 189, 190, 243, 329, 359, 360, 371, 379, 380, 382, 392, 397, 399, 457, 458, **8,** 342, 355, **9,** 8, 92, 183, **10,** 330, 331, 395, 396, 408, 421, 423, **11,** 34, 35, 44, 45, 64, 117, 118, **177, 12,** 108, 190.

Birds' eggs, gems, **4,** 268, 269; an addled egg, **8,** 10, 11; mortality of, **14,** 167, 168.

Birds' nests, adaptation of material used in, **3,** 102; unidentified, **7,** 390, 442, **8,** 10, 23, 73, 74, 89, 90, 108, 109, 113, 114, 359, **11,** 140, **12,** 17, 18, 237, **13,** 40; the time to study, **8,** 73; linings of, 368.

Bittern, American, or stake-driver (*Ardea minor*), **1,** 138, 141, **3,** 5, 46, 54, 69, 76, 4, 28, 233, 234, **5,** 367, **8,** 350, **10,** 60, 498, **11,** 68, 148, 446, **12,** 266; pumping of, **2,** 255, **4,** 107, 123, 124, **5,** 152, 193, **9,** 421, **13,** 331, 332; flight of, **2,** 304, **7,** 380, **11,** 139; homeward plodding of, **4,** 334; standing like a stake, 334; in hiding, **7,** 456; protective coloring of, 453, **13,** 250, 251; eggs of, **10,** 444; nest of, **11,** 134; different names for, 251; croak of, **12,** 248, 249, **13,** 346; a dead, **14,** 110; contents of stomach of, 133, 337.

Bittern, green, or green heron, **8,** 435, **14,** 61; notes of, **6,** 377; the bird of the Musketicook, **8,** 440.

Bittern, least (*Ardea exilis*); **13,** 421.

Bitternuts, **4,** 361.

Bitter-sweet, berries of, **4,** 308.

Black Horse Church, **6,** 94.

Blackberries, **8,** 419; price of, 436.

Blackberry, varieties of, **8,** 460. *See also* Rubus.

Blackberry, high, **5,** 366, 377, **11,** 139; superiority of, **4,** 316; leaf of,

Boon, killed by Indians, **2**, 458.

Boon's Pond, walk to, **2**, 452–458.

Boots, **5**, 51, 52; varieties of, used by T., **6**, 115; suggestive of walks, **9**, 150; purchase of, 156; heels on women's, **13**, 52, 53. *See also* Shoes.

Boston, dealings of, with slavery question, **2**, 175.

Boston Academy's Reports for 1785, **14**, 224.

Boston Court-House, attack on, **6**, 328.

Boston Harbor, islands in, **2**, 344, 345; frozen over, **9**, 226, 232.

"Boston Herald," **2**, 179, 181, 182.

"Boston Journal," **2**, 179, 181, **14**, 313.

"Boston Times," **2**, 179, 181, 182.

Botanies, the prose of flowers, **3**, 257.

Botanists, the early and the modern, **14**, 92.

Botany, worth of, **2**, 409; early history of, **3**, 118; advice for reading, 308, 309; scientific terms easily learned, 347; poor descriptions of species in, **5**, 188, 189; study of, **9**, 156–158.

Botany-box, made of hat, **4**, 133.

Botrychium lunarioides, **9**, 124, 125.

Botta, Paul Émile, quoted, **1**, 343.

Bougainville, Louis Antoine de, quoted, **2**, 246.

Boutwell, Mr., of Groton, **14**, 86.

Boutwell, Gov. George S., and the Sims case, **2**, 174; as a lecturer, **3**, 190.

Bowels, **3**, 165; and brains, **5**, 264, 265; and stars, **13**, 22.

Bowers, Matthias, **9**, 356.

Box, life in a, **3**, 240, 241.

Boxboro, churchgoing habit of, **4**, 467; Inches Woods in, **14**, 224–231, 241–249, 304; history of, 275.

Boys, a boy asks about "old-agers," **1**, 413; a little Irish boy, **2**, 117, 118, **3**, 149, 150, 241–244; smoking cigars, **2**, 341; four little Irish boys and a horse, **9**, 98; the boy and the bound, **10**, 172, 173, 177.

Bradford, George P., **2**, 365, **5**, 316, **8**, 461, **10**, 14, **11**, 18, **13**, 428.

Bradford, William, his "History of the Plymouth Plantation" quoted, **9**, 164, 169, 170, 177.

Bradley, Joseph, **3**, 284.

Bradshaw, of Wayland, ornithological collection of, **13**, 419–421.

Brady, Miss Kate, **7**, 467, 468, **9**, 335, 336.

Brady house, the, **7**, 467, 468.

Brahma, **2**, 4.

Brahmans, in early times, **2**, 32.

Brain, size of, at birth, **4**, 349.

Brakes, root of, **5**, 506, 507; autumnal decay of, **6**, 437; fallen in ranks, **11**, 207.

Brand, John, his "Popular Antiquities," **13**, 159, 240.

Brant, **7**, 25, **8**, 31, **14**, 167.

Brash, grating noise of, **10**, 304.

Brasenia peltata, **4**, 168.

Brassica, **14**, 55, 75, 158.

Brattleboro (Vt.), T.'s visit to, **9**, 61–74.

Bravery, **1**, 96–99, 164; qualities of, 172; of facing one's own deeds, 285.

Bread, art of making, **1**, 430, 431.

Bream, **1**, 475, **12**, 83; as food, **4**, 82; nests of, **4**, 149, 165, 171, 212, **5**, 261, **8**, 376, **9**, 460, **10**, 486, **12**, 261, 262, **13**, 323, 324; schools of, **4**, 261; young, **5**, 252, **9**, 460; an aboriginal fish, **5**, 314; food of, 325; effect of drought on, **6**, 481; over nest, **8**, 376; building a nest, **13**, 323, 324.

Bream, striped, **11**, 346–350, 358–360, 363, 364, **13**, 273.

Breathing, importance of proper, **2**, 251.

Breed's location, **1**, 420; tragedies of, 424.

Breeze, undertone of, **8**, 309.

"Breeze's Invitation, The," verse, **1**, 86.

Brewer, Thomas M., quoted, **7**, 399, **8**, 387, **10**, 449, 456, **11**, 167, 397, 398, **13**, 422.

Brewster (Mass.), **9**, 435, 436.

Brewster, Sir David, his Life of Newton, **8**, 362.

Bricks, old, **2**, 7, **9**, 259, 260.

Bridge, aspect of traveller on, **4**, 152.

Brigham, the wheelwright, **4**, 166.

Briney, talk with, **10**, 220, 221.

Brister, Sippio, **1**, 420; grave of **2**, 20.

Brister's Hill, **1**, 420.

"British Reptiles," quoted, **10**, 486, 487.

British soldiers, killed April 19, 1775, **2**, 19.

Cato the Elder, his ":De Re Rustica" quoted, 2, 442, 444, 445, 450, 3, 61, 6, 68, 69, 71–73, 106, 107.

Cat-tail (*Typha latifolia*), 3, 226, 7, 435, 8, 80, 10, 6; down of, 5, 43, 44; pollen of, 6, 369, 370; remarkably tall, 12, 267, 273.

Cattle, excited by grubs, 4, 72, 73; familiarity of, with man, 102; neat aspect of, 134; their alertness to perceive a step, 137; good behavior of, 189; endurance of young, 5, 527; swimming, 9, 418; sportiveness in, 10, 193; song of the dying bullock, 12, 301. *See also* Cows.

Cedar, red, northern limit of, 2, 200; apples of, 5, 173; berries of, 173, 530; buds of, 482; fragrance of, 6, 221; pollen of, 7, 332; forms of leaves of, 13, 311.

Cedar, white, 2, 200 ; large trees, 5, 502, 503; a dense growth of, 7, 90; pollen of, 332 ; a railroad sleeper of, 14, 256, 257.

Cedar of Lebanon, 2, 200.

Celandine, 7, 267.

Celastrus, 10, 281.

Celestial phenomena, undue importance attached to, 12, 390, 391.

Cellini, Benvenuto, 2, 494, 495.

Celtis occidentalis, 5, 170, 9, 383; berries of, 8, 423.

Cerastium, 8, 352, 353, 360, 366, 367.

Cereus, night-blooming, 8, 378, 379.

Chaldæans, 2, 35, 4, 469, 470.

Chalmers, Rev. Thomas, D.D., 3, 173; Life of, 5, 58.

Chamberlain Lake (Me.), 9, 494.

Chamberlin, Mr., of Brattleboro, Vt., 9, 73.

Chamberlin, Mr., of Worcester, 2, 225.

"Chambers's Journal," quoted, 12, 377, 378.

Channing, William Ellery, the younger, 3, 97, 98, 6, 16, 7, 214, 237, 263, 319, 333, 395, 411, 414, 417–421, 434, 454, 9, 343, 10, 9, 26, 30, 323, 327, 336, 337, 11, 32 note, 108, 283, 356, 393, 12, 9, 39, 71, 86, 109, 152, 153, 167, 169, 184, 187, 394, 402, 441, 449, 13, 14, 95, 165, 167, 175, 177, 183, 197, 201, 285, 294, 306, 337, 357, 14, 87 note, 95, 98, 294, 320, 324, 325, 334; acquires the boat built by T., 1, 136 note; quota-

tion from his "Walden Spring," 2, 156; a moonlight walk with, 297; to Boon's Pond with, 452; trip to Pelham's Pond with, 3, 72; quoted by Emerson, 85; to Long Pond with, 92; in bantering mood, 96; his notebook, 98, 99; his method of learning, 108; a good discipline for, 118; to Saw Mill Brook with, 160, 161; on the study of lichens, 184; his respect for McKean, 197; a remark on dogs and pups, 225; as a lecturer, 249, 250; on Conantum with, 356; fame of, 399; "riparial" excursions of, 418; watching wild geese with, 434, 435; a walk in a storm with, 440–446; scene of his ":Woodman," 464; on arches, 4, 152; on the sky, 192; on dogs, 294; to Billerica with, 419; on "angle of incidents," 421; to Second Division Brook with, 5, 84; to Bedford with, 99; to Nobscot with, 178; accused of boorish behavior, 189, 190; a sail to Carlisle Bridge with, 201; the "Hogepen" walk with, 238; meeting with a "lurker" in the woods, 247, 248; to Sudbury meadows with, 317; to Sudbury with, 379; a sail with. 436; to Fair Haven Hill with, 490; a moonlight sail with, 503–505; his visit to Rome, 6, 61, 62; incident of cat and poker, 75; on idealistic vision, 129; his remark to Minott on death, 152; on the stars, 7, 22; looking like a bandit, 23; a sail to Ball's Hill with, 70; up bank of Assabet with, 82; as a skater, 87; to Pantry Brook with, 99; out in the snow with, 117; his tracks in snow, 125; collecting specimens of lichens, 187; chasing a squirrel, 398; to Cape Cod with, 431; to Tarbell Hill with, 451; visits old Hunt house, 457; to Conantum with, 458; supper with, 460; visits circus, 461; collecting old rails, 486; to Tarbell Swamp Hill with, 8, 406; on the partridge's drumming, 9, 347; to Owl-Nest Swamp with, 10, 17; round Walden with, 35; tells of an amusing advertisement, 174; to Grackle Swamp with, 308; to Clematis Brook with, 309, 312, 315; at Clamshell with, 11, 64; his ideas for names of places, 103; on country life, 120; on the meadow-hen,

minders of the north, 138; notes of, 345, 350, 468, **4,** 17, 22, 41, 204, 386, **5,** 38, 76, 97, **7,** 66, 262, 275, **8,** 28, 53, 196, 264, **9,** 119, **10,** 171, 242, 316, **12,** 386, **13,** 87; inquisitiveness of, **4,** 396, 482, **6,** 3; sociability of, 86, 110, 122; on a sumach, **8,** 153, 154; on nest, 364; nest and eggs of, 364; scraping acquaintance, **9,** 119; winter habits of, 152; good cheer of, **11,** 290; at home in the snow, 320; antics of a, 380, 381; companion to a nuthatch, 391; a wood-bird, **12,** 453; roosting-place of, in a birch, **13,** 20; and pine seed, 95; and hemlock seed, 97.

Chickweed (*Stellaria media*), **3,** 469, **4,** 487, **5,** 32, 33, 36, 367.

Child, the, **1,** 213; playing with natural forces, **10,** 170.

Child, Mr., of Concord, **2,** 19.

Childhood, dreams of, **1,** 217.

Children, **1,** 94; of the poor, **2,** 117; senses of, 291; importance of berries to, 308; city-bred, 342; an innocent child, **3,** 150; observant, 364; their love of noise, **4,** 85, 86; reminders of God, **12,** 171; obedience in, 298, 299; precocious, **14,** 217.

Chiloe, surf on coast of, **2,** 261.

Chimaphila. *See* Wintergreen, umbelled.

Chimneys, old stone, **8,** 388; an old chimney with an inscription, **9,** 256–261.

China, hospitality in, **4,** 15.

Chinese, use of magnet by, **2,** 168; a Chinese funeral, **3,** 194.

Chinese inscriptions, **4,** 205.

Chinese novel, a, **11,** 65, 66, 81.

Chinquapin, catkins of. **6,** 278.

Chiogenes hispidula. **4,** 302, **11,** 43.

Chiogenes tea, **11,** 31.

Chip-bird. *See* Sparrow, chipping.

Chipmunk. *See* Squirrel, striped.

Chivin, **8,** 359.

Choke-berry (*Pyrus arbutifolia*), buds of, **4,** 71, **7,** 332; berries of, **4,** 281, 329, 330, **9,** 51, **11,** 97.

Choke-cherries, **5,** 345, 387, **8,** 446.

Choke-cherry, **6,** 290.

Cholmondeley, Thomas, presents T. with Indian books, **8,** 36; visits T., **11,** 402 and note.

Christ, the world's attitude toward, **3,** 119; supposititious appearance of,

in modern times, **12,** 407; discussion regarding foresight of, **14,** 291, 292.

Christian, the modern, **12,** 419.

Christianity, the laws of, **3,** 263; respectable, **11,** 357; not a matter of education, **13,** 15.

Christians, compared with Mahometans, **3,** 20, 21.

Chrysosplenium, **10,** 32 and note.

Chub, **2,** 16.

Church, the, *versus* out-of-doors, **1,** 53; a hospital, 309; and slavery, **2,** 178; a rotten institution, 400; police power of, **3,** 120; funerals and, 102; the dust of truth in, 335; undermining of, **9,** 188; the "true," **10,** 233; a baby-house, **11,** 324; hypocrisy and timidity of, 324, 325; excommunicating Christ, **12,** 404.

Churchgoing, **4,** 467.

Cicada, Anacreon's ode to the, **1,** 66. *See also* Harvest-fly.

Cicuta bulbifera, **5,** 338.

Cicuta maculata, **5,** 346, **10,** 18, **12,** 364.

Cider-drinker, a, **4,** 463.

Cinnamon stone, **6,** 48.

Cinquefoil, common, **5,** 154, 229, **10,** 415.

Cinquefoil, Norway, **2,** 430, 431.

Cinquefoil, silvery, **4,** 80, **5,** 157, **9,** 18.

Cinquefoil, three-toothed, **10,** 457, **11,** 18.

Circæa, **8,** 406.

Circæa alpina, **4,** 196, 219, **8,** 466.

Circulation, in plants, **2,** 121, 122.

Circumstances, **1,** 77.

Cirsium horridulum, **5,** 346.

Cirsium lanceolatum, **8,** 443.

Cirsium muticum, **4,** 355.

Cistuda Blandingii. See Tortoise, Blanding's.

Cistus, *or* frostweed, **4,** 88, 90, 110, **5,** 200, **7,** 518; frost-crystals on, **4,** 428, **5,** 483, 484; untouched by cows, **4,** 429; effect of frost on, **7,** 518, **8,** 10, **11,** 316, 317.

Cities, compared to swamps, **2,** 47; a city built on the site of a more ancient city, **6,** 15; maritime, 25, 26.

Citizen, of the world, **1,** 350, 351.

City, the, not now a ninth-day town, **6,** 111, 112.

Civilization, among brutes, **1,** 396; progress of, **3,** 321, 322; and architecture, **4**, 153; its effect on fish, **9**, 327; levelling tendency of, **11**, 78; its effect on the forests, **14**, 229; the division of labor entailed by, 295.

Cladonia. *See* Lichen, cladonia, *and* Lichen, reindeer.

Clam, fresh-water, **4**, 178, 215, **5**, 46, 376, **6**, 383, 406, **7**, 68, 214, 215, 295, 488, **8**, 258, **12**, 274; furrows made by, **4**, 213, **6**, 461, **7**, 466; moving, **4**, 213, **5**, 495; rising to shore, **6**, 327; description of a new kind of, 459; moving into deep water, **7**, 463; eels said to "gender" into, **10**, 399, 429; as a food, **11**, 375; moving toward middle of river, **13**, 270, 271.

Clams, **2**, 355–359; their method of taking food, **4**, 178; various species of, **7**, 436; fed to pigs, 439; the "worm" in, **10**, 247.

Clamshell field, the, **2**, 292.

Clamshells, fresh-water, **6**, 7, 8, **7**, 7, 471, **8**, 21; colors of, **4**, 58, **6**, 7, 8, **7**, 352, **8**, 297, 343; heaps of, **7**, 447; floating, **12**, 283.

Clarionet, **10**, 296, 297.

Clark, Alvan, **6**, 167.

Clark, Brooks, **10**, 109, 110, 167.

Clark, D., **7**, 224.

Clark, D. B., **12**, 200.

Clark's Island, visits to, **2**, 349–363, **9**, 415–419.

Claudian, **1**, 260.

Clay, used for mortar, **9**, 259, 263, 276.

Cleanliness, **3**, 246.

Clematis, *or* virgin's-bower, feathery fruit of, **2**, 446, **5**, 395, **11**, 292, 293.

Clematis Brook, **2**, 411.

Clematis Pond, **4**, 208.

Clergy, the, **1**, 240.

Clergymen, limitations of, **9**, 283, 284.

Clethra alnifolia, season of, **4**, 268, **9**, 9, **13**, 44.

"Cliffs," verse, **1**, 51.

Climate, **6**, 130; our adaptation to our, **9**, 343.

Clinton, mills at, **2**, 134–136.

Clintonia borealis, **4**, 95, **5**, 218, 219, 222, 329, 354, **9**, 29, **10**, 148.

Clock, Minott's old, **10**, 54, 59.

Clothes, old, **1**, 418, 419.

Clothing, convention regarding, **4**, 225.

Clouds, in June, **1**, 142; grandeur of, 171; suggesting lines of Milton, 183; art-galleries in the, **2**, 258;

a melon-rind arrangement of, 473, 474, **3**, 148, 312, **8**, 117, **13**, 23; uniformity in shapes of, **2**, 297; at and after sunset, 378; their war with the moon, 383, 384; the forces of the west, 484; making a heaven below, **3**, 66; crimson, 155, 156; a cloud like fire, 176, 177; spun from rainbows, 178; scenery in the, 181; mother-o'-pearl, 186; mountains, 189; texture of, 202; a new disposition of, 235; need of, in the sky, 272; prows of vessels in, **3**, 333, 334; shadows and motion of, 387; a battalion of, 389; a trembling in sky caused by, 468; drama of moon and, **4**, 78; description of, 106; thunder-clouds likened to fireflies, 129; philosophy of, 138, 139; make sport of the moon, 145; reflections from, 223; in afterglow, 240; at sunset, 248–250; drifting and downy, **5**, 145; attendant on sun at rising, 258; in the mind, 305; a celestial Sahara, 306; transiency of, 498, 499; fleecy, 520; a thunder-cloud, **7**, 16, 17; at sunset at Clamshell Reach, 57; mackerel sky, 125, **11**, 410, 411; lining of, **7**, 231; over the water, 307; shadows of, 404, **10**, 474, 475; sketch of, **9**, 338; a storm-cloud, 385–387; measuring distance of, **10**, 264; thunder-clouds likened to a flower, 414; 415; above the, **11**, 30; scenes on earth corresponding to, 295; snow from a single cloud, 354; summer and winter, compared, **12**, 146, **13**, 109; thunder-cloud likened to a steamer, **12**, 306; biography of a cloud, 307; bows and arrows in, **13**, 61, 62; in long bars, 94; asbestoslike wisps, 109, 110; ripple-marks, 110; web-like, 160, 161; like roundtopped hills, 271; seen from Mt. Monadnock, **14**, 46–48.

Clover, rabbit's, **12**, 303.

Clover, red, **2**, 269, 286; a field of, **5**, 255.

Clover, white, **2**, 271, 272, **8**, 311.

Club-moss. *See* Lycopodium.

Coal, in Pennsylvania, **2**, 463.

Coal-pit, an old, **2**, 95.

Coarseness, inexcusability of, **1**, 299.

Coat, T.'s new, **6**, 69, 70; of a drowned man, **9**, 442.

Coats-of-arms, proposed, **2**, 345, 433.

weather, 512, 513; a humbler rain, 515; beauty of, **13**, 290; after sunset, 401; on Mt. Monadnock, **14**, 48, 49.

Dewdrop, the wonders of a, **10**, 239, 240.

Dew-grass, **14**, 76, 77.

Dharma Sacontala, **2**, 193.

Dherma Sástra, **1**, 267.

Diana, **4**, 472; apostrophe to, **2**, 78.

Diapensia Lapponica, **11**, 17, 18.

Dickens, Charles, **2**, 482.

Dictionaries, **10**, 290.

Diervilla, **6**, 408.

Diet, its relation to employment, **6**, 20, 21. *See also* Food.

"Dildees," **12**, 149.

Dill, **12**, 341.

Diogenes, **3**, 196.

Dioscorides, **3**, 118, 281.

Dipper, the theft of a, **3**, 198.

Dipper (bird), **7**, 37, 491, **10**, 140, 208, 209, 225, 322, 323, 503, **11**, 153, 187; following tame ducks, **14**, 96, 97; the time to shoot one, 103. *See also* Grebe.

Dirca palustris, **9**, 67, 68.

Dirt, defined, **3**, 246.

Disappointment, **1**, 75.

Discovery, the joy of, **4**, 292; its effect on observation, **9**, 232; mental attitude requisite for, 466.

Disease, cannot coexist with a raindrop, **1**, 95; rupture with nature, 234; the rule, not the exception, **2**, 440, 449; often beautiful, **4**, 91; diseased organisms in nature, **5**, 21; analogy with sap of trees, **7**, 239; prevalence of, among men, **8**, 56; in the spring, 269; in flowerbuds, 423. *See also* Sickness.

Dish-washing, **10**, 56.

Distance, charm of, **4**, 346, 347.

Distribution, law of, **12**, 155.

Ditches, flowering of the, **9**, 82.

Diversion, different from amusement, **1**, 225.

Divine service, **1**, 53.

Divinity, in men, **1**, 185.

"Doab," meaning of word, **14**, 296, 297.

Dock, common, in New Zealand, **2**, 263.

Dock, yellow, **2**, 292.

Doctor, village, **9**, 163.

Dodge, Luke, **8**, 323.

Dodge's Brook, **5**, 206, 207.

Dogs, barking of, **1**, 227, **10**, 226, **227**, 252, 253; hunting moose, **2**, 113; a dog following a wagon, 275; effect of darkness on, 371; worrying cows, 397, 398; a dog returning to his vomit, **3**, 74; on a river voyage, 75; and pups, 225; without masters, 294; a dog snapping at waves, 383; the "lawing" of, 419; distribution of white on tails of, **4**, 401; among Indians, 491; a dog barking at a stump, **5**, 20, 21; a dog following a boat, 262; a dog killed by an otter, 353; a mad dog in town, 522; the story of a mad dog, 522-525; a dog running on ice, **7**, 88; a dog drowned by a fox, 154, **11**, 387; a dog catching ducks, **7**, 353; hunting at night, **8**, 138; stealing pork, **9**, 180; Wheeler's terrier, 198; Esquimau, 299; Ricketson's "Ranger," 320; Baker's Lion, squirrel chasing, 356; the civilization of the dog, **10**, 252, 253; how to anger a dog, 342; and carrion, 499; tracks of, in snow, **11**, 321, 322, 353, 354; T.'s grandmother's dog, **14**, 325, 326; an instance of a dog's sense of decency, 339; a meeting between a spaniel and a fox, 339, 340.

Dog's-bane, **2**, 313, **4**, 116, **5**, 308, **9**, 5; pod of, **8**, 306.

Dogwood, autumn foliage of, **4**, 360, 361, 367. *See also* Cornel, *Cornus florida, and* Sumach, poison.

Donati, Vitaliano, **3**, 122.

"Dong, sounds the brass in the east," verse, **1**, 259.

Donne, Dr. John, **1**, 467; quoted, **2**, 150.

Doolittle, A., pictures by, **9**, 502.

D'Orbigny, Alcide, **2**, 242.

D'Orsay, Count, **6**, 70.

Dor-bug, **4**, 12, 100, **5**, 195, **7**, 213, **13**, 340.

Dorr, Capt. E. P., of Buffalo, **9**, 290.

Double consciousness, **4**, 291.

Doubt, handmaid of faith, **1**, 346.

Douglas, Gavin, **1**, 294.

Dove, Professor, **3**, 278.

Dove, ring, cooing of, **10**, 226, 227.

Dove, turtle, **4**, 68, **5**, 85, **6**, 18, **8**, 329; flight of, **4**, 62; attitudes of, 365; nest of, **8**, 377, **10**, 444.

Doves, domestic, trodden upon by oxen, **4**, 283; noise of, alighting on a roof, **7**, 317.

Floods, **1**, 121, **3**, 447, **6**, 239–241, 243, 244, 246–248; the wreck of the river, **5**, 485, 486; mechanical force of, **6**, 160; dangers and inconveniences of, in Concord, **7**, 195; as preservers of meadow land, **9**, 19, 20; high-water record of, 152.

Flowers, the true lore of, **3**, 252, 253; as seen by child and by botanist, 279; want of popular account of, 281; unexpected appearance of, in spring, 473, 476, 477; lists of, 474, 475, **4**, 49, 50, 257, 258, 414, 415, **6**, 229, 230, **12**, 132, 133, 305; expression of character by, **4**, 92; express the beautiful and the ugly, 96, 149; made to be seen, 99; the ideal flower, 104; showy, and odorless, like many mortals, 126; one for every mood of man, 142; suggestive value of names for, 154; pursuit of, and pursuit of thought, 289; necessity of, to bees, 374; never idle, **5**, 98; female, colors of, 103; a method of searching for, 139; out in advance of the rest of their kind, 170; the colors of the sunlight, 185; white, at night, 277; emblematical of purity, 283; and the scythe, 339; of August and September, character of, 355; few perfect specimens of, 361; widely dispersed, 410; preparing for spring, 475; prevalence of yellow in late summer, **6**, 433; colors of, on cloudy days, **7**, 34; the earliest, 295, **8**, 240, **9**, 283; their dependence on the season, **8**, 241; fertile and barren, **9**, 361; effect of man's life on, **12**, 343. *See also* Plants.

Flume, the, in Franconia Notch, **1**, 91, **4**, 303.

"Flusterer," **8**, 308.

Flute, sound of, on the river, **1**, 271, 272; echo of, 375; a beautiful communication, **2**, 12; fit sound at evening, **4**, 108; foreign to trading world, 144.

Flycatcher, olive-sided, *or* pe-pe (*Muscicapa Cooperi*), **7**, 379, 415, 416, **8**, 370, **9**, 408, **13**, 313; notes of, 8, 353, 365.

Foam, in a brook, **3**, 300; on a pond-shore, **14**, 62, 63.

Foes, not dangerous, **1**, 213.

Fog, the season of morning fogs, **2**, 333; ambrosial, 334; the fairest days born in a, 334; the dreams of the meadow, **3**, 40; bird-songs in, **4**, 197, 198; touchstone of health, 198; battalions of, 254; cows in, 254; topography established by, 255; a sea of, 255; levelling effects of, 256, 257; at the end of May, **5**, 209; on Wachusett, 216, 217; a peculiar, 233, 234; an ocean of, **6**, 361; sounds in, **7**, 187; composition of, **8**, 247, 248; on the Cape, **9**, 448, 449; deceptiveness of, 455; in the White Mountains, **11**, 21–23; crystallizing, 398, 399; origin of, **12**, 39; phenomenon of, over water, **13**, 65; a local, 349; seen from Mt. Monadnock, **14**, 23, 24; the geography of, 23, 24.

"Fog," verse, **1**, 457.

Fogg, landlord at Moosehead Lake, **9**, 489.

Folger, Peter, **7**, 97.

Foliage, reflections from, **4**, 151; appearance of, in August, **6**, 448; effect of drought on coloring of, 478; transparent, **7**, 372. *See also* Leaves.

Food, nature's bill of fare, **12**, 398. *See also* Diet.

Fools, singing of, **1**, 237.

Foot, track of a bare human foot in the dust, **2**, 328.

Footpaths, the charm of, **2**, 455, 456.

Foreigner, tracks of, **7**, 202.

Forest, the cathedral of the, **11**, 353; origin of the word, 386.

Forest trees, investigations of the succession of, **8**, 315, 335, 363, **10**, 40, 41, **14**, 70–73, 104. *See also* Woodlots.

Forester, Frank, quoted, **7**, 440, **9**, 300, 301.

Forestry, in England and in New England, **14**, 71.

"Forever in my dream and in my morning thought," verse, **10**, 144.

Forget-me-not, mouse-ear, beauty of, **4**, 91.

Formalist, a, **2**, 465.

Fort Independence, **2**, 81.

Fortifications, air of antiquity of, **2**, 399; a bungling contrivance, 400.

Forts, at Hull, **2**, 344.

Forum, the Roman, **1**, 84.

Foss, A. D., **5**, 263–265.

Foster, Rev. Daniel, prays at the wharf at the time of the rendition of Sims, **2**, 176; Dr. B. and R. Rice

Gods, the, favors of, **1**, 365; communications from, **8**, 269.

Goffstown (N. H.), **14**, 39.

Gold, the true value of, **3**, 291; the false and the true, **7**, 491, 492, 496; the value attached to, **14**, 117–119.

Gold-diggers, **3**, 329, 330, **7**, 491; the finder of the great Australian nugget, 500, 501.

Gold-diggings, the Australian, **7**, 491.

Golden-eye, *or* whistler, **6**, 183, **7**, 314–316, **12**, 71.

Goldenrod, **2**, 103, 104, **5**, 340, **7**, 48; preaches of the lapse of time, **4**, 225; list of, in order of blooming, **5**, 396, 397; fruit of the sun, 403, 404; unidentified species of, 420, 422; radical leaves of, in May, **6**, 258; status of various species, Sept. 24th, **9**, 89; status of various species, Oct. 8th, 106; tenderness of, **12**, 209; heads of, in winter, 442; of Mt. Monadnock, **14**, 31.

Goldenrod, blue-stemmed, **4**, 361, 401, **11**, 307; fungus spots on, **14**, 93.

Goldenrod, early (*Solidago stricta*), **5**, 363, **9**, 35.

Goldenrod, gray, in October, **5**, 484; fuzz of, **6**, 51.

Goldenrod, seaside, **9**, 135.

Goldenrod, sweet-scented (*S. odora*), **2**, 220, **5**, 361, 362, 403.

Goldenrod, tall rough, in winter, **8**, 73.

Goldenrod, white, **4**, 401.

Goldenrod (*S. arguta*), **5**, 362, **6**, 445, **9**, 65.

Goldenrod (*S. nemoralis*), **5**, 391, 408, 455, **11**, 306, **12**, 321.

Goldenrod (*S. puberula*), **5**, 398, **12**, 363.

Goldenrod (*S. rigida*), **10**, 30, 31.

Goldfinch, **2**, 350, **4**, 251, **6**, 236, 440, **7**, 224, 292, **8**, 342, 424, **9**, 31, 10, 99, **11**, 374, **12**, 80, 145; on grass stems, **3**, 29, 30; notes of, **4**, 278, **5**, 150, 357, 365, **6**, 430, **8**, 458, **10**, 377, 378, **11**, 93, 374, **12**, 266; in the White Mountains, **11**, 7; nest of, 85, 86, 88, 89; flight of, 103; feeding in the snow, 395; a "lettuce-bird," **12**, 446; food of, **13**, 79 and note.

Gold-thread, **4**, 57, **9**, 78.

Goodman's Hill, view from; **2**, 26, 27.

Goodness, **1**, 119; as an investment, **5**, 293.

Goodnow & How, store of, **6**, 94.

Goodwin, John, **5**, 444, 447, 507, **6**, 163, **8**, 168, 197, 307, **9**, 170, 199, **10**, 384, **11**, 309; hunting propensities of, **6**, 233, 240; back from Cape Cod, **7**, 43; shooting muskrats, 131, 132, **8**, 256–259, **10**, 140; out shooting, **8**, 38; on rabbits, 78; tells a fish story, 115, 116; and a partridge, **9**, 272; fishing, **11**, 109; the one-eyed Ajax, 283, 284; guessing ages with, 289; tells of a suicide, 294; cheeriness of, 351; talks of Therien's tea-drinking, **12**, 455.

Goodyera pubescens. See Rattle-snake-plantain.

Goosander, a male found dead, **7**, 287, 288; description of, 288–290; skinning and stuffing the bird, 291, 292, 295; a pair, 291, 329; like a paddlewheel steamer, **12**, 77. *See also* Sheldrake.

Goose, wild, **1**, 130, **3**, 436, 439, **5**, 53, 511, 518, **7**, 71, 72, 299, 322, **8**, 31, **10**, 169, 170, 376, 377, **11**, 242; honking of, **1**, 401, 402, 422, **7**, 258; at Walden, **3**, 360; the spring and autumn flocks of, 418; watching a flock of, 434, 435; swept north on storms, **4**, 19; William Wood on, **7**, 136; three harrows uniting, **8**, 22; flying over cities, 46; large flocks of, **9**, 447; the air full of geese, **10**, 216, 217; Minott and the box of wild geese, 265; caring for their wounded, 378; Channing's description of a flock, **12**, 80; on the meadow, 94; flocks in flight, 94, 95; migration of, 99; experienced in gunning matters, 99.

Goose Pond, **2**, 87.

Goosefoot, **7**, 443.

Gordon, Mr., of Concord, his boundary dispute, **10**, 172, 173, 176, 177.

Goshawk, American, **5**, 114, **6**, 184.

Gosnold, Bartholomew, **3**, 373.

Gossamer (spider's web), **3**, 87, **9**, 128, 268, 269, 271, **10**, 327, **11**, 311, 322, **13**, 197, 198.

Gosse, Philip Henry, his "Letters from Alabama," quoted, **14**, 311.

Gould, John, **5**, 110.

Government, the best, **2**, 412, 413; functions of, **6**, 355–358.

Hemlocks, the Leaning, **5,** 388.

Hemp, Indian. *See Apocynum cannabinum.*

Henbane, as a symbol, **12,** 341.

Hen-harrier. *See* Hawk, marsh.

Hen-hawk, **3,** 426, 427, **7,** 455, **8,** 436, **11,** 313, **13,** 194, 195, 426; hunting, **2,** 480; guarding nest, **5,** 341; caught in a trap, **7,** 27; on perch, 285; preying on a cat, 353; shot by Minott, **9,** 122; scream of, **10,** 135, 296; flight of, 135, **12,** 74, **13,** 255, **14,** 61; indifferent to crows, **10,** 398; a young one shot by Garfield, **11,** 302, 303; lament for the death of a, 304–306; a remarkable feat of, 398; friend of the pine, 450; wildness of, 450; pursued by crows, **13,** 291.

Hens, ennui of, **1,** 350; domesticity of, **2,** 302; stealing nest, 309; object of, in following cows, 319; companions for men, **3,** 192; ducks hatched by, **4,** 197; legs of, 197; track of, **7,** 212; feeding by the river, 282; their love of an early salad, 319; a crazy hen, **9,** 239; a hen eating a mouse, 419; drawling note of, **10,** 298.

Heraclius, **2,** 189.

Herbert, Mr., on the humming of the snipe, **4,** 495.

Herbert, Edward, Lord, **14,** 344.

Herbs, aromatic, **8,** 466.

Hercules, and the twelve labors, **1,** 78, 427.

Herd's-grass, **4,** 199.

"Hero, The," verse, **1,** 403.

Heroes, real and ideal, **1,** 22, 23; insanity of, **2,** 11; imaginary and real, **12,** 405.

Heroism, the seeds of, **1,** 52; music and, 188.

Heron, great blue, **2,** 63, **3,** 427, **5,** 381, **9,** 23, **11,** 113, 114, 165, **12,** 267, 268; flight of, **3,** 443, 444, **5,** 153, 156, 157, 380, 391, **6,** 228, **7,** 40, 41, **11,** 109; feeding-places of, **6,** 465, 466; a fine view of a, **7,** 310; on a buttonwood tree, 450; at Westport Pond, 482; droppings of, 527; slate-colored expanse of wing of, **8,** 4; note of, **11,** 138; a deceptive, **12,** 284, 285; sketches of head of, 286; sounding the river, 287; skeleton of, **14,** 110.

Heron, green. *See* Bittern, green.

Hesperian Isles, **4,** 402, 403.

Hewit, Captain, of Marshfield, Daniel Webster's nearest neighbor, **2,** 361, 362.

Heywood, Dr., and "Perch" Hosmer, **8,** 365.

Heywood, young, of Concord, catches a large trout, **11,** 433.

Heywood, Abel, **4,** 202.

Heywood, George, **10,** 224, 225; his character, 230.

Heywood's Gazetteer, quoted, **14,** 44.

Heywood's Meadow, a tragedy in, **2,** 13–15.

Hibiscus, **4,** 297–299, **5,** 373; flowers of, ornament of river, **4,** 301; escaping the mowers, **5,** 362; seed of, **9,** 99.

Hickory, *or* walnut, **2,** 9, 3, 228, **6,** 136, **7,** 378, 512 ; buds of, **2,** 12, **5,** 149, **6,** 280, **9,** 390; on a hill-slope, **2,** 459; sap of, **3,** 292; by moonlight, **5,** 322; autumn colors of, **9,** 108, **11,** 197; fallen leaves of, **10,** 120; a remarkable, 210; a burnt stick of, **11,** 402; prolonging the autumn, **12,** 384, 385; planting of, **14,** 93, 94; love of, for hillside, 281. *See also* Wood-lots.

Hickory-nuts, *or* walnuts, **5,** 457, 463, 487, **11,** 337; aroma of green, **4,** 300, 301; variety in form of, **5,** 482; gathering of, in snow, **9,** 177; on the tree, **12,** 379.

Hieracium. *See* Hawkweed.

Higginson, Storrow, **10,** 387, 497, 500, 501, 507, **11,** 151, **12,** 166.

Higginson Thomas Wentworth, as a lecturer, **3,** 213; talks with, **7,** 102, **9,** 254; his collection of rare plants, **8,** 382.

Highland Light, visits to, **7,** 433–443, **9,** 441–449.

Highway robbery, **2,** 332, 333.

Hill, Mr., of Bangor, "Walden" and, **7,** 102, 103.

Hillocks, stone-capped, reminiscent of mountains, **4,** 209.

Hills, and vales, **4,** 263; range of, seen from Billerica, 422; near the water, **7,** 11; explanation of barrenness of brows, **12,** 62; common form of, **13,** 339.

Hillside, the floral history of a, **4,** 127.

Hindoos, the, book of, **1,** 266, 267; conception by, of man, 275; austerity of, 278, 279; religion of, **2,** 3, 4; rites

different objects in, 196; value of imagination to, 445; vegetable and animal, akin, **12**, 23; improving the opportunities of, 159, 160; measured by enjoyment, **13**, 159; small things of, **14**, 104; the successful, 281, 282; valued in money, 284; the narrow, 306.

Life, future, **3**, 107.

Life-everlasting. *See* Everlasting.

Light, vitality of, **1**, 451; reflections of, from leaves and grass, **4**, 98, 115, 151; reflected from ferns, 217; reflected from sunset clouds, 223; reflected from water, 422; reflected from fields, **6**, 411; laws of, **11**, 52, 53; reflections of, in November, 307, 308, 331, 336; reflected from grass stems, 426; reflected from snow-crystals, **13**, 112, 114; reflected from awns of a grain-field, 383.

"Light-hearted, thoughtless, shall I take my way," verse, **1**, 95.

Lighthouses, **2**, 36.

Lightning, destruction of ash by, **4**, 155, 156; inscrutability of, 156, 157; compared to a flower, **8**, 349; effect of, on atmosphere, 450, 451; heat of, **9**, 399; green, **10**, 36; striking a tree, 441, 442 ; telegraph-posts struck by, **14**, 415, 416.

Lightning-rod, uses of, **4**, 157.

Lights, November's silvery, **11**, 307, 308, 331, 336.

Lilac, **1**, 420, 421.

Lily, great yellow, *or* spatterdock (*Nuphar advena*), **5**, 9; expresses the fertility of the river, **4**, 163, 185; a rich yellow, 185 ; roots of, **7**, 490; fruit and seeds of, **12**, 326; in a newly dug pond, **14**, 109, 110.

Lily, kalmiana (*Nuphar lutea* var. *Kalmiana*), **4**, 111, **8**, 431, **12**, 230; in a newly dug pond, **14**, 109, 110.

Lily, red, **4**, 195, 206, 207, **6**, 381, **8**, 409.

Lily, white. *See* Water-lily.

Lily, yellow (*Lilium Canadense*), **4**, 219, **6**, 392, **10**, 13, 14; pods of, **13**, 69.

Lily, yellow (*Nuphar*), **3**, 357, **4**, 201, **5**, 152, **7**, 296, **13**, 204; roots of, **4**, 413, **5**, 528, **6**, 465, **7**, 302, **8**, 302; at river-bottom, **7**, 71; color of, **12**, 323; pads of, **13**, 409.

Lily pads, **5**, 124; like turnover platters, **6**, 266; shadows of, **11**, 98, 99; abundant, **13**, 405; insects on, 408; open spaces amid, 409; crowded, 409.

Lime, price of, **10**, 167.

Limestone, **2**, 16.

Lime-tree, a great, **4**, 87.

Linaria. *See* Redpoll, lesser.

Lincoln (Mass.), graveyard in, **2**, 19, 20; altitude of, 26; inhabitants of, **3**, 3; church in, **9**, 356.

Lincoln (N. H.), **1**, 91.

Lincoln Bridge, fatal accident at, **9**, 151; a modern Dragon of Wantley, 175, 176.

Lindley, John, on the Linnæan system, **3**, 250, 251.

Line of beauty, **5**, 531.

Linnæa borealis, **7**, 401, 405, **11**, 47.

Linnæan system, **3**, 250–252.

Linnæus, preparing for a campaign, **1**, 95; his revenge on his enemies, **3**, 120, 121; on Tournefort's compliment to Hermann, 122; Haller on, 181; nomenclature of, 257; and plant affinities, 286, 287; on character, 288; recommended to students of botany, 308, 309; on propagation of flowers, 324; on scientific terms, 326 ; classification of soils and plants by, 346–348; "man of flowers," **4**, 99; on hawks, **5**, 83; account of *Andromeda Polifolia*, 316.

Lint, on surface of water, **6**, 326, 327.

Lion, the king of beasts, **2**, 271; in "New England's Prospect," **7**, 134; the balls to kill lions with, **8**, 403.

Liquidambar, **9**, 136.

Liquor, old-fashioned conveniences for storage of, **13**, 247–249.

Literature, classical, how formed, **1**, 370, 371; indispensability of classical, 371; the wild in, **2**, 97; tameness of English, 144; comment on official, **11**, 456.

Little & Brown's bookstore, **13**, 30.

Little John, **1**, 298.

Little Quitticus Pond, **9**, 327, 328.

Littleton Giant, the, **3**, 202, 203, **10**, 131, 132.

Living, by self-defense, **1**, 478, 479; simplicity in, **5**, 410–412; and getting a living, **7**, 80.

Living, a, means of procuring, **2**, 164, 319; getting, **8**, 7, 19, 120, 121;

INDEX

ents of, 192; limitations of their knowledge, 246; a man of the old school, 465; dreaming of impracticable things, **9,** 169; world-ridden, 362; lack of enterprise of, 390; poor crack-brains, **10,** 53; effect of place of residence on, 70; at home, 190, 191; association with, unprofitable, 204; fatality governing, 251, 252; a man's relations to Nature, 252; indoor and outdoor, 326; gregariousness of, 350, 351; too great ambitions of, **11,** 304; tracks of, in snow, 321, 322, 353, 354; appetite of, for novelty, **12,** 65, 66; mercenary minds of, 111; industry of, 242; promising, 329; growth of, in different zones, 334, 335; effect on nature of baseness of, 343; infinite promise of a man, 369 ; thoughts of, corresponding to the man himself, **13,** 69, 70; receptivity of, 77, 78; stupidity of, 145; easily imposed on, **14,** 278; success and failure of, 281, 282; narrow life of, 306.

Men, white, the colors of, **4,** 92, 93.

Menagerie, a visit to a, **2,** 271; music in a, 356; an ill-managed, 367–369.

Menan, Louis, **9,** 199.

Menhaden, back fins of, **8,** 398.

Menu, **1,** 268; quoted, 229, 263; the "Laws of Menu," 264, 266, 267, 279, 280.

Merchant, and farmer, **1,** 78.

Merganser, red-breasted, **6,** 215. *See also* Sheldrake.

Merman, discovery of a, **9,** 337.

Merriam, Francis Jackson, **13,** 3 and note, 4.

Merriam, Joseph, **2,** 167; duck-shooting, **9,** 466, 467.

Merrimack (N. H.), **1,** 91.

Merrimack River, boat journey on, **1,** 91; wildness of parts of, 451; buttonwood trees on the banks of the, **2,** 10; in spring, **5,** 111; walk by, **9,** 189; reaches of, **11,** 4.

"Methinks all things have travelled since you shined," verse, **1,** 243.

"Methinks that by a strict behavior," verse, **1,** 457.

Mexico, table-land of, **2,** 243.

Michaux, F. Andrew, quoted, **2,** 142, 195–201, 211, **9,** 396 note, 414, **11,** 385; on the Ohio, **2,** 230–232.

Michigan, wild horses of, **2,** 38.

Mickle, William Julius, **1,** 288.

Microscope, **7,** 61.

Middleborough, **7,** 472–474, 477, 478, 484.

Middleborough ponds, the, **7,** 465–467, 471–479, **9,** 327–330.

Mikania scandens, **5,** 337, **14,** 73, 74; married to the button-bush, **12,** 336.

Mildew, on ground, **9,** 267, 269.

Miles, Charles, his swamp, **1,** 270, 271, **4,** 280, 281.

Miles, Martial, **6,** 147, **8,** 192; a talk with, 191; his cider, 193.

Miles, Warren, **12,** 277; and his mill, **8,** 190, 191, 303, 304, 310, 326–328, **9,** 201.

Milk, Captain Minott's nightly quart, **14,** 329.

Milkmen, early risers, **2,** 386.

Milkweed, pods and seeds of, **3,** 57, 58, 63, 128, **11,** 246, **14,** 63; flowers of, **4,** 284; unidentified species of, **6,** 404.

Milkweed, common (*Asclepias Cornuti* or *Syriaca*), **8,** 400; pods and seeds of, **3,** 17–20, 23, **4,** 396, **9,** 96, 126.

Milkweed, water (*A. incarnata*), **5,** 323; fibre of, **2,** 314, **8,** 119; pods and seeds of, **8,** 71, 72, **9,** 99; flowers of, **11,** 70.

Milky Way, **4,** 470.

Miller, Hugh, quoted, **2,** 172, **3,** 30.

Millers, black-winged, **7,** 409.

Mills, gingham, at Clinton, **2,** 134, 135; coach-lace, 136; a wire-rolling mill, **7,** 101, 102; cobweb drapery at a mill, **11,** 224, 225, 363. *See also* Sawmills.

Millstones, primitive way of getting out, **10,** 246.

Milton, John, quoted, **1,** 183, **7,** 28; lack of moral discrimination in, **1,** 218.

Milton (Mass.), **2,** 46.

Mimulus ringens, **4,** 285, **9,** 5.

Min, the Thoreaus' cat, **8,** 158, **9,** 141; playing the prodigal son, **8,** 192, 193; and a mouse, **9,** 154, 155.

Mind, the sovereign of nature, **1,** 488; development of, **2,** 203–205; chastity of, 289–291; moods of, 340; in winter and summer, **3,** 70; the sky and, 201; in youth and age, 203, 204; during sleep, 354; loses adipose tissue in America, **4,** 20; atmosphere of, in the evening, **5,** 254.

Minds, should echo to music, **4,** 144.

Mine, lead, **4,** 54.

Miner, Lewis, **8,** 170.

Ministerial Lot, surveyed, **3,** 122 ff.

Mink, **3,** 160, **4,** 421, **8,** 40, 194, 259, **9,** 346, **12,** 43, 67, **13,** 267; gnaws off legs in trap, **1,** 481; tracks of. **5,** 10, 11, **7,** 163; swimming, **5,** 492, **6,** 17; preying on frogs, **7,** 207; value of skin of, 248; enemy of birds, 252; hunting at night, 270; carrying a muskrat, **8,** 22; Minott's account of, 31, 32; money value of, 34; odor of, 36; a near view of a, **10,** 369; not eaten by other animals, **13,** 205; feeding young, 259.

Minnesota, trip to, **14,** 339, 340.

Minnows, **1,** 475, 476, **5,** 14, **7,** 207, **8,** 414, 415, **10,** 392, **11,** 346, 347, 454; swallowed by pickerel, **5,** 307, **11,** 75; leaping out of water, **8,** 3; method of keeping alive, **9,** 308, 309; muscular vigor of, 477. *See also* Shiner.

Minos, **1,** 391.

Minott, Captain, second husband of T.'s grandmother, **14,** 329, 330.

Minott, George, **3,** 87, 128, **5,** 221, **6,** 211, **7,** 239, **8,** 25, **11,** 374; a poetical farmer, **3,** 41–43; his methods of farming, 67; a hunting adventure of, 69; a walk with, 108, 109; on snow-shoes, 193; on the care of hay, 358; on stake-drivers, **4,** 124; on the striped squirrel's bark, **5,** 12; tells a mad-dog story, 522–525; the site of his house, **6,** 147; his attitude toward death, 152; his visits to Boston, 175; on foxes, **7,** 154, 155; on the rabbit, 169; on partridges, quails, etc., 211, 212; tells an owl story, 380; a story about ants, 398; on the migration of swallows, 449; his cats, **8,** 31; tells a story of a September gale, 150, 151; as a story-teller, 194, **10,** 56, 266; Emerson and, **8,** 195; talks of Uncle Charles, 245; talks with, 308, **9,** 129–132, 212, 213, 273, 274, 356, **10,** 54, 163, 164, **11,** 108, 109, 190, 191; on meadow-grass, **9,** 6; on General Hull, 94; on meadow-hay, 94, 95; on the relation between strong drink and mowing,

95, 288; tells hunting story, 122. tells anecdote of bacon-eating, 141; 142; on wood-cutting, 177, 178; tells story of song sparrow, 230; on the Cold Friday, 230; tells story of crazy hen, 239; on ducks, 467; discovers a squirrel's storehouse, **10,** 41; in his wood-shed, 51–53; tells peach tree story, 63; recollections of an old grist-mill, 87; in accord with nature, 168; his house, 207, 208; his ear for bird-notes, 265; tells story of a slave, 284, 285; on Indian creels, 313 note; his hunting stories, **11,** 108, 223, 224; criticises Shattuck's History of Concord, 110; on meadow-haying, 128, 129; his reminiscences of the Great Meadows, **12,** 281, 282; tells animal stories, **13,** 103, 104; ill with dropsy, 410.

Minott, Deacon George, brother of Captain M., **10,** 219.

Minott, Miss Mary, **7,** 239, **8,** 127, 150; talks of her brother George, **9,** 212; her old furniture, 274; death of, **14,** 321.

Minott, Thomas, secretary of the Abbot of Walden in Essex, **10,** 219.

Mirabeau, **1,** 429; as a highwayman. **2,** 332, 333.

Miracles, **2,** 33; attitude of Hindoos toward, **4,** 250.

Mirage, **3,** 290, 291; sets landscape in motion, **4,** 39; on Buzzard's Bay, **10,** 15.

Mirick, B. L., **3,** 282 note.

Misfortune, a beneficent, **11,** 196.

Missionaries, **9,** 208.

Mississippi River, panorama of the, **2,** 146, 147.

Mist, **4,** 105, 239, **5,** 257, **8,** 316, **9,** 174; formation of, **5,** 513; silvering the water, **7,** 294; like a roof, **8,** 14; reflections from, 16; frozen, 46. *See also* Fog and Vapor.

Mitchell, Henry, **14,** 343.

Mitchella repens, or partridge-berry, **4,** 129, 265, **6,** 12, **12,** 386; appropriately called "checkerberry," **2,** 100, **3,** 89; scent of flowers, **6,** 372, **12,** 217.

Mob, rests on air, **4,** 16.

Mocker-nut, nuts of, **5,** 486, 487, 518, **9,** 414, **11,** 334, **12,** 326; autumnal foliage of, **10,** 90.

course with, 193; slow processes of, 257; marriage of the soul with, 413; present in her working, 416; delight in fruitfulness of, 431; propagation secured by, **3**, 65; a plain writer, 233; publishes her secrets, 255; not found in books, 271; in youth and age, 378; odors of, **4**, 27; demands virtue, 80; her love of variety, 145; reveals itself to the vigorous 155; her demand to be viewed humanly, 163; reveals herself to the lover of life, 174; her enmity toward the debauchee, 195; intimacy with, compels to solitude, 258, 259; revolutions of, 350; learned by perception, 351; comparison of, to humanity, 445, 446; duplex character of, 459; innocent purposes of, 461; roominess of, 478; the observation of, **5**, 45; as a language, 135; amount of fertility in, 139; interpreted only by life, 323; furnishing man's food, 330, 331; doubleness in, 343; a kind of gall, 349; a Bacchanal, 356; unused abundance in, 368; health and, 395; as interpreter of life, 472; nutriment offered by, 478; acceptance of gifts of, 487; her closed door, 499; effect of intercourse with, 506; preserving relation to, 517; message of, compared to books, **6**, 40; touch of, transmutes to beauty, 66, 67; correspondence of, to almanac, 145; disappointments in the study of, 293, 294; inspiration in, 294, 295; serenity of, 329; purity of, 352, 353; beauty of, destroyed by evil, 358; genial attraction of, 486; stung by God, **7**, 10; calling for her fan, 321; healing her wounds, 407, 408; overbounteous, 504; secrets of, 514; confidence and success of, **8**, 43; beauty and wonder of, 43–45; economy of, 110; doing her planting, 198; primitive, 221; eternity in, 224; Sardanapalus-like, 315; her grandest voice, 349; impartiality of, **9**, 55, 56; reflection of man, 121; devices of, 127; winter colors of, 153; epic of, 168; a musical instrument, 191; daily intercourse with, a necessity, 200; foresight of, 205; effect of her society, 205, 208–210, 215; abhors a

straight line, 281; love of, very rare, 336, 337; still unexplored, 490; as described by Ruskin, **10**, 69; the lover of, and the lover of art, 80; as a banker, 92, 93; repetition in, 97; correspondence of, to man, 127; Ruskin and, 147; an artist, 159; healing her wounds, 160; in November, 203, 204; relations of, to man, 252; her love for gradation, 260; indulgence of, 301; glorified by man, 364; the mysteries of, 430, 431; displaying her beauty, **11**, 77; careless observation of, 148; sameness of, 155; confident of future, 207; likened to an athlete, 260; phenomena of, concealed, 285, 286; blush of, 300; gradation and harmony of, 319; deliberateness of, 449; man's interest in phenomena of, **12**, 65, 66; feasts prepared by, 96; carrying out her plans, 160; avoiding unbroken lines, 352; bill of fare of, 398; amusements offered by, 400; equilibrium of, **13**, 38; her care for her creatures, 99; an unprejudiced view of, 169; regularity of her phenomena, 279; extracting beauty out of foulness, 400; leisureliness of, **14**, 311, 312.

Naumbergia thyrsiflora, **9**, 411.

Nauset Lights, **9**, 437.

Naushon, **8**, 392, 393.

Nautical terms, **2**, 361.

Nawshawtuct, view from, **1**, 57, **2**, 18, **9**, 81; seen over a lake of fog, **2**, 486.

Nealy, after partridges, **9**, 107, 108.

Nebraska Bill, speeches on, **6**, 129.

Necessaries, **1**, 398, 486.

Negro, a, his idea of heaven, **9**, 215; picked up at sea, 337.

Neighbors, appreciation of, **9**, 151; bad, **11**, 338; distances between, **12**, 417.

Neottia. *See* Rattlesnake-plantain.

Nepeta Glechoma, **5**, 134.

Neptune, Governor of Penobscot tribe, **5**, 427 and note, 428.

Nestor, **1**, 61.

Nettle, **12**, 341.

New Bedford, visits to, **7**, 89, 470, **8**, 384–397, **9**, 315–330; spring climate of, 330.

New England, question of decrease of woods in, **3**, 215; love of, **7**, 104,

Orator, most eloquent when most silent, **1**, 67.

Orchidaceæ, seeds of, **12**, 326.

Orchis, dwarf (*Platanthera flava*), **4**, 128, **6**, 369.

Orchis, great purple fringed (*P. fimbriata*), **4**, 103, 104, **5**, 244, **6**, 337, 338.

Orchis, purple fringed, **4**, 117, 122, 128.

Orchis, ragged (*P. lacera*), **4**, 229.

Orchis, round-leaved (*P. orbiculata*), **4**, 302.

Orchis, small purple fringed (*P. psycodes*), **4**, 268, 271, 273, 285, **5**, 337, 345, **6**, 401.

Orchis, white fringed, **5**, 345, **6**, 408, **11**, 83.

Orient, luxurious idleness of the, **1**, 343.

Originality, tariff on, **11**, 343.

Orinoco River, **2**, 11.

Oriole, Baltimore, *or* golden robin, **4**, 35, **7**, 376; notes of, **4**, 35, **5**, 136, **7**, 388, **8**, 336, **10**, 412, **13**, 296; a herald of hot weather, **5**, 133; nest of, **7**, 218, 240, **8**, 119, 120, **13**, 38; young of, **7**, 430, **9**, 461.

Ornithology, **1**, 125.

Orrock, Hannah, **11**, 381.

Osborn, Sherard, **4**, 320.

Osier, red. *See* Cornel, river.

Osiers, **8**, 208, 244; Evelyn on, **4**, 86; brightening of, **7**, 212, **13**, 170, 171; brilliance of, in winter, **7**, 255; attractiveness of, **8**, 49; like flames, 82.

Osmunda, **5**, 478; wool of, **4**, 33. *See also* Ferns.

Osmunda regalis, **10**, 495.

Ossian, landscapes of, **8**, 51.

Ossoli, Marquis of, **2**, 43.

Ostriches, eggs of, **2**, 131.

Ostrya. *See* Hop-hornbeam.

Otter, **8**, 191, **12**, 139; tracks of, **3**, 338, **4**, 474, **6**, 40, **7**, 169, 170, 174, 479, **8**, 183–185, 200, **9**, 162, 163, **13**, 126; dog killed by, **5**, 353; retired life of, **6**, 86; sliding down a bank, **7**, 174, **9**, 162; jelly-like substance left by, **8**, 200; skins of, sold by the Pilgrims, **9**, 163, 164; roaming habits of, 247.

Outdoor life, its effect on the character, **3**, 104; a ballast to thought, **4**, 409, 410; degrees of, **12**, 324.

Ovn, on rocks in river, **12**, 250, 251.

Oven-bird, *or* golden-crowned thrush, **1**, 145, **6**, 368, 369, **7**, 355, **9**, 90, **10**, 426; song of, **2**, 9, **6**, 251, **10**, 411, 412; nest of, **2**, 35, 36, **5**, 310, **7**, 414; running from nest, **5**, 229, **10**, 501. *See also* Night-warbler.

Ovid, quoted, **2**, 144, 145.

Owl, Acadian (*Strix Acadica*), **11**, 392.

Owl, barred, a captive, **11**, 373.

Owl, cat, **3**, 122; hooting of, **10**, 227; with nest and young, 438; nest of, 499.

Owl, hawk, **6**, 14.

Owl, hooting, hooting of, **3**, 122, 123, **4**, 5, 130, 191, **5**, 85, **6**, 52, **9**, 172, 182, 191, **11**, 378, 390; hoot of, a sign of rain, **3**, 131; rarely seen, **6**, 52, 53, **9**, 172.

Owl, long-eared, **13**, 421, 422; with nest and young, **9**, 457, 458; notes of, 458.

Owl, red. *See* Owl, screech.

Owl, screech, **7**, 12, **9**, 458; lament of, **1**, 378, 379; notes of, **6**, 439, **7**, 457, **13**, 325, 374; on its nest, **7**, 364–367, 371, 372, 375, 390; spied at by a thrasher, 387; a captive, 521–525; a pair with young, **8**, 405, 406; red, **14**, 294; fitted to withstand winter, 294, 295; gray, 314.

Owl, short-eared, **6**, 14.

Owls, **7**, 380, **8**, 96, **14**, 93; fowls eaten by, **6**, 60; feathers of, **10**, 248; fitted to withstand the winter, **14**, 295.

Owls, unidentified, **6**, 13, 14; notes of, **7**, 12.

Ownership, public and private, in natural objects, **14**, 305.

Ox-Bow, in Concord River, **12**, 268, 269.

Oxen, with loads of hay, **2**, 53; majestic sleep of, 258; brass-tipped horns of, 270; working for themselves, 310; action and reaction between the farmer and his, 453; chased by an ox, **3**, 94; a tired team, 158; a wounded farmer and his, 276; horns of, 305, 306; their relation to man, 306, 307.

Oysters, **2**, 42; William Wood on, **7**, 137; at Perth Amboy, N. J., **9**, 142.

"Packed in my mind lie all the clothes," verse, **1**, 291.

Page, a White Mountain collier, **11**, 15, 16.

375; a visit to Walden as a child, 380; leaves the Walden house on account of plastering and returns in three weeks, 387; making bread, 430, 431; as a town officer, 434–436; visits Haverhill and the Dustin house, May 12, 1850, **2,** 7, 8; sets fire to the woods, 21–26; goes to Fire Island to search for Margaret Fuller's remains, July, 1850, 43 note; at Patchogue, L. I., 49–51, 78–80; practice work of, 52 note; the Canadian excursion, Sept. 25–Oct. 4, 1850, 73–77, 417, 418; visits the Clinton gingham-mills, 134–136; his love of chastity, 186; gets false teeth, 194; taking ether, 194; humility of, 285, 286; his thoughts on reaching the age of thirty-four, 316, 317; considers embracing huckleberry-picking as a profession, 319; excursion to Clark's Island and Plymouth along the South Shore, July 25–Aug. 1, 1851, 341–367; goes mackerel-fishing, 351–353; fears he is becoming too scientific, 406; perambulating the bounds, 498, 504, 505, **3,** 3–5; aids a fugitive slave, 37, 38; goes to an evening party, 115; his coldness, 147–149; a misunderstanding with a friend, 167, 168; shames impudent persons, 199, 200; why he left the woods, 214, 215; invited to read his papers to a friend, 216; the use of his Journal, 217; his failures and offenses, 293; hypothetical Norse ancestry of, 304, 305; a visit in Plymouth, May 22–24, 1852, **4,** 68–70; refuses to engage in an unprofitable occupation, 252, 253; excursion to Peterboro and Monadnock, Sept. 6 and 7, 1852, 342–347; receives a circular from the secretary of the Association for the Advancement of Science, **5,** 4; describes himself as a transcendentalist, 4, 5; a water-owner, 45; men's use of, 46; a visit in Haverhill, 109–115; conducting huckleberry parties, 358 note; comforting a troubled child, 359 note; the second excursion to the Maine woods, Sept. 13–27, 1853, 424–433; carries a subscription paper for a charitable object, 438, 439; receives and stores the unsold remainder of his first

book, Oct. 28, 1853, 459, 460; a proposed speculation in cranberries, 512; paying for the "Week," 512; settles the account with his publishers, 521; surveying, **6,** 20, 21; not employed as a lecturer, 21; gets a Christmas-tree for the town, 22, 24, 25; tempted to certain licenses of speech by a companion, 165; buys a telescope, Mar. 13, 1854, 166, 167; criticising his compositions, 190; receives a specimen copy of "Walden," 419; "Walden" published, Aug. 9, 1854, 429; his yearning for solitude, 439; his faults as a writer, **7,** 7 note, 8 note; sends Fields copies of the "Week," 8 note; thinks of writing lectures and going abroad to read them, 46; the advantages of his obscurity and poverty, 46· goes to Plymouth to lecture and survey, 62, 63; an excursion to Wachusett Mountain, 64–66; to Philadelphia, Nov. 20, 1854, 72–75; calls on Greeley in New York, 76; lecturing in Providence, 79; his lecturing, 79, 80; visits Daniel Ricketson in New Bedford, Dec. 25 and 26, 1854, 89–91; a trip to Nantucket, 91–97; lectures in Worcester, Jan. 4, 1855, 99, 100; walks to Quinsigamond Pond *via* Quinsigamond Village, 100–102; climbing trees, 362, 363; to Provincetown and Highland Light and back with Channing, July 4–18, 1855, 431–443; goes to the circus, 461; visits Ricketson in New Bedford, Sept. 29–Oct. 5, 1855, 463–482; to the Middleborough ponds, 465–468, 471–479; Ricketson drives him to Plymouth, 483, 484; returns to Concord, 484; his lack of sympathy with his neighbors, 527; recalls the houses and towns in which he has lived and some events of his life, **8,** 64–67; stories of his childhood, 93, 94; his journal, 134; consciousness under ether, 142; Jones ancestry of, 187, 188; with Brown and Blake in Worcester, 377–382; accompanies Ricketson back to New Bedford June 23, 1856, 384; to the Middleborough ponds, 385, 386, 395–397; to Sconticut Neck, 388–392; to Naushon, 392, 393; returns to Concord, 398; chasing and capturing a runaway pig, 451–456; spends a successful afternoon in a cranberry swamp, **9,** 35–41; excursion to Brattleboro, Vt., and to Alcott's at Walpole, N. H., Sept. 5–12, 1856, 61–80; a dextrous barberry-picker, 85; sets out for Eagleswood, Perth Amboy, N. J., Oct. 24, 1856, 133; at Barnum's Museum in New York, 133, 134; visit at Eagleswood, 134–139; buying a pair of boots, 156; his botanical studies, 156–158; lectures at Amherst, N.H., 186–189; his poor success as a lecturer, 214, 215; finds good society in solitary woodland walks, 215, 216; lectures in Fitchburg, 235, 236; loses a friend, 249, 250; dines with Agassiz at Emerson's, 298, 299; visits Ricketson again, Apr. 2–15, 1875, 315–330; a member of the "Walden Pond Society," 331; singing "Tom Bowling," 393 and note; sets out for Cape Cod, June 12, 1857 413; at B. Marston Watson's in Plymouth, 414, 415; visits Clark's Island, 415–419; in Plymouth again, 419, 420; down the Cape on foot, 420–440; at Highland Light, 441–449; the walk to Provincetown, 450–452; a night in Provincetown, 452–454; by steamer to Boston, 454, 455; the third excursion to the Maine woods, July 20–Aug. 7, 1857, 484–503; his varied employments when living at Walden, **10,** 61–63; his dream mountain, 141–144; lectures in Lynn, 243; visits Nahant and drives about Lynn, 244–247; to Worcester on the way to New York, May 22, 1858, 440; walks to Quinsigamond Pond with Blake, Brown, and Rogers, 440–442; to New York, 442, 443; visits William Emerson on Staten Island, 443; returns to Concord, 443; excursion to Mt. Monadnock with H. G. O. Blake, June 2–4, 1858, 452–480; White Mountain excursion with Edward Hoar, July 2–19, 1858, **11,** 3–62; meets Blake and Brown on Mt. Washington, 29; sprains his ankle, 32; a Cape Ann excursion, Sept. 21–24, 1858, 170–180; loses his father, 435; walks about Lynn, **12,**

164, 165; studies the physiography of Concord River, summer of 1859, 219 and note; his first address on John Brown, 400 note; a visit from Ricketson, 449 note; a member of a committee to ask liberty of the selectmen to have the town bell tolled on John Brown's death, 457; assists one of John Brown's men on his way to Canada, **13,** 3 note, 4; Monadnock excursion with Channing, Aug. 4–9, 1860, **14,** 8–52; takes the cold that results in his last illness, Dec. 3, 1860, 290 note; his journey to Minnesota, May, 1861, 339, 340.

Thoreau, Jane, aunt of H. D. T., **5,** 58, **11,** 436; birth of, **11,** 381.

Thoreau, Jennie Burns, grandmother of H. D. T., **10,** 252.

Thoreau, John, brother of H. D. T., **2,** 12; death of, **1,** 321 note.

Thoreau, John, father of H. D. T., **2,** 81; enumerates old Concord houses, **7,** 505, 506; some biographical notes of, **8,** 64–66; disastrous results of his attempt to milk the cow, 93; dispute with, on the use of making maple sugar, 217; and a lost pig, 451; his reminiscences of his father, **9,** 132, 133; on the former price of wood, 271; birthplace of, **11,** 381; death of, 435; biographical comment on, 435–437.

Thoreau, John, grandfather of H. D. T., a privateersman, **5,** 242, 243; death of, **7,** 325, **9,** 132; his son's reminiscences of, 132, 133; Mrs. William Monroe's recollections of, **10,** 252, 278; a religious man, 278.

Thoreau, Maria, aunt of H. D. T., **4,** 462, **5,** 58; and old family letters, **7,** 325–327.

Thoreau, Peter, great-uncle of H. D. T., letters from, **7,** 325–327.

"Thoreau, Peter, on Book-keeping," **7,** 434.

Thoreau, Sophia, sister of H. D. T., **8,** 403, **9,** 142, 455, **10,** 363, 489, **11,** 149; her herbarium, **4,** 360; up Assabet with, **5,** 176, **8,** 24, **9,** 105; to Nawshawtuct with, **5,** 319; back from Wachusett, **7,** 43; to Conantum with, 344; barberrying with, 460; a letter from, **8,** 377; to Hermitage Woods with, 378; to Shrewsbury with, 380;

early in fall, 67; buried in streams, 87; a graveyard of, 276; flattened by snow and wind, **11**, 32; marked by ice, 105; value of, to a village, 218–221; dense masses of bare, 295; destruction of, in Concord, 299, 300; frostwork on, 398–400, 403–407; symmetry of those growing in the open accounted for, 442, 443; blooming before May 1st, **12**, 133; dispersion of, **13**, 305; vivacity of roots of, **14**, 121; list of those which grow in masses, 134. *See also* Forest trees.

Tree-toad, **12**, 399; marked for concealment, **4**, 162; called out by warm weather, **5**, 162; notes of, 195, 196, 253.

Trench, Richard Chenevix, **4**, 466, 467, 482.

Trichostema dichotomum. See Blue-curls.

Trientalis, **5**, 164.

Trillium, nodding, scent of, **4**, 73, **5**, 164.

Trillium erythrocarpum, beauty of, **10**, 454.

Trilliums, fruit of, **2**, 440, **4**, 304.

Troopial, cow. *See* Cowbird.

Tropics, effect of, on man, **12**, 365.

Trough, for cattle, **10**, 210.

Trout, **1**, 475, 476, **3**, 57, **7**, 113, **8**, 303, 327, **9**, 201; in early March, **6**, 155; agility of young, 159; running up brooks, **7**, 283; concealing himself, 293; antics of, **9**, 293; in a Maine pond, 503; a ten-pound, **10**, 180; attacking a pickerel, 399; in Walden, **11**, 433.

"True friendship is so firm a league," verse, **1**, 248.

"True, our converse a stranger is to speech," verse, **1**, 50.

Trumpet-flowers, **4**, 284. *See also Eupatorium purpureum.*

Truth, in the abstract, **1**, 52; evasiveness of, 117; has no opponent, 118; paradoxical, 153; God's concern, 213; unattained, 236; grounded in love, 332; kinds of, **2**, 403; power of, to communicate itself, **3**, 172; sweetness of, **4**, 129; compared to cocoanut milk, 146; publicity of, 290; spoken out of bitterness, **6**, 169; the eternal plains of, **9**, 237, 238; view-points of, **10**, 165; concealment of impossible, **11**, 449.

"Truth, Goodness, Beauty, — those celestial thrins," verse, **1**, 51.

Truths, the perception of a new truth, **3**, 441, 442; roundly represented, 465; higher and lower, **10**, 153.

Tub-maker, shop of a, **9**, 187.

Tuckerman, Edward, quoting Fries, **3**, 286; on Linnæus, 288; on rock-tripe, **6**, 158; on potamogetons, 449; on lecheas, **8**, 423.

Tuckerman's Ravine, visit to, **11**, 21–37; slides in, 57.

Tulip-tree, **9**, 136.

Tullus Hostilius, **6**, 28.

Tunison's Bookstore, **9**, 138.

Tupelo, **6**, 253, **10**, 238; at Scituate, **2**, 349, 350; leafing of, **4**, 58; leaves of, **6**, 393, **7**, 14, 15; fruit of, 61, **12**, 319; in "New England's Prospect," **7**, 133, 134; an umbrella-shaped, **8**, 395; a large, **10**, 27, 28.

Turdus aquaticus. See Water-thrush.

Turkey, wild, **7**, 135.

Turkeys, **2**, 83, 430, **8**, 165.

Turkey-shooting, a, **9**, 130, 131.

Turnips, raw, **2**, 305, 306.

Turpentine, **7**, 237.

Turritis stricta, **5**, 192, 228.

Turtle, an unidentified, **9**, 328 and note, 329, 330, 484, 485.

Turtle, musk, *or* stinkpot (*Sterno-thœrus odoratus*), **4**, 222, **6**, 271, **7**, 451, **8**, 423, **11**, 80, **12**, 119, **13**, 407; eggs of, **6**, 349; development of an egg of, 388; hatching, **7**, 28, 29; a newly hatched, 32, 33; young, liberated, 382; shell of, **8**, 361; sluggishness of, 399; scent of, **10**, 340; climbing willow stems, **11**, 80, 81; time of laying, **13**, 357.

Turtle, snapping *or* mud (*Chelonura serpentina*), **8**, 25, 310, 311, 328, 403, **9**, 361, 362; catching a horned pout, **2**, 14, 15; young in egg, 102, **6**, 414, 473, 474, **7**, 4, 5; protective color of, **4**, 222; taken into the boat, **6**, 270, 271; beauty of outline in shell of, 271; description of one captured and dragged home, 271–274; snapping of, 276; method of excavating, 334, **13**, 355; after excavating, **6**, 334; a method of catching, 337; nest and eggs of, 367, 368, 454; hatching of, 474; the irresistible necessity for, 474; used as food, 475; the catching and killing of, 475, 476; some large ones, 475,